Skills for Success

The Personal Development Planning Handbook

Visit our free study skills resource at **www.skills4study.com**

Palgrave Study Guides

Authoring a PhD
Career Skills
e-Learning Skills
Effective Communication for
  Arts and Humanities Students
Effective Communication for
  Science and Technology
The Foundations of Research
The Good Supervisor
How to Manage your Arts, Humanities and
  Social Science Degree
How to Manage your Distance and
  Open Learning Course
How to Manage your Postgraduate Course
How to Manage your Science and
  Technology Degree
How to Study Foreign Languages
How to Write Better Essays
Making Sense of Statistics
The Mature Student's Guide to Writing

The Postgraduate Research Handbook
Presentation Skills for Students
The Principles of Writing in Psychology
Professional Writing
Research Using IT
Skills for Success
The Student's Guide to Writing
The Study Skills Handbook (2nd edn)
Study Skills for Speakers of English as
  a Second Language
Studying the Built Environment
Studying Economics
Studying History (2nd edn)
Studying Mathematics and its Applications
Studying Modern Drama (2nd edn)
Studying Physics
Studying Psychology
Teaching Study Skills and Supporting Learning
Work Placements – A Survival Guide for Students
Writing for Engineers

Palgrave Study Guides: Literature

General Editors: John Peck and Martin Coyle

How to Begin Studying English Literature
  (3rd edn)
How to Study a Jane Austen Novel (2nd edn)
How to Study a Charles Dickens Novel
How to Study Chaucer (2nd edn)
How to Study an E. M. Forster Novel
How to Study James Joyce
How to Study Linguistics (2nd edn)

How to Study Modern Poetry
How to Study a Novel (2nd edn)
How to Study a Poet (2nd edn)
How to Study a Renaissance Play
How to Study Romantic Poetry (2nd edn)
How to Study a Shakespeare Play (2nd edn)
How to Study Television
Practical Criticism

Skills for Success

The Personal Development Planning Handbook

Stella Cottrell

First published 2003 by
PALGRAVE MACMILLAN
Houndmills, Basingstoke, Hampshire RG21 6XS and
175 Fifth Avenue, New York, N.Y. 10010
Companies and representatives throughout the world

PALGRAVE MACMILLAN is the global academic imprint of the Palgrave
Macmillan division of St. Martin's Press, LLC and of Palgrave Macmillan Ltd.
Macmillan® is a registered trademark in the United States, United Kingdom
and other countries. Palgrave is a registered trademark in the European
Union and other countries.

ISBN 1–4039–1132–0 paperback

This book is printed on paper suitable for recycling and made from fully
managed and sustained forest sources.

A catalogue record for this book is available from the British Library.

10   9   8   7   6   5   4   3
12 11 10 09 08 07 06 05 04

Printed in China

Self-evaluation sheets, planners and activity sheets may be photocopied
by individual students for their personal use only.

Contents

Introductory notes for university staff

What is Personal Development Planning (PDP) and what do we have to do?

The Dearing Enquiry (1997) recommended that progress files be introduced by universities as 'a means by which students can monitor, build, and reflect upon their personal development'. The Quality Assurance Agency (QAA) now expects all universities to use the progress file initiative to ensure that students undertake personal planning throughout their time as undergraduates. Progress files consist of three elements: (1) personal development processes, (2) student records that guide personal reflection and planning, and (3) the formal university transcript.

The processes of Personal Development Planning (PDP) are at the heart of the progress files initiative and are the most important aspect of it. PDP brings together the three concepts of personal development, 'improving learning and performance', and forward planning to achieve goals, whether academic, personal or professional. There are formal requirements for universities to deliver PDP. These include:

- informing students about PDP when they first make contact and at each stage of their learning;
- providing structured opportunities for reflection and PDP at all stages of university education;
- enabling students to keep records of their personal progress to aid reflection and planning;
- providing formal records of achievement (transcripts) that students can use to assist their planning.

PDP refers to much more than career planning, although that is one important aspect of the initiative. It is about creating structured opportunities for students to develop a wider range of skills and personal qualities that will benefit them in life, work and study. These might include inter-personal skills, team work, problem-solving, self-management skills and similar skills. At its best, PDP develops rounded, reflective individuals who are responsible, emotionally mature, forward thinking, and capable of working well with others. Such skills and attributes take time, practice, support and encouragement to develop. Where possible, it helps students when these are made relevant and accessible by being provided through their programme and linked to the curriculum rather than left to occasional and last-minute sessions with the Careers Service.

How can this book help university staff to deliver PDP?

This book provides information and structured activities that will assist universities in meeting QAA expectations for PDP. It includes a broad range of approaches so that lecturers and other staff can select aspects that they feel are most relevant. There are activities within the text that some tutors have found useful when considering how to deliver PDP, either through workshops or tutorials. In addition, academic staff can direct students to materials within the book that:

- inform them about personal development planning;
- structure reflection on a broad range of PDP issues;
- help them to evaluate current levels of competence and confidence;

- include activities that develop specific skills and attitudes;
- relate PDP to academic study;
- enable aspects of PDP to be incorporated into the curriculum;
- enable them to record different kinds of goals and achievements for their personal records.

Over time, you will probably want to adapt some activities to suit your own programme. However, for those starting out in this area, activities are written in a generic way in order to enable time-pressured staff to use them with minimum alterations.

Using *Skills for Success* with students

The book is designed for use either as a key text to support PDP within a programme of study, or to be used as a stand-alone text. It is not designed for students to read from cover to cover. Not every aspect of the book will be relevant to all students for their particular programme or level of study. It is likely that many students will find it very difficult to think about their future and to plan the development of personal skills and qualities over a three- or four-year period unless they receive support. This is why Dearing and the QAA lay emphasis on 'structured opportunities' for PDP. Tutors can assist students by:

- identifying which materials and activities are most useful at their stage of the programme;
- creating workshop opportunities for students to undertake the activities in a supported way;
- providing opportunities for discussion, activities and reflection;
- if possible, developing skills and qualities (such as team work, problem-solving, self-evaluation and action-planning) through the curriculum over the length of the programme so that these are nurtured and reinforced over time.

The following activities are suggested for each level of an undergraduate programme. They are not exhaustive, and there are other activities in the book that you may wish to use at each level.

Level 1 PDP activities

Introduce PDP

The Introduction to the book (pp. 1–13) will help introduce the concept of PDP to students in line with QAA expectations. It specifies some of the benefits of PDP. Students can be invited to personalise these so that they see the relevance of PDP to themselves. At level 1, students may need lecturers to make explicit the links between PDP and their programme, clarifying how developing skills and personal qualities can assist academic progress on their particular programme.

Personal engagement

Some students find it difficult to grasp the importance of forward planning. 'The future' can seem a long way off. This book provides many activities to assist students to focus on themselves, their ambitions and their motivation from a number of angles. Some activities focus more on self-understanding, some on life planning, and some on learning styles and habits. Tutors can help students by guiding them towards activities from Chapters 1–3 that suit their programme, interests or personality.

Employability

Students who make the wrong choice of degree are the most likely to leave early and may not be preparing adequately for jobs that interest them. You may like to invite the Careers Service to offer a session early on about career options and subject choices. Students also need to be informed early on about the kinds of skills, qualities and experiences that employers are looking for, so that they can plan their development. These cannot usually be gained 'at the last minute': personal, inter-personal and task-management skills can take years to develop.

Identify local opportunities

Identify what kinds of structured activities students can expect from the university over their time as a student. Clarify what, if anything, will be offered through the programme or through academic staff, and how the procedures will work. Invite in representatives from central units that provide some of those opportunities, to make a brief introduction, or ask them to provide a flier. Students may have met some of these staff in an advisory capacity during induction, but they would have a different role from a PDP perspective. Other sources for input are staff offering subjects that students can take to supplement their main subject or broaden their studies.

Link to study skills

It can be helpful to link PDP to academic development, especially at level 1. An initial PDP self-evaluation could be linked to the early identification of study skills needs. Students benefit from being involved in diagnostic and self-evaluation processes, even if objective testing is also used. Once areas for improvement are identified, these can be followed up by guidance, a personal action plan and specific targets. It is useful for staff to monitor student action plans. However, students should be able to show how they have monitored and evaluated their own development. Students could also support each other in achieving development plans, such as through the action sets described in Chapter 5. Materials for supporting specific study skills can be found in *The Study Skills Handbook* (Cottrell, 2003, 2nd edn, published by Palgrave Macmillan).

Introduce self-management

This can link quite easily with study skills such as time management and working with others. Some or all of Chapter 3, 'Successful Self-management' and Chapter 5, 'People Skills', will be useful at level 1.

Look forward

School-leavers may find it difficult to think ahead towards a career, even at level 3. The earlier this is raised, the more time students have to plan towards a job they will want. Activities in Chapter 1, 'The Vision: What is

Success?', encourage students to explore what is important to them for their futures. It can be useful to discuss different concepts of success and achievement, especially if student retention is an issue. Not all students will be as academically successful as they would like. This can be difficult, especially in a university culture where the academic focus is a major part of everyday life. For some students, aspects of personal identity and family duty, not to mention personal finances, are bound up with very specific ideas of what constitutes success. Whilst every attempt should be made to support improvements in academic performance, it is important that students think through what is really important to them beyond their degree, and the contribution that academic study can make towards achieving personal goals, irrespective of degree classification.

Start early with skills of reflection

Introduce the concept of reflection as early as possible. Many people find it takes time to develop reflective skills, so it is important to build this in early to ensure plenty of practice. Chapter 7, 'The Art of Reflection', gives examples of types of reflective activity. Draw attention to those used for your subject at each level. If possible, give brief examples of reflective writing from your subject discipline. Let students know from the outset whether reflective journals will be collected in for tutors to see, so the students can make decisions about information they prefer to keep private. If you neither mark nor make use of reflective materials, then students will soon stop using them, however valuable they might be. Some ways of incorporating reflection into programmes are:

- set reflective activities drawn from various chapters to discuss in class or tutorial;
- set a reflective essay or position paper for an assignment (see Chapter 7, 'The Art of Reflection');
- ask students to submit a summary from their reflective journal and a photocopy of certain pages (by negotiation);
- ask students to reflect upon specific issues which they then discuss in class;
- make clear that reflective journals or logs must be handed in as part of a final

assignment in order for a mark to be received (even if the journal is not marked);

- provide a reflective cover sheet for students to complete and hand in with assignments; examples of these are given in Cottrell (2001, pp. 237–8, 300–2, 319–21);
- make clear whether journals will be marked and what percentage of the mark is allocated to this;
- give time in class for comments to be recorded in journals after an activity has taken place;
- invite comments based upon reflective work, as relevant opportunities arise.

Record achievement

Encourage students to begin the process of recording achievement. This should arise naturally out of writing action plans, setting targets and monitoring these. At level 1, you may prefer to focus such action plans entirely on skills development or planning for a particular assignment. The aim is to help students to become systematic in thinking ahead, making plans, executing a plan and reflecting how the plan and their performance could have been improved.

Level 2 PDP activities

It is likely that the bulk of PDP activity will take place at level 2. At this level, tutors can usefully establish a base line. This could include:

- students identifying progress to date, based upon work undertaken at level 1 and outside of university study;
- updating personal goals and action plans;
- making specific links between academic skills and their application and adaptation to non-academic contexts.

Management skills

The four skills areas covered between Chapters 2 and 6 are loosely referred to here as 'management' skills as they enable students to:

- manage themselves;
- manage their working relationships;
- manage tasks, projects and problem-solving;

- manage their minds and their thinking.

These skills are mutually reinforcing, and together form the core of what is needed for the kinds of jobs graduates can expect to enter. A weakness in any one of these skills can impact upon the others. Together the four skills establish a solid basis for working in most situations with confidence, irrespective of the context. Students will be better prepared to address any problem from a strategic and creative standpoint, identify their own development needs, take responsibility, cope with pressure, and work with others to arrive at a solution.

Academic staff can assist students by creating opportunities to develop the four 'management' skills, using the materials in the book as well as subject-specific examples. The emphasis on each skill will vary depending on the kinds of careers usually associated with the programme and with what it is feasible to cover either through the programme or alongside it. 'People skills', for example, will mean different things depending on whether the skills most frequently needed within the discipline are primarily for working on an individual basis with clients, working in a research team, managing other people's work, or coping with the public. Tutors can guide students to the appropriate skills within the chapter and use naturally occurring situations to evaluate, discuss and reflect upon relevant skills. However, it is worth noting that over 40 per cent of graduates enter professions that are not related to their subject discipline, and where 'management' skills are likely to be at a premium.

Career planning

In their penultimate year, which is usually level 2, students need to prepare more seriously for employment. Employers are now much less likely to offer intensive training after employment than was the case in the past. They prefer to take on graduates who already show relevant skills in areas they want. The skills required are especially those of self-management, working with others, and being able to 'hit the ground running' to solve problems, especially as part of a team. This means that students who lack experience of team working, employment culture, applied problem-solving or project work are likely to be at a disadvantage when they apply for jobs. Students need to be much more alert to career planning than was the case several years ago and need to be active in searching out opportunities to develop and apply skills.

The Careers Service is obviously the first port of call for guidance about career planning. As a personal tutor, you may identify those who have not yet seen a Careers Adviser and prompt a visit early in the penultimate year of study. Academic staff can also promote career planning by activities such as inviting alumni and professionals to talk to students about how they used subject skills in particular work situations. Assignments that focus on applying subject knowledge to work or 'real life' contexts can also encourage work-related reflection.

Experience

Students can be reluctant to take on extracurricular activities in case they affect their degree grades. It can be helpful if academic staff give guidance on this and encourage those who would benefit from broadening their experience to look for opportunities of gaining this. Some programmes have developed links with businesses, agencies, schools and community groups to generate work experience that enables students to explore themes or develop skills relevant to their programme. These can be used to produce assignments for formal assessment, and provide opportunities for students to gain feedback on their skills from people other than their tutor.

Recording achievement and attributes

It is not enough for students to have developed skills and gained experience, they also need to be able to talk about their experience, drawing out its relevance to different contexts. This is one reason for the emphasis on structured reflection. 'Transferable skills' and 'transferable experience' are not always readily recognised. It is helpful if academic staff make explicit the ways that skills developed within the programme could be transferred or adapted to the world of work.

In addition, employers are interested to know about personal qualities, how these have been acquired and demonstrated. They may be keen to see whether the student is aware of the relevance of their skills, qualities, experience and knowledge to the workplace, and how good they are at spotting and using opportunities. This means that 'recording achievement' is not simply about writing a list or even a curriculum vitae (CV). Some jobs do not accept CVs. Useful records are now more analytical, evaluative and reflective. The materials provided in Chapter 9, 'Recording Achievement', encourage students to draw out the significance of their achievements. This puts them in a better position to address competence-based job application processes.

Level 3 PDP activities

Projects and dissertations

PDP at level 3 is likely to consist of fine-tuning and updating work undertaken at level 2. Some universities are linking level 3 PDP to the dissertation. For example, students are encouraged to map the development of their project planning skills when they undertake their dissertation. Students are sometimes introduced to dissertation skills at level 2, such as through early project planning. Chapters 4 and 6 are likely to help in developing these skills. These would need to be supplemented by materials relating to the research methodologies used for different subjects.

Recording achievement

Although, ideally, students would have been recording achievement throughout their programme, records will need to be completed and updated during level 3. The key time for interviews is early in the final year, so record maintenance should be encouraged at the end of level 2 and the start of level 3.

Applying for jobs

The Careers Service will provide the main support for job applications. However, if you are aware that students are soon to attend an interview or have not visited the Careers

Service, you may wish to draw their attention to Chapter 8, 'Successful job applications'.

How are universities addressing progress files and PDP?

PDP is still a mutable entity. It will take shape over time as different disciplines and universities adapt it in ways that are meaningful for their own students. Across the country, a broad range of approaches is developing. Some universities are integrating PDP and career planning into the core curriculum; others have adapted the personal tutor system as the vehicle to carry PDP; yet others are investigating on-line delivery for some aspects of progress files. Some universities have integrated several or all of these approaches, along with other initiatives such as student volunteering, mentoring, and increased opportunities for work experience.

Feedback from academic staff approached by Palgrave Macmillan during 2002 reveals differing views about the potential of PDP. The majority of respondents felt that the most important aspect was in relation to graduate 'employability', emphasising the 'planning' aspect of PDP. However, other academic staff stressed the 'personal development' angle, arguing strongly in support of this new opportunity to develop students as rounded people, as creative individuals or as 'radical thinkers'. Subject disciplines are likely to develop their own emphases for PDP, identifying areas where aspects of students' personal development are likely to enhance academic performance and improve achievement of subject skills.

It is hoped that this book will assist busy university staff to deliver PDP – and help their students to achieve their ambitions.

Stella Cottrell

List of abbreviations

CEO	chief executive officer
CPD	continual professional development
CV	curriculum vitae
CVCP	Committee of Vice Chancellors and Principals
HE	Higher Education
IiP	Investors in People
PDP	personal development planning
PI	performance indicators
QAA	Quality Assurance Agency
SHAPE	Style, Habits, Attitudes, Preferences and Experience
SWOT	Strengths, Weaknesses, Opportunities, Threats

Acknowledgements

Acknowledgements and thanks are due to the many people who contributed to the development of activities and ideas presented in this book. In particular, very warm thanks are given to the reviewers, drawn from several universities, who made suggestions for improvements to the first draft. Their comments and guidance not only encouraged me to proceed with the book, but also added considerably to the final version of the text, making it more relevant to a wide range of higher education contexts.

Thanks are also due to the lecturers and professional support staff at the University of Luton for pioneering work in introducing personal development planning into the curriculum. Special thanks goes to Mark Atlay, Roger Woods and Valerie Shrimplin for their contribution to that work; to all the staff who pointed out that lecturers needed materials to work from, and to Dai John for his encouragement and support.

I should also like to thank everyone at Palgrave Macmillan who contributed to the production of the book and made it such a pleasant experience, and especially to Suzannah Burywood.

Finally I should like to thank my partner for countless good ideas, for such 'open-handed generosity', and for supplying me with endless cups of tea without my even asking.

Stella Cottrell
2003

Introduction

Think positively and masterfully with confidence and faith, and life becomes more secure, more fraught with activity, richer in achievement and experience.

Eddie Rickenbacker

What's it all for?

- What do you really want?
- Do you know what you can really aim for in life?
- What will trip you up?
- What can you do now to put yourself in charge of your own future?

More than just a degree

When students leave university, they usually have a good understanding of their subject discipline. This has been the focus of their lives for a number of years. Although this is good, it is only part of the story.

Being at university provides opportunities for you to mix with a wide range of people, to learn skills, to take part in new activities, to manage positions of responsibility, and to broaden your outlook. Most of these opportunities lie outside of the taught curriculum. Many programmes also include opportunities to develop skills, undertake work experience, and to engage in voluntary and community work. Students are being encouraged to adopt a broad-based approach to the university experience and to use their time and the university curriculum imaginatively.

university. That is to be expected. However, the planning that is needed to achieve success and reduce problems later needs to start from the beginning of the first year.

This book is designed to support you to:

- shape your own ambitions;
- identify the skills and qualities needed to achieve your goals;
- develop skills, qualities and attitudes that will help you to find a good job as a graduate;
- develop skills that will help you in your studies, in your career and in life more generally;
- make strong job applications;
- use your time at university effectively;
- manage the personal development agenda that is becoming an important part of university life.

Create your own horizon

It is up to you to plan ahead towards your dreams – and to have those dreams in the first place. Many students do not have a clear vision of their future when they first arrive at

Why was PDP introduced into universities?

The kinds of jobs that most graduates want to enter require a range of qualities and skills that take time, support and good planning to develop. These include people skills, problem-solving, project work and self-management. Such skills cannot be suddenly acquired in isolation or at the last minute. In the past, many graduates felt disappointed that they had not been better prepared for when they left university. It has now been recognised that students need structured opportunities to think about, and plan towards, their future.

In 1997, a major report by Dearing recommended that students receive structured opportunities to become:

● more aware of themselves;
● more aware of how to learn;
● more aware of how to improve personal performance;
● better able to cope with the transition to their chosen careers.

As a result, universities are now required to introduce progress files for all undergraduates.

What are progress files?

Progress files consist of three aspects.

1. Personal Development Planning process (PDP)

The Quality Assurance Agency for Higher Education describes personal development planning as:

> Structured and supported processes to develop the capacity of individuals to reflect upon their learning and achievement, and to plan for their own personal education and career development.   (QAA, 2000)

This is the most important aspect of the Progress File initiative. The PDP process is something that has to be lived, thought about, discussed and experimented with over several years.

2. Personal records of learning and achievement

These can contain details of personal goals, plans, reviews and achievements. They are a source of material for you to draw upon to monitor your own progress and to prepare job applications.

3. A formal transcript provided by the institution

The formal transcript will be provided by the university, usually in addition to a degree certificate. It records more information about your learning and achievement than the traditional degree certificate.

As a student in a British university, you can expect to see some or all of these elements introduced before 2005, and to experience all three elements after 2005–6.

PDP – why bother?

Benefits of PDP to academic performance

When undertaken in supported and structured ways, PDP gives you a much deeper under-standing of the learning process and your own learning. You develop the ability to evaluate your own performance, rather than being reliant upon the views of others. Instead of being locked into a routine learning cycle, you enter into an upwards learning spiral. PDP puts you in charge.

The advantages of taking a personal development approach to your learning are:

✓ a clearer focus to your learning;
✓ more control over your personal motivation and the ability to direct this to achieve your goals;
✓ developing essential skills in self-management;
✓ greater independence and confidence about yourself as a learner, through gaining a better understanding of how you learn and how to improve your performance;
✓ more enjoyment and less stress from your learning as you become consciously skilled;
✓ more awareness of how to apply your learning to new problems and contexts;
✓ reflective, strategic, analytical and creative thinking skills that strengthen academic performance.

The personal planning approach presented in this book will have a positive effect upon your academic work, especially when combined with the development of study skills. Study skills for university-level study form a separate but related area. These are covered in a companion volume, *The Study Skills Handbook* (1999, 2003).

Benefits of PDP to professional life

✓ Gaining strategies for improving personal performance;
✓ gaining a much better sense of the kind of life and work you want;
✓ developing confidence in the choices you make;
✓ developing confidence in the skills, qualities and attributes you bring to the career of your choice;
✓ being in a better position to compete for jobs;
✓ being better able to discuss your skills and competences with employers;
✓ developing the positive attitudes, creative thinking, and problem-solving approaches associated with successful professional life.

Continuous professional development is expected within many professions. It is now quite usual for employers to ask candidates at job interviews about the steps they have taken to identify and address their own development needs.

Benefits of PDP to personal life

✓ Gaining a better understanding of yourself and how you 'tick';
✓ being in a better position to make appropriate choices to meet your own aspirations;
✓ gaining a better sense of yourself as an individual;
✓ greater awareness of your needs and how to meet these;
✓ greater awareness of the unique contribution you can make;
✓ developing a positive, forward-looking approach;
✓ developing skills such as reflection, strategic thinking, self-direction and self-evaluation, useful in most life contexts.

Activity

● Browse through the benefits listed in the three lists above. Which of these are most important to you?
● Choose between three and five of these and jot down in your own words what these mean for you.

Opportunities for PDP at university

Each university offers a different set of opportunities for personal and professional development. These may include:

Opportunities through the curriculum

- PDP as a core subject or as optional modules;
- career-planning modules;
- credit for work experience;
- credit for voluntary work or mentoring;
- skills development built into the curriculum;
- electives or subsidiary subjects that enable you to broaden your perspective by learning about something outside of your main subject.

Opportunities provided through programme staff and support services

- personal tutors: interviews or tutorial sessions on an individual or small group basis;

- academic guidance: specialist advisers who give advice on academic choices;
- careers advisory services: these offer a range of individual, paper and on-line resources;
- job-shops and information about work opportunities;
- learning development units: support for academic or language skills;
- voluntary work experience;
- skills programmes offered by the student union or a central department;
- employer-led skills sessions;
- chances to meet with employers.

Other opportunities

Universities offer a selection of other opportunities, some with training and certification:

- entrepreneurship prizes or awards;
- positions of responsibility such as student representative for the programme, posts within the student union or for student clubs;
- contributing to a student magazine or radio;

Jamila's efforts at personal development knew no bounds.

- mentoring other students;
- mentoring or coaching children in local schools;
- setting up your own club or support group;
- taking part in activities in the local community;
- pursuing a new interest;
- projects for employers;
- various graduate schemes with employers.

Activity

Look through the three lists above. Jot down any of these opportunities that appeal. Check whether these are available at your university.

Improving learning and performance

Learning and performance

Learning is an integral part of the process of improving performance. Learning is what we do from before birth: it is how we arrived at a point where we could sit or walk or talk, or identify objects or use tools or cook an egg. However, few of us have been taught how to learn or to think. Indeed, we have usually developed habits and beliefs that make learning more difficult than it needs to be.

The way we learn best is likely to change throughout our lifetime. It will vary depending on the activity, our circumstances, the time-scale and resources, or the people around us. As we change, the way we approach our learning also needs to change. The methods appropriate for school, for example, are not always suitable for university-level study.

In this book, you will be given tools which help you to explore the conditions that affect your own learning and influence your current levels of achievement. You can then apply this knowledge to improve your performance in most contexts.

Lifelong learning and the workplace

Many employers now expect employees to understand their own performance, and to know how to adapt to meet times of increased workload, stressful situations or conditions of change. Employees are expected to respond well to change. Although some employers offer training, it is more typical for employers to expect graduates to arrive ready to manage both their own performance and the performance of other people. Time devoted to understanding the influences upon your own performance is, therefore, very well spent.

Whereas education used to end at 18 or 21, it is now recognised that formal and informal learning will be needed throughout life: hence the term 'lifelong learning'. Successful employees are expected to show personal commitment to their continual professional development (CPD), actively seeking out information, training and events that will keep their skills and knowledge up-to-date. Knowing how to learn, and how you learn best, will be invaluable skills to carry into such work environments.

Do I need Personal Development Planning?

Self-evaluation

For each of the following statements, rate your responses as outlined below.
Note that *strongly agree* carries no score.

Rating: *0 = strongly agree   1 = agree   2 = sort of agree   3 = disagree   4 = strongly disagree*

Rating

1.	I am certain that I can keep myself motivated towards achieving my degree for the next few years	0	1	2	3	4
2.	I am very clear what my goals are for the next seven years	0	1	2	3	4
3.	I am confident that I have planned sufficiently to enable me to achieve my goals	0	1	2	3	4
4.	I am very clear how my degree fits into my life plans	0	1	2	3	4
5.	I am clear which skills employers are looking for	0	1	2	3	4
6.	I am confident I have the skills employers are looking for	0	1	2	3	4
7.	I am very clear about the importance of reflective activity to professional life	0	1	2	3	4
8.	I am confident that I am able to undertake structured reflection without guidelines	0	1	2	3	4
9.	I am confident that I can develop an effective strategy to meet most circumstances	0	1	2	3	4
10.	I am confident that I can set well-formed targets	0	1	2	3	4
11.	I have a clear understanding of how to evaluate my own performance	0	1	2	3	4
12.	I am confident that I know how to improve my performance in most circumstances	0	1	2	3	4
13.	I know how to apply my expertise in one area to a very different field	0	1	2	3	4
14.	I am confident that I can see myself as others see me	0	1	2	3	4
15.	I am confident that I have effective listening skills	0	1	2	3	4
16.	I am an assertive person	0	1	2	3	4
17.	I am a good 'self-starter'	0	1	2	3	4
18.	I am aware of the best roles for me to fill for team work	0	1	2	3	4
19.	I am confident at problem-solving	0	1	2	3	4
20.	I am confident that I know how to make best use of my mind	0	1	2	3	4
21.	I am confident that I will take a creative approach to most problems	0	1	2	3	4
22.	I am confident about making competence-based applications for jobs	0	1	2	3	4
23.	I am always very clear about which skills I am developing	0	1	2	3	4
24.	I can see clearly how my skills apply to a wide range of other situations	0	1	2	3	4
25.	I know where my own 'developmental edge' lies	0	1	2	3	4

Add up your score out of 100.   **Total score** _____

Although this is only a rough guide, you now have a personal development 'needs' score. If this is more than zero then you would benefit from some personal development. The higher your score, the more likely it is that you need to undertake personal development. Even if you do not need any personal development today, this is likely to change within a few months or even weeks, as your circumstances change.

What are my PDP priorities?

- Identify in column A which aspects of personal development are important to you at present. Give a rating between 5 and 0, giving 5 for *very important* and 0 for *not important at all*.
- In column B, consider how essential it is that you develop this aspect soon. Give a rating between 5 and 0, giving 5 for *very essential* and 0 for *not essential at all*.
- By adding scores in columns A and B, you will gain an idea of where your priorities lie (column C).

Aspects I want to develop further I want to . . .	A How important is this to me? *Rate from 0 to 5*	B How essential to develop it now? *Rate from 0 to 5*	C Priority score *Add scores for columns A and B*	See chapter
1. Clarify my vision and goals for my life				1 and 10
2. Clarify my values				1 and 10
3. Identify a source of inspiration				1
4. Clarify what 'success' means to me				1
5. Clarify what I want to achieve from university				1
6. Strengthen my motivation				1
7. Understand myself better				1, 2, 3 and 10
8. Understand what reflection is about				7
9. Identify ways of approaching reflection				7.
10. Evaluate my learning goals				7
11. Develop a reflective journal				7 and wherever you see 📖
12. Write about my personal development planning				7 and 9
13. Develop a strategy for improving performance				3 and 4
14. Develop a strategy to address problems				4

Aspects I want to develop further I want to . . .	A How important is this to me? Rate from 0 to 5	B How essential to develop it now? Rate from 0 to 5	C Priority score Add scores for columns A and B	See chapter
15. Make sense of my life story				2
16. Understand the effect of my personal choices				2
17. Gain a sense of my strengths and areas for improvement				2, 9 and 10
18. Make better use of my own expertise				2 and 9
19. Know more about my learning styles and preferences				2
20. Identify personal qualities				2 and 9
21. Know how to make a SWOT analysis				3
22. Improve my time management				3
23. Develop more constructive attitudes to achieve my goals				3
24. Develop my self-confidence				3
25. Understand more about emotional intelligence				3
26. Manage change and uncertainty more effectively				3
27. Understand what prevents me from achieving my potential				2, 3 and 6
28. Complete tasks more effectively				4
29. Improve my problem-solving skills				4
30. Know how to set effective targets				4
31. Be better at getting down to tasks				4
32. Become a good 'self-starter'				4

Aspects I want to develop further I want to . . .	A How important is this to me? *Rate from 0 to 5*	B How essential to develop it now? *Rate from 0 to 5*	C Priority score *Add scores for columns A and B*	See chapter
33. Develop project management skills				4
34. Identify my 'competitiveness' in task management				4
35. Develop better rapport with others				5
36. Develop my listening skills				5
37. Develop team-work skills				5
38. Set up a support group (or action sets)				5
39. Be better at giving and receiving criticism				5
40. Be more assertive				5
41. Deal well with difficult people				5
42. Develop negotiating skills				5
43. Develop leadership skills				5
44. Develop creative thinking skills				6
45. Understand more about the brain and how to use it				6
46. Develop skills in applying for jobs				8 and 9
47. Make use of personal records when applying for jobs				8 and 9
48. Develop my personal records				8 and 9

Development priorities
- Look back over the priorities table above.
- Identify the three aspects that you gave the highest scores. If there are more than three with the same score, select three.
- Write the three priorities in words that are meaningful to you.
- If you are ready to start on these, you may find it helpful to use the Action plan on p. 102.

The approach taken by this book

Personal Development Planning

This book emphasises the idea of PDP as a structured reflective process which gives individuals greater insight into their own development. The book provides:

- opportunities to explore what is valuable to your own personal, professional and academic development;
- activities to help achieve personal goals;
- different methods of structured reflection;
- resource materials to support the processes of reflection, planning, recording and evaluation;
- information about what employers are looking for;
- guidance in developing the skills associated with success;
- support in making effective job applications.

A solution-focused approach

The book takes a solution-focused approach. This approach is characterised by a belief that people are usually capable of arriving at their own solutions, even if this requires some guidance and support. People usually have far more knowledge and expertise than they believe. Guided reflection can encourage people to consider the same issue from many perspectives, allowing different insights and personal solutions to emerge.

The book also provides practical strategies and guidance for addressing problems and managing tasks, in both the short and long term. It provides the tools to assist you in arriving at the best solutions.

The contents of the book

Your success

Chapter 1 takes as its starting place the notion that all students want to experience success. Most make sacrifices to put themselves through college or university and expect a better future as a result. However, many students are very vague about how to plan for a future they really want. This chapter helps you consider questions such as:

- What does success mean to you?
- What motivates you?
- What are your ambitions, goals, values?
- Who or what inspires you?
- Which goals are you likely to achieve?
- What kind of life do you want to find yourself living 10 or 20 years from now – and what would be your worst nightmare?

You can travel a long way if you have a good idea of who you are and what you really want.

Focus on you

Chapter 2 encourages you to look in detail at you – and what helps you to achieve. Use Chapter 2 to:

- explore your learning strategies, habits, attitudes, preferences and experiences;
- identify the optimum means of improving your own personal performance;
- identify your own areas of expertise and use these to solve problems in new contexts.

Taking charge

Success begins with knowing and managing the self. Whilst the first two chapters focus on knowing yourself, Chapter 3 looks at successful 'self-management'. Check whether you could increase your personal success by improving:

- your emotional self-management;
- your attitudinal responses;
- your understanding of your own life story;
- your internal narratives;
- your time management;
- your 'emotional intelligence';
- how you manage change, confusion and uncertainty.

Managing solutions

Good problem-solving strategies will enable you to take on almost any task and will greatly increase personal confidence when you enter new situations. Use Chapter 4 to:

- organise time and tasks effectively;
- learn basic problem-solving strategies;
- select and apply problem-solving strategies to more complex tasks and problems;

- develop planning skills, such as identifying priorities, setting targets and finding good solutions;
- learn skills useful to project management;
- gain familiarity with concepts such as performance indicators and benchmarking.

The chapter invites you to audit your personal 'competitiveness'.

People skills

How good are your 'people skills'? Good people skills mean that teams work better, and that individuals gain the consideration and support that they need. People skills create more effective and manageable work environments, which is why employers place such a high value upon them. Use Chapter 5 to consider ways of developing your people skills whilst still at university. The chapter addresses such issues as:

- developing rapport;
- listening skills;
- team work;
- assertiveness and negotiation skills;
- leadership;
- giving and receiving constructive criticism.

Creative thinking

Creativity isn't simply for artists. The most elusive aspect of problem-solving and task completion is in the 'spark of creativity' that brings the right idea to mind at the right time. Chapter 6, 'Thinking Outside the Box' looks at ways of building confidence in your individual creativity. Use Chapter 6 to:

- develop confidence in your creative abilities;
- harness a basic knowledge of how the mind works in order to improve your thinking skills;
- try out a range of activities to develop creative thinking skills.

Reflection

Many professions now want 'reflective practitioners'. Lecturers may require you to 'reflect upon your performance'. But what is 'reflection'? How do you go about it? How do you write about it? As you work through the book, you will find many opportunities for structured reflection. Chapter 7 outlines

different methods for structured reflection. You are unlikely to need all of these so browse through the chapter and select methods that suit you and your programme. Your tutors may direct you to certain kinds of reflection. The chapter also gives guidance on the structured reflection required for marked assignments.

Just the job

Surveys of students show that their main goals in entering university are associated with finding a graduate job or improving their work prospects. The skills developed throughout the book are those associated with graduate careers. Chapter 8 focuses on the processes of applying for jobs. It looks at such issues as:

- what employers are looking for;
- choosing a job that suits you;
- using the PDP process to plan towards a career;
- making successful job applications;
- preparing for interviews.

The chapter aims to equip you to make good choices and strong applications for the jobs that interest you most.

Personal records

Chapter 9 provides a range of pro formas for recording your skills, personal qualities, experience, education and training. There are structured opportunities to reflect upon what you have learnt from different experiences. A series of resource sheets are also provided (pp. 257–91) to record essential information about a range of key competences. When completed, these records will provide an invaluable resource when applying for jobs and preparing for interviews.

Raise your game

Finally, Chapter 10 draws together and updates the learning and reflection undertaken throughout the book. If you have followed through on the skills development introduced throughout the book, you will have noticed changes in yourself. The chapter encourages you to recognise personal change and to review your values and goals. It encourages you to build connections between different skills, areas of expertise and personal development so that you can more easily transfer your skills from one context to another. You are invited to assess your readiness for taking higher risks and are challenged to identify your own 'working edge' for future development.

Using this book

Experiment

The strategies and skills developed in this book can be applied to a wide range of circumstances.

● Combine and adapt these to suit you;
● experiment with applying the different strategies to your studies, job and personal life;
● find out what works best for you.

Keep a journal

This book uses self-evaluation questionnaires, question-based activities and other activities in order to structure personal reflection. Spaces have been provided in the text where brief and immediate responses are most useful. For more detailed responses, find a light notebook that is easy to carry around. The book refers to this as a 'reflective journal', but you may prefer to call it a diary, log, notebook, ideas book or whatever suits you.

Thandi struggled under the weight of an active imagination, carefully noted on a daily basis.

Use the journal to develop ideas, capture your insights and inspiration, work through your thoughts, identify helpful and unhelpful responses to events, and so forth. If you find something is puzzling you, write out your thoughts or feelings. You will probably find that giving the matter attention in this way helps to clarify what is going on. Put time aside regularly to make entries in your journal, and to look back over previous entries. Note the changes in your thinking and personal development.

This symbol reminds you to note down your reflections in your journal when working through the book.

Be selective

Each chapter contains a wide range of activities. Don't feel you have to undertake them all. Different activities will appeal to individual students. Select those that look most relevant to you. On another occasion, you may prefer a different set of activities. However, do notice whether you resist undertaking particular activities. The personal development activities we resist are often those that we need the most.

Read out of sequence

Browse through the book and identify chapters and sections that are relevant to you. It is not important to read the chapters in the order presented, except for parts of the last chapter.

● Use Chapter 8 if you are applying for a job now.
● If you feel uninspired about life or study, try Chapters 1 or 6.
● If you are struggling with an assignment, look at Chapters 4 and 6, and use these to supplement a study skills book.
● If you are finding it difficult to deal with a particular person at present, use Chapter 5.
● If you feel your life or study needs better management, look at Chapters 2, 3 or 4.

However, most aspects of personal development, improving performance and problem-solving are closely interlinked. What you need for any particular situation may be spread across several chapters.

Keep records

Chapter 9 and the competence sheets in the Appendix provide a wide range of resources to record your experiences. Look at this early on rather than waiting until you have read the other chapters.

Students may photocopy blank sheets such as self-evaluation questionnaires and planners for their personal use. This will enable you to compare your responses to the same activity at different times and to monitor your own development.

Do it again!

Return to the activities at different times throughout your studies, and even beyond. The basic concepts covered in this book are applicable to many circumstances. When you enter a new situation, you will interpret the material differently.

Enjoy the book and good luck with all your ambitions!

Chapter 1

The vision: what is success?

To accomplish great things, we must dream as well as act.

Anatole France

Learning outcomes

This chapter offers opportunities to:

- reflect upon the nature of success
- understand the importance of personal vision to successful outcomes
- formulate a personal definition of success
- gain insight into personal motivation, inspiration and values, and see how these can assist with current study
- formulate a personal vision of the future and consider how current study contributes towards that vision.

Introduction

Choosing to go to university is a major life decision. Students invest a great deal in attending university: time, money, effort, personal risk. For some people, a great deal of courage is involved, as they leave a familiar world of friends and family. Some travel a long way to study, opening up to new places and ways of living as well as studying. Others decide to study subjects they have already found difficult, determined to be successful nonetheless. Many are worried that they will not succeed at their studies or will let down their family.

Such a decision is not made lightly. It is accompanied by high hopes. Everybody both gives up something but also aims to gain something. There is a goal, a plan, an ambition, an expectation of success. Working towards 'success' is highly motivating: it is what keeps people going, what makes it possible to make the sacrifices that university demands.

For some people, success at university is a goal in its own right. A degree is carried with you

through life. Greater knowledge of the subject discipline is the goal for other people: they value knowledge for its own sake. Mature students, for example, sometimes take time away from work for a number of years simply to gain a deeper appreciation of a subject that fascinates them.

However, most students want more than knowledge and a degree. Although they may enjoy the subject they have chosen, they regard a degree as a necessary passport to other kinds of success: to a career, to financial security, to highly paid work, to specialist skills needed for particular work, to more interesting work, to management-level work. For some, a degree is regarded as the first small step towards high office, big-business success or to fame.

Success means different things to different people. The kinds of success characterised by David Beckham, Indira Gandhi, Nelson Mandela, Whoopi Goldberg or the people next door are all very different – but not necessarily any less valuable to the people concerned. The following activities aim to sharpen your thinking about your own ambitions and concepts of success.

Defining success

There are many ways of looking at 'success'. Some people value success in terms of objective material criteria (how much money, how high a position in a company, how big a house).

However, successful athletes may win world records, even fame, without earning a great deal of money. Successful artists may measure their success by how true they are to their artistic endeavour. Other people judge success by the integrity they bought to a task: the confidence that they did their best in an honest way and can live with their consciences. It used to be a sign of success to still have your own teeth at an advanced age.

In other words, 'success' is a very subjective matter. It depends on what is meaningful to you and the people around you.

There is only one success – to be able to spend your life in your own way.

Christopher Morley

● What would it mean for you to 'live your life in your own way'? What would this involve?
● What, if anything, stops you from doing this?

Activity: A personal definition of success

Complete the sentence below. In doing so, consider what personal success would be in your own case. Don't worry if you find this much more difficult than you imagined. You will be asked to return to this statement later in the chapter, when you may wish to change or refine it.

For me, being successful means . . .

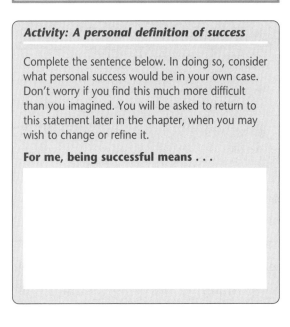

Activity: Personal ambitions

Sometimes we come up with different answers if we frame the question differently. This activity invites you to give some initial thought to your ambitions for different areas of your life. Later activities explore this in more detail.

My ambitions for my academic work are:

My ambitions for my professional life or career are:

My ambitions for my personal life are:

Personal influences

Some of the definitions of success that you use were probably adopted originally to please other people – or are those you have inherited, or picked up from peers and the media. This is not necessarily a bad thing: these may be influences that you respect or that matter to you. External influences can be very valuable and help us to form our sense of who we are.

However, sometimes, we live out ideas of success that we pick up from other people, without thinking through what they really mean for us. It can be easy to lose ourselves in the values and interests presented by others, especially if we are surrounded by these for much of the time. We can 'forget' that there may be alternatives that are better suited to our personal circumstances, character and beliefs.

As so much personal investment is likely to be involved in working towards your concept of success, it is worth considering how your own view of success has been influenced by others – and how far you can say 'This is really me'.

📖 *Reflection*   Personal influences

Who do you consider to be the greatest influence on your life? How far do your ideas of 'success' reflect the influences of that person or group?

● Look again at your responses to the above activities about success.
● What values and beliefs are associated with your responses?
● Are these influences still valuable to you or do you need to develop more independence?

Owning the influence

Your goals may have been strongly influenced by others but ultimately, when you decide to act upon them, you have made those goals your own. The important thing is to be clear that your action is a personal choice no matter who influenced it. This means recognising your own role in the action you take, rather than saying later, 'Well, I only did that because my parents/teacher/friend/children/boss, etc., wanted me to.'

Inspiration

Sometimes influences act as positive inspiration, moving us to achieve things we value. Many people have used a role model from their personal life, history or public life to inspire them.

📖 Reflection   Inspiring people

Look back to the list of successful people you jotted down in activity 1. Do any of these inspire you? If you answered 'No', think of at least one person who does inspire you. If you answered 'yes', which person from your list do you find most inspiring?

Consider the person that you selected as inspiring. What is it about them that most inspires you:

- What they achieved?
- Hurdles they overcame?
- Their level of skill or ability?
- Their personal qualities?
- Their effect on the lives of other people?
- Something very individual they bring to life?

In what way has that person already inspired you? In what other ways could you use that person as an inspiration towards achieving your goals?

Other sources of inspiration

Anything may be a source of inspiration. For some people, a piece of music, a rap, a poem, a painting, a postcard, a view of the sea, an episode in history, a personal event, can be inspiring. Alternatively, doing something for a cause or to bring about change can be a source of inspiration. Traditionally, artists and thinkers used to write, paint or compose for a 'muse' – a real or a mythological person to whom they dedicated their lives or their work.

Thinking about your sources of inspiration can be like receiving a burst of energy – it can boot you back into action when your spirits are flagging, and keep you focused. Inspiration, in other words, is another tool you can use to achieve your objectives.

📖 Reflection   Sources of personal inspiration

Consider:

- Apart from people, what has inspired you most in life? This could be a book, music, etc. What was it about this that inspired you?
- What things inspire you to feel good about life?
- What things inspire you to go beyond yourself, to do more than you thought you were capable of?
- What else would you consider to be a source of inspiration to you?

📖 Reflection   Inspiration to succeed on your course

- What, if anything, inspired you to come on this course or to return to study?
- What inspiration can you draw upon to increase your motivation to succeed?

Values

You will probably already have noticed that thinking about personal success raises questions about values, beliefs and ethics. It is not always easy to square our desires with our values and beliefs. It can also be hard to identify what we really value – sometimes this is not possible until we are faced with a life-or-death challenge. However, if we work against our values, we are likely to experience self-conflict, which can undermine our chances of success. The following activities aim to help you identify what things you hold important relative to other things.

Activity: The Zed box (1)

Imagine that you are given a 'smart' or magical box, known as the Zed box. If you open the Zed box, you may be given the thing that you want or value most in life. (The box cannot change the past.) You have five seconds to jot down the one thing you would most want the box to give you.

The thing I would want most is:

Activity: The Zed box (2)

However, as the Zed box is 'smart' and magical, it can read your most secret wishes. It may give you what you wish for in your deepest heart, even if this is something you are not aware that you do want. For example, you may think you want most to be a football champion but deep down want to be creative or helpful. The Zed box would know that. It would give you an opportunity to be of service to others rather than making you a football star. The choice the Zed box makes may come as a shock to you. You have one minute to jot down an answer to both of the following questions:

1. What would you most fear that the Zed box decided you really wanted?

2. What do you most fear the Zed box would take away from you, thinking it knew best?

You may have found this activity difficult if you have not spent time thinking about what you feel you *ought* to do with your life as well as what you *want* to do with your life. You may find it useful to reflect upon this over some time or on a long walk. Consider:

● What do I want to do with my life?
● What do I feel I ought to do with my life?
● What are the key characteristics of the lives of people who inspire me?

Layers of the onion

Knowing what we 'really' want is not easy. There are many layers to our 'wanting' and 'needing' and 'valuing', like skins on an onion. It is worth taking time to reflect on the things we value, asking why we value them, following each answer with 'And what is it about this that I value?' For example, do you value celebrity because you are excited by the lifestyle that it represents? What is it about that lifestyle that you value? Is it being in the public eye? In which case, how many other ways are there of being in the public eye? Is it about the money celebrities earn? If so, what other ways are there of earning that money? Is it because famous people seem to gain recognition? If so, are there other ways of gaining recognition that you would value as much or more? Is it really popularity that you are seeking? Keep going until you run out of questions.

Sometimes it is easier to aim for the surface of things (money, power, celebrity) rather than looking at what is creating a need for such things. Whether those things are good or bad in

their own right is a value judgement – and may depend on the circumstances. It is worth remembering that what we need in order to survive is usually very little. In your reflective journal, jot down your ideas on:

● What is at the 'core of the onion' for you? What is really driving you towards the things that you want?
● How far are your values being shaped by your wants and needs (for yourself, others or the world?)

Activity: Personal values 1

What I value most is . . .	Important to me (✓)			Important to me (✓)
1. A good car	☐	22.	Leadership and authority	☐
2. Challenge	☐	23.	Leaving something for posterity	☐
3. Contributing to society	☐	24.	Making a difference to the world	☐
4. Feeling I am in control of my life	☐	25.	Money	☐
5. Creativity	☐	26.	New experiences	☐
6. Fairness	☐	27.	Personal qualities such as kindness	☐
7. Fame and celebrity	☐	28.	Physical appearance	☐
8. Family and home life	☐	29.	Popularity	☐
9. Friendship	☐	30.	Good-quality possessions	☐
10. Having a good time	☐	31.	Power	☐
11. Health	☐	32.	Being needed	☐
12. Help received from others	☐	33.	Security	☐
13. Helping others	☐	34.	A feeling of self-worth	☐
14. Honesty	☐	35.	Social Life	☐
15. A big house	☐	36.	Solitude	☐
16. Independence	☐	37.	Spiritual life	☐
17. Influence	☐	38.	Sporting ability	☐
18. Integrity	☐	39.	Being wanted	☐
19. Intellectual abilities	☐	40.	Other things: (state what)	☐
20. A good job or career	☐			
21. Justice	☐			

Activity: Personal values 2

Select the ten items you value most and list these in order of importance, where 1 is the most important, 2 for the next in importance, and so on.

1.		6.	
2.		7.	
3.		8.	
4.		9.	
5.		10.	

Consider the top ten items that you valued. What themes can you identify? For example, do your choices suggest you place a high value on any of the following:

- personal qualities (character);
- control over something;
- people;
- material objects;
- power and influence;
- mind and body;
- personal recognition.

Are you comfortable with your responses or do you feel you 'ought to' value other things? If so, what does this response tell you about yourself?

Compliments

What three compliments do you most want to hear from other people?

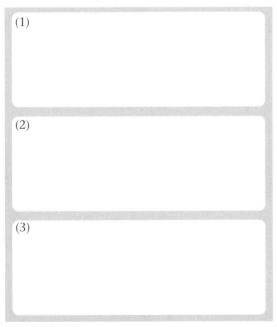

(1)

(2)

(3)

Vision

It helps to get to the top of a mountain if we have seen the pinnacle and know where we are headed.

This does not necessarily mean that we should have very clear life goals, with every detail planned out. Successful people seem to be characterised by not having very rigid life plans (Taylor and Humphrey, 2002).

However, it is important to have a vision of the general direction in which we are going, the kind of life we want to lead, and the levels of personal investment we want to make in different kinds of activity. It is this vision that keeps us going when the inevitable unexpected setbacks occur. Even if we are assembling a bookcase or doing a jigsaw puzzle, it helps to have the picture before us of what we want to achieve, so that we can see the end goal as a realistic possibility. A vision of what we want to achieve is even more important when we are undertaking a project that lasts for several years, such as working towards a degree or a career.

Ambitions

An obvious starting place is to clarify your current sense of what your ambitions might be. Some people have very clearly formed ambitions and even well-formed goals by the time they enter university. However, many students have given little thought to what they want after university. It is not necessary to have clearly defined goals, but it is useful to start clarifying personal ambitions, so that you can check both how important these really are to you – and how far you are working towards what matters to you.

The dream

Dream lofty dreams, and as you dream so shall you become. Your vision is the promise of what you shall at last unveil

John Ruskin

When we are young, we are often told to stop day-dreaming. However, many great inventors and scientists attribute success to the combination of their analytical work with the inspiration that came through dreams or day-dreams.

Activity: The dream

This activity is linked to the next activity.

First, undertake an activity that uses up any surplus energy and leaves you alert and awake. Taking a walk or doing housework is ideal, but any moderately strenuous activity will do. This will get the blood flowing to your brain (so you think better) but work off excess adrenalin (so you are open to being creative rather than defensive).

Then, find a comfortable seat where you will not be disturbed. Read the quotation by Ruskin (above) a few times and let your mind wander over what this means for you.

● What dreams have other people had for you (if any)?
● What are the dreams and ambitions of people you know well?
● How are your dreams different from those of people around you?

Your 'dream' does not have to be the same as anyone else's, and it does not need to be well defined. It may be something as simple as 'happiness'.

Clarifying the dream

To gain a clearer view of the 'dream', come back to the above activity and repeat it from the beginning once you have undertaken the 'Vision' exercise below.

You may find that the more analytical nature of the 'Vision' activity focuses the mind. Let go of particular details when you return to the 'Dream' activity.

Your mind will automatically play with the ideas you had and feed them back, either straight away or at some time in the future. However, as our relaxed brain likes to play with images and metaphors, it may return the ideas to you in a way that is hard to recognise at first.

Whatever images come to mind on this second occasion, however unexpected, hold them in mind for a few days, and see what emerges.

The long-term vision

For the activity on pp. 23–4, imagine yourself travelling forward into the future, to a time approximately 10 or 20 years from now. This activity is not about laying down a rigid plan for your future but, rather, is to help you form a sense of what general circumstances you would like to experience, as far as you can tell now. The aim is to gain a sense of the type of life you want, so that you can make the right kinds of choices to achieve it.

Activity: The Long-Term Vision

Ten years from now, I see myself . . .

Aspect	Write your own vision of this aspect below	How important is this aspect to me?
Living in which part of the world?		
Living in what kind of place (city, town, village, countryside, by the sea, etc.)?		
Considering the most important things in my life to be . . .		
Solitary? Or surrounded by people?		
Working with colleagues who are . . . artistic? intellectual? practical? down-to-earth? caring? active? thoughtful? kind?		
Working to stress levels which are . . . Pressurised? Reasonable? Very low level?		
Enjoying privacy? Public attention? Celebrity?		
Working 20, 30, 40, 50, 60, 80, 100 hours a week?		
Taking a lead? Being a good second in command? Happy to be part of a team? One of a large crowd?		
Wanting to 'get by' unnoticed? Gaining reasonable recognition for my work? Gaining the attention of management? Being top management? World-famous?		
Based mostly in an office? On the road? In the field?		
Working for myself? Working for a large company? Working for a small company?		
Doing work which is very varied? Very routine? Predictable?		

Ten years from now, I see myself . . .

Aspect	Write your own vision of this aspect below	How important is this aspect to me?
Likely to stay in the same job for years? Changing job occasionally?		
Living with a large/small/minimal family. With strong/weak/some family connections?		
Considering my work to be central/ important/not very important in my life?		
My contribution to my community or society will be through . . .		
My time outside work will be spent doing . . .		
My friends will be the kinds of people who . . .		
I will be the kind of person who . . .		
My main achievements in life are likely to be . . .		
Other important aspects of my vision of the future are . . .		
The main influences, inspirations and values on this vision of my future derive from . . .		

Look again at the third column, *How important is this aspect to me?* Consider what this tells you about the kind of lifestyle and career that you are likely to enjoy?

If you found it difficult to answer many of the questions above, this suggests that you are either very flexible or that you need to spend more time thinking through what sort of things you want to aim for. This will help you to make certain decisions about programme options, work experience, extracurricular activities and early job applications.

Return now to the 'Dream' activity and 'Clarifying the Dream' (on p. 22).

Using the vision and the dream

- In what ways can you make use of the 'Vision' or 'Dream' that emerged through these activities to motivate you further?
- In what ways do your current study and extracurricular activities contribute towards taking you towards your 'Vision'?

Goals

The long-term vision gives us a sense of how well we know ourselves and a goal at which we can aim. Some people are very good at 'deferring gratification': that is, at making personal sacrifices in order to achieve a goal many years down the line. They usually have a very clear vision of what they want to achieve.

However, it is not easy to 'defer gratification' unless there are lots of small successes along the route. It is difficult to put effort and energy into study, work, research or exercise if we do not have mini-goals towards which we are working. Success at these spurs us on to greater triumphs. If we are not successful, this can also be valuable, providing time to take stock and re-evaluate how important something really is to us.

Smaller goals enable us to experience success along the way and test us in the short term. For example, we can:

- perform in concerts whilst training to become a professional musician;
- put on exhibitions if we wish to be an artist;
- publish material if we want to be a writer;

Activity: What do I want to gain from my time at university?

On the table below, indicate with a (✓) if the item is something that you want to gain from your time at university. Put more than one tick if you feel this is very important. (✓✓✓)

Go through the items you ticked and rate them in order of importance (1 for the most important, 2 for the next in importance, and so on).

From my time at university I want to:	Important to me?	Order of importance	From my time at university I want to:	Important to me?	Order of importance
'Get the piece of paper' (the qualification)			Develop technical skills		
Achieve a good classification of degree			Develop a wide range of skills		
Gain a deeper understanding of my specialist subject			Work with a wider range of people		
Enhance my thinking ability			Develop problem-solving skills		
Broaden my mind			Develop people skills		
Stretch myself intellectually			Try out new things		
Know myself better			Develop a broader set of interests		
Learn to believe in my own abilities			Gain work or volunteering experience		
Gain the confidence to speak in public			Make friends		
Experience student life			Make contacts for my career		
Enhance my career opportunities			Take on positions of responsibility		
Be able to get a well-paid job			Other things:		

Activity: Short-term goals

Select the three items to which you gave the highest rating in the previous activity. Consider what short-term goals you can set in order to give you an initial taste of success. You may need several short-term goals for each item you select. These goals are 'milestones' along the road to success. Copy out this table and keep it where it will remind you to complete the goal. An alternative action plan can be found on p. 102.

Item	Short-term goals	When I will do this	How I will know I have achieved this
1	(a)		
	(b)		
	(c)		
2	(a)		
	(b)		
	(c)		
3	(a)		
	(b)		
	(c)		

- make a speech at a wedding if we are likely to work in the public eye;
- take on voluntary work if we are anxious about working after graduation.

Assessed coursework and exams offer the experience of 'being tested' and can develop a range of qualities that go with such 'testing'.

University offers many opportunities for developing a more rounded portfolio of experience and broadening horizons. It is difficult to over-estimate the number of ways that extracurricular activities can benefit you in later life. The activity on p. 25 encourages you to take stock of the ways that you could make best use of university life, depending on your circumstances and what is important to you.

Motivation

Success is associated with high levels of motivation. For this reason, it useful to be clear about what is likely to motivate you the most. Each of us is motivated by different things. Below are some techniques people use to keep themselves motivated.

Being realistic

Little is achieved without setbacks, effort and hard work and even moments when you feel like giving up. Although positive thinking is an asset, unrealistic thinking sets you up for failure as you will be unprepared to meet hurdles that are set in your way. Think through what setbacks you may face and make plans to deal with these. Take them in your stride as part of the natural process, rather than as disasters which mean you will fail.

Setting high expectations

Success is linked to high expectations. These may take the form of very specific things which you wish to achieve, or a more general vision or ambition. If you set low expectations, you will probably achieve very little. Once you set high expectations, you need to plan accordingly, making sure you create the right opportunities

for yourself. If your expectations are low, you are likely to be unprepared to make good sense of any opportunities that may arise.

Setting realistic milestones

The section above, on goals, refers to the importance of setting milestones so that you can chart your progress. The more challenging the overall goal, or the longer it takes to achieve, the more important it is to set yourself intermediate targets to check you are moving in the right direction.

Rewarding achievement

Promise yourself a reward for reaching your intermediate targets – something you would really appreciate but which is appropriate to the size of the task – and then make sure you really do take that reward when you reach the target. You can set rewards such as a break, a coffee, a special meal, a phone call to a friend, for small targets on a single day.

Harnessing support

If you feel it will be difficult to keep yourself on track, ask a friend or mentor to check at set, regular intervals that you are keeping to plan. You may work better if you set up a support group to encourage you to keep going. These can work best if you set clear targets and your support team is given a specific date on which to check whether targets have been met.

Recording success

It is easier to monitor and reward your successes if you keep a record. This can be useful for the task in hand and also in retrospect when you reflect back upon what you achieved. A record of past successes can be very motivating for future enterprises.

Hunting out the interest

It is much easier to succeed at a task if we find it engaging. We often react towards things we find difficult as if they were inherently boring.

However, we can make something appear interesting even if, at first, we do not think it is. For example, we can make it a personal challenge to complete the task, or set up challenging time targets for each stage. Perhaps paradoxically, if we find out more than we need to know about something, we are more likely to find it interesting: feeling we have expertise can increase our interest.

The important thing is to know what kinds of motivational spurs work for you

---

Activity: Sources of motivation

When the going gets tough, I am most likely to be motivated by . . .
(*tick all that apply to you*)

- [ ] my long-term vision
- [ ] lots of short-term goals
- [ ] my values
- [ ] my belief system
- [ ] my will to win
- [ ] my sources of inspiration
- [ ] people who are close to me
- [ ] my desire to do good for others
- [ ] my desire to prove something
- [ ] achieving lots of small successes along the way
- [ ] giving myself a reward for completing a stage
- [ ] enjoyment of the activity
- [ ] finding something in the activity to interest me
- [ ] the support of other people
- [ ] having another person monitor my progress
- [ ] recording my successes

Personal investment: benefits, costs and commitments

Put your heart, mind, intellect and soul into even your smallest acts. This is the secret of success.
Swami Sivanandi

The person who makes a success of living is the one who sees his goal steadily and aims for it unswervingly. That is dedication.
Cecil B. DeMille

You can be an ordinary athlete by getting away with less than your best. But if you want to be great, you have to give it all you've got, your everything.
Duke P. Kahanamoku

📖 *Reflection*   Commitment

- Do you agree with the comments quoted above?
- What, if anything, are you willing to commit to in such dedicated ways?
- What phrase would you find more motivating than those in the quotations?

For some people, success is measured by the achievement of a goal at any cost. For others, success is measured by overall outcomes. For example, the building of a new dam may be regarded as a successful outcome (it got built). On the other hand, some may view the event as a limited success or even a failure (it was built but at too great a cost financially, or to local inhabitants, or to the environment).

What is success to one person (those who benefit from the dam) may be a loss to others. This is an extreme example, but it illustrates the point that each act is accompanied by benefits and loss. Each of us has to weigh up, for ourselves, what 'costs' we are willing to bear in order to achieve what kind of outcome. Often, we proceed without even considering the full picture – without considering what we already have, really want and value.

To be successful, it helps to know certain things about yourself, such as:

- What you really want – your vision of your life.
- Your assets: what you have to bring to the task in hand, that you are willing to 'invest' or risk. This includes such things as time, effort, money and material resources, friends and family, practice, endurance, willingness to wait or to try again.
- Your limits: what sacrifices you are really prepared to make and where your limits lie. In this respect, the cost to others, the opinion of others, your values and your sense of self may all be relevant.

Activity: Benefits and costs of achieving a personal goal

Identify one personal goal. Using the chart below, consider what a successful outcome would mean to you. What is it really worth to you? Write your responses in the boxes on the right.

Your goal	
Perceived personal benefits of achieving this goal?	
Perceived benefits to other people if the goal is achieved?	
What would you need to invest to achieve this goal (time, money, possible loss of self-confidence, friendship, etc.)?	
What level of such costs would you consider unacceptable?	
What costs would there be to others (time, money, possible loss of trust, etc.)?	
What level of such costs would you consider unacceptable?	
How would other people's opinion of you change if you were successful? Would this differ if the 'costs' were different?	
Would other people's opinion matter to you?	
How would your opinion of yourself change if you succeeded? Would this be different if the 'costs' were different?	
At what point would the benefits outweigh the costs for you? (or at which point would the costs outweigh the benefits?)	

Ingredients of success

Taylor and Humphrey (2002) analysed interviews made with 80 UK and US business leaders, drawn from a wide range of businesses. They identified the skills and attributes which were most common amongst those who had been successful at Chief Executive level. Although most (91 per cent) had a degree and relevant technical skills, success was not closely linked to a level or type of knowledge: few had business degrees or outstanding technical ability.

Characteristics of successful chief executives

The chief executive officers (CEOs) worked very long hours – but loved their work. They enjoyed leadership and recognition. They were noticeably self-confident, good at communicating with others and putting the interviewers at their ease. Their excellent inter-personal skills included patience and tolerance, often learned through the job itself. They were energetic, but took care to manage stress levels and stay healthy. Male directors were more sensitive to variations in their emotional lives and needed emotional stability in order to succeed. Most had a wide range of interests and part of what they brought to a company was 'breadth of vision developed from a wide range of experience'. Most of these are self-management and people skills rather than unusual abilities or technical skills.

Attributes associated with success

The surprising outcome of Taylor and Humphrey's survey was that the range of personal skills and qualities associated with success were ones that most people could nurture. The researchers wrote: 'Board directors are not a race apart . . . we found ourselves in the presence of bright, hard-working people, but not creatures from another planet. They had a variety of IQs, expertise, and backgrounds. In other words, directors are just like the rest of us – and their positions are up for grabs.' The skills and attitudes of successful people can be developed by others. The main skills valued by the CEOs included:

- self-knowledge and self-awareness – this was especially noticeable, and the directors were frank about their skills and their short-comings;
- inter-personal skills, especially the ability to work with, and lead, teams;
- problem-solving ability, using creative approaches and positive attitudes;
- a desire to win, especially on behalf of the company or team;
- a willingness to work very long hours and to 'do what it takes';
- emotional intelligence, especially when relating to others;
- the ability to manage stress and to take care of their health;
- a love of change;
- confidence;
- a broad range of personal interests;
- readiness to seize opportunities rather than making rigid personal plans.

Many of these skills have long been recognised as essential in the caring professions. It may be surprising to find this list associated with business success. However, similar skills are likely to be required across a very wide range of professions. Increasingly, employers expect employees to be able to work in project teams on complex problems. This requires many of the other skills listed: good people skills, emotional intelligence, self-knowledge, a positive attitude, a willingness to put the team's interests first. Negative-thinking, selfish people who lack confidence, who get easily stressed, fear change or who are not aware of how they are coping with their own emotions, are unlikely to be a great asset to a team.

However, the qualities needed for different kinds of success may vary from the above list. Academic success requires a willingness to refine analytical thinking skills. Successful relationships may require a willingness not to work very long hours outside of the home, but are still likely to require a willingness to 'do what it takes' to achieve a successful outcome for the relationship. High levels of success in any field tend to require long hours, hard work, practice, and a willingness to keep going towards achieving the goal even when you do not feel like it, or when you are tired or want to give up. There are few areas of life where an individual is unlikely to benefit from the characteristics associated with chief executives, as listed above.

Where are you now? Self-evaluation of personal qualities associated with success

On the chart below, identify whether each of the personal qualities associated with success are ones that you already possess, wish to develop or are not relevant. The final column of the activity indicates where in the book you can find out more about this skill or aspect.

Skills and qualities needed to achieve your goals

It is worth comparing the list of the attributes associated with successful outcomes at chief executive level with the attributes you regard as necessary to achieving your goals and ambitions. You may find that your personal goals call for a very particular set of skills and qualities. However, it is important to think through all the kinds of situations and problems that you may have to address in order to achieve your goals. What qualities would help you in those circumstances.

Activity: Self-evaluation of personal qualities associated with success

	Good	Wish to improve	Not relevant to me	See chapter
Self-knowledge and self-awareness	☐	☐	☐	1 and 2
Problem-solving ability	☐	☐	☐	4 and 6
A creative approach	☐	☐	☐	6
Positive attitude	☐	☐	☐	3
People skills	☐	☐	☐	5
Team-working	☐	☐	☐	5
Leadership	☐	☐	☐	5
Negotiating skills	☐	☐	☐	5
A desire to succeed	☐	☐	☐	1
A willingness to 'do what it takes'	☐	☐	☐	3 and 4
Emotional intelligence	☐	☐	☐	3 and 5
The ability to manage personal stress	☐	☐	☐	3
The ability to cope with and/or promote change	☐	☐	☐	3
Self-confidence	☐	☐	☐	3 and 5
A broad range of personal interests	☐	☐	☐	1
Self-knowledge (reflection, self-analysis)	☐	☐	☐	1 and 2
Risk management	☐	☐	☐	4
Ability to cope with uncertainty	☐	☐	☐	3

Activity: Attributes needed to achieve a particular goal

The goal or ambition analysed here is:

To achieve this goal or ambition, the following attributes will probably be needed:

Attribute	Highly relevant	May be relevant	Not relevant	Don't know
Self-knowledge and self-awareness	☐	☐	☐	☐
Problem-solving ability	☐	☐	☐	☐
A creative approach	☐	☐	☐	☐
Positive attitude	☐	☐	☐	☐
People skills	☐	☐	☐	☐
Team-working	☐	☐	☐	☐
Leadership	☐	☐	☐	☐
Negotiating skills	☐	☐	☐	☐
A desire to succeed	☐	☐	☐	☐
A willingness to 'do what it takes'	☐	☐	☐	☐
Emotional intelligence	☐	☐	☐	☐
The ability to manage personal stress	☐	☐	☐	☐
The ability to cope with and/or promote change	☐	☐	☐	☐
Self-confidence	☐	☐	☐	☐
A broad range of personal interests	☐	☐	☐	☐
Good health	☐	☐	☐	☐
Self-knowledge (reflection, self-analysis)	☐	☐	☐	☐
Risk management	☐	☐	☐	☐
Ability to cope with uncertainty	☐	☐	☐	☐

Other skills needed to achieve this goal or ambition:
1.

2.

3.

Personal qualities needed to achieve this goal or ambition:
1.

2.

3.

Any other attributes needed to achieve this goal or ambition:
1.

2.

3.

Is there a good skills 'match'?

At this point, it is useful to compare the attributes that you identified as necessary for achieving a successful outcome of your goal (p. 32) with the attributes you ascribed yourself in the activity on p. 31. Is there a good match? If not, which skills and qualities will require further development? What will you do to develop these?

If you added further skills, goals and attributes to your list, which of these would benefit from being further developed whilst at university? What will you do to develop these?

Breadth of vision and experience

📖 *Reflection*   Extending experience

In your reflective journal, jot some thoughts on the following questions.

- In what ways do you already have a breadth of experience drawn from different contexts?
- In relation to your current goals and career aspirations, what opportunities are open to you for extending your breadth of experience? Consider, for example, work experience, travel, taking on a position of responsibility, joining a student society, community or voluntary work, sporting activity, mentoring schemes, etc.
- What opportunities are offered through the curriculum for designing a personal programme that extends your range of skills and experience?

In the section on successful CEOs above, Taylor and Humphrey (2002) identified 'breadth of vision developed from a wide range of experience' as an important characteristic of successful people. It is easy to see why this would be the case. Experience gained from many different settings brings you into contact with a more diverse range of people. This provides opportunities for learning about people, developing inter-personal skills and networking. Each context provides knowledge, skills, opportunities to develop personal qualities, as well as new perspectives and information.

Congruence

Congruence refers to consistency in our thoughts, actions, behaviours and beliefs. It is about all our energies flowing in the same direction. It takes less effort to achieve goals if there is a high level of congruence between the different factors that influence, inspire and support those goals. If you are struggling to see the way towards success, it is worth checking whether there is a high level of congruence (or a 'good fit') amongst the following:

- your vision;
- your motivation;
- the 'influences' you value;
- your sources of inspiration;
- your short-term goals, targets or milestones;
- your values and beliefs;
- the attitudes of the people around you;
- your means and resources;
- your current situation.

In particular, it is worth checking that your 'vision' is still relevant to you. New experiences can change your vision, either reinforcing it, modifying it, or making it irrelevant. If you have 'vision inertia' or 'goal inertia', you continue to work towards a vision which may seem appealing but, in reality, no longer inspires or motivates you. This is especially true if your values change in the light of your experience.

Activity: Does it all add up? Checking for congruence

Are your vision, ambitions, values and inspiration in alignment? Where might there be sources of internal conflict that could be undermining your efforts? On the chart below, jot down a response to the questions, using the space boxes.

Goal (e.g. what I want to achieve from my time at university)?

What is my vision of success in relation to this goal? What would success look like?	
How does this goal fit into a bigger 'vision' for my life and my longer-term ambitions?	
What motivates me to pursue this goal – what do I want to gain from achieving this goal?	
What has influenced me, perhaps over many years, in forming this goal?	
What inspiration can I call upon to help me achieve this goal?	
What are my short-term goals? How do these support my main goal?	
How does this goal fit with my beliefs and values?	
How do the attitudes of people around me support me in working towards my current goal?	
What resources do I have to support me towards my current goal?	
What else in my current situation supports or undermines me in working towards my goals?	
Conclusions	

Opportunities

Forks in the road

If you know what you want, either generally or in fine detail, are you taking and making opportunities that advance your aims? Are you somebody who looks for the opportunities in whatever comes your way or are you more likely to wait, hoping for the perfect moment to arrive? In every moment of the day, we make decisions that create a 'fork' in the path of our life. By acting one way or another, or by not acting at all, we make a choice to move in one direction and not another.

For example, at 15, Paulette decided to leave her part-time job at a local shop and work part-time in an electronics company. At the time, she just wanted a 'change of scene' that allowed her more flexible hours. From that decision, she met new people, overcame a fear of 'technical things', and travelled to China. These changes affected her choice of subject and friends at university.

Example   Paulette's decision

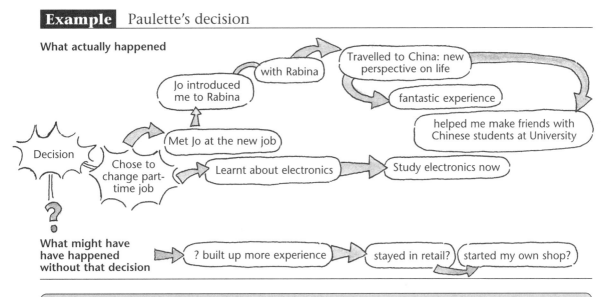

What actually happened

- Jo introduced me to Rabina
- with Rabina
- Travelled to China: new perspective on life
- fantastic experience
- helped me make friends with Chinese students at University
- Met Jo at the new job
- Decision
- Chose to change part-time job
- Learnt about electronics
- Study electronics now

What might have have happened without that decision

- ? built up more experience
- stayed in retail?
- started my own shop?

Activity: The road walked

Take approximately three minutes to brainstorm choices you have made that you look back on and feel good about. This may include significant friendships, work, how you dealt with difficult situations, saying or doing the right thing, presents given, offers that you accepted or turned down, your dedication to your learning or to resolving a problem, the benefits from learning a new skill, acts of kindness, and good decisions you made. Focus on your role – what you did or did not do – rather than on what others did to you.

Read through your list and select your best use of an opportunity. It may appear small, such as giving somebody a card and seeing their face light up, or it may have been a major event such as saving a life.

Take a piece of paper and write the example at the top of the paper, as in the example above under 'Paulette's decision'. Spend a few minutes brainstorming all the ways the one occasion had an impact upon other aspects of your life. What opportunities, large or small, arose for you from seizing that first opportunity?

The following activities aim to tease out your recognition of opportunities that have and do present themselves to you – and the way you respond to these.

What if I . . .

What ideas emerge if you keep asking yourself the same question and have to give a different answer each time? The obvious answers tend to get used up after a while so that you draw more on your imagination to find new responses. Some of your responses may become rather far-fetched. However, sometimes, unexpected and useful responses can emerge. For the following activity, let your mind range broadly. Avoid censoring your thoughts, even if an idea seems unlikely. Be imaginative. See what emerges.

When engaged upon a long-term project such as gaining a degree or developing a career path, it is important to stay focused on what you want to achieve. This may be very different for each person. It is for you to decide what 'success' means for you, what you would consider to be an 'achievement', and what you want to gain from the experience. For some, the 'travelling' is as important as arriving: the journey may be the goal.

This chapter has encouraged you to think deeply about the things that influence, motivate, inspire and guide you. Long-term goals require commitment. It is unlikely that everything will run smoothly over a period of several years. It is quite common to feel like giving up when things feel difficult. However, you can take action to increase your motivation and keep going until the path gets easier. Motivation is the key to success. It provides the energy and the drive. That is why the goal or 'vision' must contain something within it that really motivates you.

It is also important that you are true to what you really believe. The obvious reasons for personal goals are not always those that motivate us the most. This chapter has encouraged you to look more deeply below the surface and examine what is really important to you. You should now have a much clearer idea of your visions for your life, your goals, your targets, values, motivation and skills.

Further reading

Covey, S. R. (1999) *The Seven Habits of Highly Effective People: Restoring the Character Ethic* (London: Simon and Schuster).

Taylor, R. and Humphrey, J. (2002) *Fast Track to the Top: Skills for Career Success* (London: Kogan Page).

Chapter 2

Start with yourself

Self-knowledge is the beginning of self-improvement.

Spanish proverb

Learning outcomes

This chapter gives you the opportunity to:

- consider the impact of your own life story upon your current performance
- make use of your experience
- identify the impact of different factors upon personal achievement
- better manage set-backs and difficulties
- identify conditions that most suit your learning and performance
- identify areas of personal expertise that can be applied to new tasks and areas of learning.

Introduction

This chapter focuses on your life story so far and the narratives that influence your life. It encourages you to investigate how your personal history, attitudes and beliefs about your ability can affect your achievement. It also enables you to examine what conditions are most likely to lead to improvements in your performance and increase your chances of success.

We all have preferences in the way we work and study. One of countless things may have a profound effect upon your performance. Dunn and Dunn, for example, isolated 21 different factors that affect learning. They found that some people are very sensitive to particular conditions, and can under-achieve if the wrong conditions are in place. This differs from one person to another. Sometimes, changing something as small as your seating position, the light, or the way you study can have a dramatic effect (Dunn et al.,1995). This chapter enables you to study your learning preferences in detail.

If you undertake the activities in this chapter with a particular goal in mind, you are likely to gain a different set of responses. If you find that a particular type of task is proving especially difficult for you, it is worth going through some of these activities again but with only that task in mind. You may uncover unexpected hindrances that you can then address.

The true story

Each time you review your life story, you will find the story changes. The events may be the same, but different things will become significant to you. If you keep a copy of your story and look back at it in later years, you will be surprised at how your attitudes, responses and the themes of your story change over time.

Life metaphor

Some people regard life as a journey. Other people treat their life as a mission or a battle. Others think of it as a burden, a gift, an adventure, a lesson to be learnt, a trial, a walk in the dark. These are their personal metaphors for their own lives. Maybe you catch yourself using expressions such as: 'My life is like a disaster waiting to happen . . .' or 'it's all part of life's rich tapestry . . .'. If so, that may indicate your metaphor for your life.

Activity: Life metaphor

- What is your personal metaphor for your life? You may need to give some thought to this. If you do not think there is *one* metaphor, just select one for this exercise.
- How does it help you to make sense of your life?
- In what ways does this metaphor offer a constructive way of approaching your life?

Activity: Significant events

Take five minutes to brainstorm a list all the events that you regard as important in your life. For example, you could include some or all of the following:

- 'first times' you did something;
- successes;
- crises;
- challenges;
- opportunities that arose;
- important events in the family that were significant in their impact upon you;
- happy memories;
- school memories;
- holidays that were important in some way;
- friendships and relationships;
- work experience;
- other things.

Your list will be used for further activities in this chapter.

Activity: The links

On your chart (see the 'Life Chart' activity below):

- Indicate the date of each event (an approximate date will suffice.)
- Indicate whether you think each event was positive, negative or neutral for you. You could write this on the chart, or use different colours to circle positive and negative events, or draw a large plus sign (+), a minus sign (-), and an equal sign (=) for 'neutral'.
- Write a brief commentary next to each item. Give a few details about the event, what you felt about it at the time, what you feel about it now.
- Mark in, with arrows or other signs, the connections between any events. Do you think that any events influenced others that occurred?
- Comment on any events you think are still significant for your life and performance today.

Activity: Narrative

You have gathered and ordered the raw material of your story. Now all you have to do is to write it out – or tell your story aloud and record it. It is tempting to cut out this step – but it is important to let the narrative develop. This will not only draw together your thinking, it will develop it. Make sure you include how you feel about the things that happened. Be honest. This copy is just for you – so you don't need to worry about writing a good introduction or about your writing style. Just tell it.

Once you have completed your story, leave it for a few days and then go on to the next activity.

Activity: Life chart

Bearing your life metaphor in mind, organise your list of events from the previous activity roughly into the order they happened to you in life – as far as you can remember. You can do this simply by tearing the list up and rearranging it on a flat surface. Glue pieces down, with space to write around them. If you did the activity on the computer, simply cut and paste on screen leaving lots of space, and print out the new 'list'. You can draw the events on a large sheet of paper, if you prefer, so that you can 'see' the events in the order they occurred. The visual aspect is important. You may have photographs that you could stick onto the chart, or you could use symbols to represent an occasion (toothbrush for first visit to a dentist, ice-cream for a holiday, etc.).

Now go to 'The Links' activity above.

Activity: The writer's voice

Read through your 'narrative' or 'story'.
On a piece of paper, or in your reflective journal, jot down your responses to the following questions:

- Have you included more positive or more negative experiences and events for your story? Could you have included more positive items?
- What themes or patterns emerge from the story? For example, is the story full of adventures? Disasters? Effort and reward? Disappointment? Seizing and creating opportunities? Meeting and losing people? Full of blame? Is it a sad or a happy story?
- What do the themes in your narratives tell you about the way you view your life? Is this the most helpful view you can take? Does it help you to achieve what you want to achieve? Does it further the 'vision' you identified in Chapter 1?

Activity: The opportunities

All experiences offer opportunities to learn and to develop strengths – no matter how wonderful or awful they may have been. Look again at your story.

- What things happened to you that would not be typical of everyone's experience? Think of a way that these can provide an advantage (such as the people you can communicate with as a result, the realism they bring to your life, the different range of skills they developed, etc.).
- What were the most difficult things you had to face? What lessons did you learn from those events that can be of advantage to you either in completing your programme or in achieving the 'vision' you identified in Chapter 1.
- How easy or difficult are you finding it to regard experiences and challenges as 'opportunities'?

Activity: The Hero

Consider the main character of the story you have written. What part do you play in the plot? Are you active, taking the lead, and making things happen? Or do you sit back and wait for things to happen? Or are you the passive recipient of other people's actions? Or do you sound like you are forever in battle, holding your ground? Have you written the story so that you sound mainly like:

- the Warrior stepping into battle and fighting your own or others' wars;
- the Saint who is always doing good and in the right;
- the Martyr who has to suffer so others can benefit;
- the Adventurer, looking for new experiences;
- the Scapegoat, carrying the blame for others?
- the Ruler, commanding the troops or the people;
- the Sportsperson, playing a good game;
- the Villain, who has been lucky not to be caught;
- the Wounded Soldier, who needs time to heal;
- the Conjuror, pulling unexpected rabbits out of hats;
- a different kind of hero?

Reflect on your 'hero':

- How far does the hero you have chosen represent the way you really think, feel and act?
- What does this choice tell you about the way you view your life or yourself as an active agent in your own story?

Activity: Create a personal caricature

A good caricaturist helps us to recognise a character by exaggerating particular features. These are often the characteristics that make the person more individual and distinctive.

Self-recognition is notoriously difficult to achieve. It is a life-long activity. However, we can use the caricature technique to help us see ourselves more accurately. We gain a great deal from such insights – although self-recognition can involve a certain degree of embarrassment or discomfort.

If you feel you are up to the task, jot down your life story again. This time, exaggerate behaviours and speech that you think are typical of you. If you are not sure about what these might be, ask a friend.

Exaggerate your story:

Consider your personal traits and mannerisms. Put these into the story, again exaggerating them. For example, if the first draft of your story had lots of references to 'beginning' and 'starting' activities, exaggerate this theme, adding in lots more things that you 'started' (real or imaginary). If your story contained many references to meeting people, then flood this next draft with more meetings, making up lots of meetings that never happened. If you travelled a great deal, triple or quadruple the amount of travel when you come to this story, making up journeys you never had. If you think a particular comment is very typical of you, write it out seven times each time you introduce it:

I was just about to do that.
I was just about to do that.
I was just about to do that.
I was just about to do that.
I was just about to do that.
I was just about to do that.
I was just about to do that.

Next:

- Read through your story, aloud. What does it tell you about yourself?
- Are you comfortable with your personal caricature – or do you want to change it?
- Were you able to laugh at your caricature?
- What do you think is the value of using this 'caricature' or 'exaggeration' technique for personal development?

Activity: The choices

Look over your life chart and mark in all the occasions when you made a choice that had an impact upon your life.

- What kinds of choices have you faced?
- What opportunities have you taken or not taken?
- What were the effects of the choices you made?

Exercise your imagination. Visualise at least two different scenarios of how your life might be different now if you had made different choices. If possible, select one choice that you consider to have been a bad choice, and one that is a good choice.

- Were all the outcomes of the good decision ones that you welcome?
- In what ways did the 'bad choice' provide a different set of opportunities for you that could be regarded as positive in some respect? The examples on p. 36 ('The road unwalked') may serve as a useful prompt.

- What do you think characterises a 'good choice'?

Activity: The next chapter

Having completed your story, thought about it and exaggerated it, consider now:

- Are you still happy with the life metaphor you chose? If not, create a new metaphor for your life now.
- How do you want the plot of your life to unravel over the next 10–20 years? What kind of story do you want to be telling in 20 years' time?
- What kind of role would you like to play in this next chapter of your life?
- What would need to change in your life now in order for you to play that role successfully?

The top forty

Look again at either your life chart or the 'True Story' you wrote. Count how many examples of personal success you included. Was there at least one for every year of your life? If not, write in some more.

Our personal success is rather like breathing: we rarely notice it on an everyday basis. However, it is hard to ignore 'hiccups' – the things that go wrong. Beaver (1998) argues that we do not spend enough time thinking of all the things we *can* do and spend too long focusing on what we cannot do. She encourages us to draw up very long lists of what we can do – and much shorter ones of things we cannot.

Activity: Top forty strong points

● Make a list of your strong points, successes, qualities, attitudes and attributes. List at least forty things. If that sounds like too many, you are underestimating yourself. Draw stars by the ten that you perform the best. Draw circles around the seven of which you are most proud.

1.	21.
2.	22.
3.	23.
4.	24.
5.	25.
6.	26.
7.	27.
8.	28.
9.	29.
10.	30.
11.	31.
12.	32.
13.	33.
14.	34.
15.	35.
16.	36.
17.	37.
18.	38.
19.	39.
20.	40.

In your reflective journal, jot down your thoughts to the following questions.

- What is the ONE thing that you do best?
- What is it like to recognise these positive activities? How often do you stop to value them?
- Are these strengths appreciated by the people around you? If not, how do you account for this? Is it, for example, because you are embarrassed about showing your strengths? Do you surround yourself with people who do not appreciate you? If you want to gain realistic recognition for your attributes, it is up to you to make that happen. What could you do to change the situation?

Activity: Seven areas for improvement

List seven areas for improvement in your life.

1.
2.
3.
4.
5.
6.
7.

- What is it like to recognise these weak areas?
- What do you do to cope with them or to work around them on a day-to-day basis? Do you hide them, develop strategies, blame other people or find help and support?
- Who or what can help you to manage better in these areas? Do you have sufficient support to do this? If not, where can you gain it?

Expertise metaphor

When confronted with new tasks, people often say things such as:

- I don't know where to start.
- I can't cope with this.
- I am no good at things like this.
- I am not good enough for such tasks.

Sometimes, the gap between previous experience and the current task can make the task too difficult. Sufficient time and support may make it more achievable. However, we can take on challenges more easily if we can recognise, value and draw upon an area of personal expertise. This can happen even if the area of expertise seems to bear little relation to the task in hand.

Examples of expertise transfer

Victor and car maintenance

Victor's challenge was in producing academic writing. He had little writing experience because he entered university from a foundation programme that did not use formal written assignments. He was very reluctant to write and was convinced that he lacked the logical, sequential skills needed for continuous prose. On the other hand, Victor identified a strong interest and practical experience in car engines – which he used as his 'expertise metaphor'.

Victor brainstormed all the skills he used to understand and repair car engines. He went on to brainstorm all the skills needed to write an essay. He then looked at how repairing an engine uses similar skills to those needed for writing essays. For example, he analysed the ways car mechanics use skills in:

- finding out information (about the engine)
- sequencing the order of tasks
- planning time to meet deadlines
- weighing up options
- forming a theory about what is wrong
- testing out ideas (about how to fix it)
- selecting between options using the appropriate methods for the job
- prioritising tasks
- testing out results
- re-evaluating the work done
- reflecting on performance.

Once he had analysed his skills in detail, he drew parallels between car repair and the skills used for academic writing. Below is his own account of this process.

© Stella Cottrell (2003), *Skills for Success*, Palgrave Macmillan Ltd

Start with yourself 43

Victor – My Engine

When I first started university, I had not worked at the academic level required by university before. When I visited the learning development unit . . . [it was] suggested that I treat an essay like a car engine. When I broke the metaphor (analogy) down, this is what I came up with:

1. Fuel – this supplies the necessary stored kinetic energy to power the engine – research at the library, lectures, seminars.
2. Battery – this stores the electrical energy – research notes, essay outline.
3. Oil – this lets the engine run smoothly – spelling and grammar.
4. The alternator – supplies electrical energy necessary for the engine to run – the essay question, unit guide, using aims etc.
5. Engine ignition system – supplies the spark to ignite the fuel, and the sequence in which the cylinders fire. Paragraphs.
6. Introduction – where this essay is going.
7. Main body – critical discussion of main points.
8. Conclusion – insights gained and mileage from essay, i.e.: 'What I have learned'.
9. Tool box – this is where the necessary tools are bought, borrowed or acquired and stored – dyslexia workshops, English workshops, Accelerated learning seminars, etc.

This can be broken down even more . . . When all the elements of the essay are integrated successfully then it should flow like a smoothly running engine.

Victor B.

This may not be how other people view an essay: the important point is that the metaphor worked for Victor. It released his potential not simply to write – but to write good essays. This was because the process of writing now made sense in terms of things he really knew about.

Roger and aircraft assembly

Roger consistently failed to produce written work. He wrote well but took a perfectionist approach. As his ideas evolved during the process of writing, he rewrote the whole of his work 'in neat', from the beginning. This meant he never reached the end. He assumed that each draft would be his final draft. In effect he was fine-tuning his work too early in the process.

Roger's area of expertise was assembling light aircraft that arrived from overseas as 'flatpacks'. He analysed the process of assembling a plane and how this might be similar to or different from assembling an essay. At this point, he recognised that if he tried to build a plane as he did an essay, it would also be impossible. If he tightened all the nuts and bolts, sanded it down, painted it and so forth on one part of the plane before going onto the next part, it would be impossible to manoeuvre the pieces into place. Nuts and bolts should be tightened, and the final touches added, only when the whole plane is in place. Roger could easily see the comparison with fine-tuning an essay too early.

Once he had drawn the initial parallel, Roger saw many comparisons between aircraft assembly and academic problems. He used his previous expertise to address these. When introduced to new information, for example, he felt he should play around with it, like pieces of the flat pack, observing roughly how to structure these. 'As you bring them closer together, you are working quite globally – with an eye on how it all fits together. Then you can home in and complete sections.' Similarly, he could see how good planning and structure was like 'glue' that held writing together: 'Keep an eye on how the sections will link. Aircraft glue is like a linking sentence, or a logical sequence that dovetails into the next item.'

Luzia and dressmaking

Luzia also had difficulties with essay writing. She had extremely low self-esteem and was very reluctant to identify any area of expertise. Finally, she settled on dress-making skills. She brainstormed all the processes that go into dress-making, and drew parallels between these and essay writing.

For example, she saw that both dressmaking and essay writing required a clear vision of the final product. She couldn't set about choosing a pattern or buying materials until she had a sense of what she was trying to achieve. She compared this to interpreting the assignment title and having a strong argument: 'Your vision is your interest in it – without which you just wouldn't get it done.'

Similarly, both newly made clothes and essays need structure. Before she began to make a new item, she would decide whether it was to have a collar, cuffs or pleats and use this to guide her choice of pattern and material. For Luzia, laying out a pattern was like drawing up an essay plan:

'the pieces of a dressmaking pattern have to be laid out in a precise way so that the cloth falls properly'. Similarly, in a well-planned essay, all the pieces of the argument fall logically into place.

She made further comparisons between tacking a dress together before the final sewing and writing drafts before a final write-up. Trying a dress on to check for 'final flaws' was compared to proofreading. For Luzia, the most important element of dressmaking was having 'equal seams'. She compared this to treating different schools of thought equally when writing an essay: 'you must ask the same questions of each'. The dressmaking analogy enabled Luzia to make sense of essay writing, calling upon her own expertise.

Make it 'make sense'

Just as Donaldson (1978) showed that young children are capable of performing tasks well above their supposed developmental level if the task is presented in a way that 'makes sense' to them, so Victor, Roger and Luzia were able to demonstrate that this is also true of adult expertise. They were able to use their own areas of relative expertise to address tasks that they had previously considered too difficult for them. They used extended metaphors – or an analogical thinking process – to accomplish this. If they can do this, so can anybody else.

It is very common for students to resist the idea that they are an 'expert' in anything. The first task, therefore, is to identify an area of expertise. This won't make you 'arrogant', as some people fear. Rather, it will provide you with a useful problem-solving tool. There will be one, or several, things you:

● perform with relative ease;
● can complete without supervision;
● feel comfortable doing – and may even enjoy;
● have several different stages or aspects to them.

Learning history

Our early learning experiences are amongst the most profound influences upon our attainment and current levels of performance. They shape our approaches to learning itself. They affect our belief in ourselves and our ability to see possibilities or opportunities for improving our performance.

Common responses

Below is a list of common responses to the activity above. The list is typical of that put together by very different groups of people within educational contexts. Check your list against it. You can add items to your own list if you think they are true of your experience.

My best learning experiences were when . . . ✓

Nature of the task

- [ ] I felt the task set was interesting, worthwhile or of value to myself or others
- [ ] the learning was relevant to the real world or had practical uses
- [ ] the work was going to be seen and appreciated by somebody other than a teacher
- [ ] it was clear what was expected from me
- [ ] I could move around or there was movement built into the activities
- [ ] there was a creative aspect to the task
- [ ] there was personal choice in some aspects of the task.
- [ ] there was a 'teaser', mystery or puzzle to be solved

Feelings and emotions

☐ there was praise and appreciation which came across as genuine

☐ I was treated like I mattered or my opinions and ideas counted

With whom

☐ I could work with my friends

☐ we did small group work or worked in pairs

☐ we taught each other

The teacher

☐ the teacher was fair

☐ the teacher thought of interesting ways of introducing new material

☐ the teacher worked beside us and inspired rather than preached at us

Timing

☐ I had time to finish what I was doing without rushing

☐ I had time to take it in

☐ there were lots of breaks so I didn't feel overloaded

Mastery

☐ I felt I understood one thing before moving onto another

☐ the tasks set were manageable but challenging so that there was a sense of both competence and achievement

Assessment

☐ I felt the way it was marked was fair

☐ I felt I had a fair chance of handing in what was expected

☐ my hard work was recognised

☐ I knew I couldn't get away with not doing my best

Special features

☐ we went on field trips or visits

☐ we had guest speakers or celebrity visits

☐ we showed our work to parents or visitors

📖 Reflection

In your reflective journal, jot down responses to the following questions.

● Is the list you completed about your best learning experiences similar or very different to the general trend? If your list is considerably different from that given here, what reasons might there be for that?

● At school, you may have been dependent upon other people to create the right conditions for your learning. Which of the items on this list could you put in place for yourself now, to enhance your current learning experience as far as possible?

The impact of educational experience upon performance

📖 Reflection

In your reflective journal, jot down responses to the following questions.

● In what ways do you consider your educational experiences have had an impact upon your performance generally?

● What positive things did the educational experience give you that you carry through life (this may not be classroom learning)?

● Look again at the items you identified as beneficial to your learning in the activity 'Positive learning experiences' (p. 46). Which of these could you bring into other situations, such as work or personal life, in order to enhance your performance, enjoyment or sense of satisfaction there?

Learning from experience

Making use of setbacks

Chapter 1 focused on success and visions of success. However, successful people often claim that they learnt more from their failures than from their successes. Sometimes, they argue that they are 'better people' because of major failures. Apparent failure often brings us face to face with realities that we otherwise try to avoid. Disasters can make us stop and take stock.

However, it appears to be less common for people to reflect in depth upon smaller setbacks, identifying what they have learnt from such experiences. It is not untypical, for example, for students to throw lecturer feedback in the bin, unread, if they are not happy with the mark given. This is a loss of a valuable opportunity.

Setbacks seem to encourage 'denial' – a pretence that nothing went wrong. Instead, setbacks and difficulties contain the seeds of our future success: they hold the secret to 'what went wrong' and 'what could be done differently'.

📖 **Reflection**   The 'best failure'

In your reflective journal, jot down responses to at least five of the following questions:

● What, on the surface of it, was the best 'mistake' of your life?
● What happened? What was your role in the event?
● What characterised this event as a failure?
● What bad choices did you make?
● When did you first realise you had made a mistake? How did you find out?
● What lessons did you learn?
● What benefits resulted from learning those lessons?
● What opportunities arose out of this event?
● How did the event spur you to action that you might not otherwise have taken?
● What does this event tell you about the nature of success and failure?

Turn it to advantage

Many people ascribe their success, relative or actual, to the way they responded to bad news or to adversity. We can all make the decision to:

● use our experience as an excuse for not doing something;
● use our experience to 'prove' something;
● use our experience to keep going as before.

It is noticeable that the stories of many successful people include a critical experience when they were dismissed, belittled, ignored, suffered discrimination, or suffered a serious setback. Such experiences can be crushing to self-esteem. It can be extremely difficult to maintain a sense of self-worth or to believe in personal achievement if we are attacked when

we are most vulnerable, or about things which are central to who we are. However, paradoxically, dealing with such events, whether at the time or later in life, can become the driving force that leads to unexpected successes.

This is very noticeable amongst students who face extreme difficulties, often facing multiple challenges from disability, pain, bringing up children, managing debt, work requirements and so forth. Often, the aspect of a person's life which appears to be the greatest challenge is the one that spurs them to action. Such students often come through as successful in completing their degree and developing a good career, when those with fewer difficulties turn back at lesser hurdles. Typically, they learn to use the apparent disadvantage as an advantage.

For example, a person with a disability could use the disability as an excuse not to take part in an activity; however, it is common for students with disabilities to develop alternative ways of addressing a problem so that they can take part. In this way, they often gain a deeper understanding of what is involved, or learn new software, or make different contacts, any of which can pay off later in life.

Similarly, students who are also parents often find that they need to develop skills in identifying priorities, multi-tasking, negotiating support and hard bargaining in order to complete their degree – skills which can stand them in good stead in other contexts. Anybody can make use of difficulty in order to emerge stronger – but not everybody does.

📖 **Reflection**   Make setbacks work for you

In your reflective journal, consider:

● What are the potential setbacks that you are likely to face in achieving your current goals?
● What things might make it difficult for you to achieve these goals?
● What kinds of things might be preventing you from achieving the 'vision' you identified in Chapter 1?
● Consider how you can turn these setbacks 'on their heads', so that they become sources of strength, inventiveness, motivation or contact with others.
● Copy this and attach it where you are likely to see it on a regular basis.

Performance styles, habits and preferences

The following activities are designed to help you explore the impact of different conditions upon your personal performance. A high score in one area does not necessarily mean that you are a certain 'type' of learner or person; it suggests that you have habits, styles or preferences that may influence successful performance.

1. Structure

The following set of questions looks at how far you prefer to work in structured or unstructured ways. Rate each pair of statements only once, depending on how true they are of you. **Rating**: 3 for 'very true of me', 2 for 'true', 1 for 'sort of true', 0 for 'no strong preference'.

Less structure		**More structure**
1. I enjoy creative chaos	3 2 1 0 1 2 3	I enjoy being very organised
2. My desk/workspace is a mess	3 2 1 0 1 2 3	My desk is always neat
3. I like to personalise my workspace	3 2 1 0 1 2 3	I keep work surfaces very clear
4. I remember things in my head	3 2 1 0 1 2 3	I write lots of lists
5. I never use bookmarks	3 2 1 0 1 2 3	I always use bookmarks
6. I leave my papers out overnight	3 2 1 0 1 2 3	I tidy my papers away at night
7. I work whenever I find the time	3 2 1 0 1 2 3	I work to a strict routine
8. I study what interests me that day	3 2 1 0 1 2 3	I work to a strict timetable
9. I have a relaxed approach to time	3 2 1 0 1 2 3	I always meet deadlines
10. I write all over my own textbooks	3 2 1 0 1 2 3	I never write on books

Score for less structure _____   *Score for more structure* _____

Total score: [   ]

Interpreting your score

- **0–10** suggests you have no strong preferences for structured or unstructured approaches.
- **20–30** suggests you have very strong preferences about the way you study.
- A score of **20–30** for the 'Less structure' column suggests you have a strong preference for working or studying in your own way at your own time. This can be a very creative and independent way of working. It is worth considering whether a more organised and structured approach would help. Danger points to watch for are missing deadlines and not fulfilling the requirements for an assignment.
- A score of **20–30** for the 'More structure' column suggests you have a strong preference for working or studying in an organised and systematic way. This can be a very productive way of working, and you are likely to be someone who gets things done. It is worth considering whether more flexibility and openness to new ideas would benefit your performance. Danger points to watch for are over-rigid ways of thinking and working.
- Scores of **10–20** for either column suggest moderate over-dependence on your personal preferences. It may be useful to experiment with features of the opposite column.

2. External direction

The following set of questions looks at how far you prefer to work with or without external direction. Rate the statements below depending on how true they are of you. **Rating**: 3 for 'very true of me', 2 for 'true', 1 for 'sort of true', 0 for 'no strong preference'. You may choose only one response for each pair of statements.

	Less external direction								**More external direction**
	I prefer . . .								
1.	lectures to be unpredictable	3	2	1	0	1	2	3	to know what to expect in lectures
2.	a lecture just to unfold	3	2	1	0	1	2	3	an agenda at the beginning of lectures
3.	to develop my own projects	3	2	1	0	1	2	3	to be given set assignments
4.	to invent my own assignment titles	3	2	1	0	1	2	3	tutors to set assignment titles
5.	to explore topics for myself	3	2	1	0	1	2	3	tutors to give clear outlines
6.	to develop my own reading list	3	2	1	0	1	2	3	tutors to give the reading list
7.	to do things my own way	3	2	1	0	1	2	3	to be told exactly what I have to do
8.	to pick up how to use computer software as I go along	3	2	1	0	1	2	3	to go on a course to learn new software
9.	to just get on with study for myself	3	2	1	0	1	2	3	the lecturer to give an early overview of the subject
10.	to work out how to solve new problems	3	2	1	0	1	2	3	clear guidance on how to approach new problems

Score for less external direction _____   *Score for more external direction* _____

Total score: [ ]

Interpreting your score

- **0–10** suggests you have no strong preferences about external guidance.
- **20–30** suggests you have very strong preferences about the way you work or study.
- A score of **20–30** for the 'Less external direction' column suggests you have a strong preference for taking control over how you work. This can be very useful in developing as an independent, autonomous learner, capable of taking on new projects and setting targets for yourself. It is worth considering whether you need to be more open to ideas from others. Danger points to watch for are possible weaknesses in team working and not fulfilling the requirements for an assignment.
- A score of **20–30** for the 'More external direction' column suggests you are very open to direction and leadership from others. This can be very useful in assuring that you are going in the right direction, for using time economically and for team working. It is worth considering whether you need to start taking more control over your own learning and being more open to exploration and risk-taking. Danger points to watch for are reliance on others to do your thinking and planning, and underdeveloped personal independence and leadership.
- Scores of **10–20** for either column suggest moderate over-dependence on your personal preferences for study. It may be useful to experiment with features of the opposite column.

3. Working with others

The following set of questions looks at how far you prefer to work with or without other people. Rate the statements below depending on how true they are of you. **Rating**: 3 for 'very true of me', 2 for 'true', 1 for 'sort of true', 0 for 'no strong preference'. You may choose only one response for each pair of statements.

Preference for working with others				**Preference for working alone**
1.	I prefer group work	3 2 1 0 1 2 3		I prefer to work on my own
2.	In a library, I prefer to sit near others	3 2 1 0 1 2 3		In a library, I prefer to sit on my own
3.	I like to go through lecture notes with a friend	3 2 1 0 1 2 3		I prefer to keep my lecture notes private
4.	I value hearing other people's ideas	3 2 1 0 1 2 3		I prefer to develop my own ideas
5.	I enjoy the interaction in group work	3 2 1 0 1 2 3		I enjoy thinking through an idea in quiet reflection
6.	I learn more through discussion than reading	3 2 1 0 1 2 3		I learn more from reading than discussion
7.	Groups come up with more ideas	3 2 1 0 1 2 3		I come up with more ideas on my own
8.	For me, team working is really useful	3 2 1 0 1 2 3		For me, team-working is a waste of time
9.	I like to discuss assignments with others	3 2 1 0 1 2 3		I prefer working alone on assignments
10.	I would find a study support group helpful	3 2 1 0 1 2 3		I work best if left to myself

Score for working with others _____

Score for working alone _____

Total score: ☐

Interpreting your score

● **0–10** suggests you have no strong preferences about working with others

● **20–30** suggests you have very strong preferences about the way you work.

● A score of **20–30** for the 'working with others' column suggests a strong social preference when working or studying. This can be very useful for gaining a wide set of perspectives and ideas, for developing social skills, for team working and for developing mutual support. It is worth considering how far you would benefit from more time studying independently. Danger points are possible over-reliance on others and not developing your own ideas in an independent way.

● A score of **20–30** for the 'working alone' column suggests a strong preference for solitary working. This can be useful for avoiding distractions, for achieving goals, and developing independence. It is worth considering in more depth what can be gained from working with others and the skills that emerge from reconciling different sets of opinions and personalities. You may lose out by not gaining access to a wide set of perspectives, especially in real life or 'applied' settings. Danger points may be failure to appreciate the work of others and under-developed inter-personal skills.

● Scores of **10–20** for either column suggest moderate over-dependence on your personal preferences. It may be useful to experiment with features of the opposite column.

4. Physical factors

The following set of questions looks at how far physical factors may affect the way you work. Rate the statements below depending on how true they are of you. **Rating**: 3 for 'very true of me', 2 for 'true', 1 for 'sort of true', 0 for 'no strong preference'. You may choose only one response for each pair of statements.

	High stimulus								**Low stimulus**
1.	I need to work in a very bright room	3	2	1	0	1	2	3	I need to work in a very dim light
2.	I need music or TV in the background	3	2	1	0	1	2	3	I need absolute quiet to work
3.	I work well when there is a lot going on in the background	3	2	1	0	1	2	3	My attention is very easily distracted
4.	I always eat when I am studying	3	2	1	0	1	2	3	I can't think about food when I am studying
5.	I need to drink a lot when studying	3	2	1	0	1	2	3	I never drink whilst studying
6.	I work best when it is either very hot or cold	3	2	1	0	1	2	3	I prefer a moderate room temperature
7.	I tend to move about or fiddle with things	3	2	1	0	1	2	3	I am quite still when I settle down to work
8.	It helps me to think if I walk about	3	2	1	0	1	2	3	I can't think if I am moving about
9.	Doodling helps me to listen in meetings and lectures	3	2	1	0	1	2	3	I focus on listening and making notes in meetings and lectures
10.	I prefer to work on several things at once	3	2	1	0	1	2	3	I need to finish one thing before starting another

Score for high stimulus _____   *Score for low stimulus* _____

Total score: ☐

Interpreting your score

- **0–10** suggests you have a high tolerance for working in most conditions.
- Scores of **0–1** for any item suggests that you have a reasonable tolerance for working without that stimulus being present.
- Scores of **2** for any item suggests that your performance might be affected if that stimulus is not present.
- Scores of **3** for any item suggests your performance might be seriously affected if that stimulus is not present. You may need to think creatively about how you can make it possible to provide that stimulus for most study contexts (for example, if you are light sensitive, by using bright lamps to increase the lighting or by wearing hats or sunglasses to dim light.)
- A score of **20–30** for either column suggests a very strong overall preference for working with or without stimulus. Given this preference, it is possible that if these stimuli were not present when you were being taught in childhood, learning may have felt difficult for you. High scores may also indicate a high level of stress. It may be helpful to speak to a counsellor or adviser about this.

Experiment

It is worth experimenting with studying with different kinds of stimuli present or absent. Monitor how far these do affect your performance. For example, many people have been surprised at how far they follow a pattern set down when they were at school as if that were the only 'right' way to study or work when alone. You will find that you learn more easily if you find the stimulus combination that suits you best.

5. Global or serialist

The following set of questions looks at how far your learning responds to 'global or 'serialist' approaches. Sometimes these are equated with 'right brain' and 'left brain' thinking. Rate the statements below depending on how true they are of you. **Rating**: 3 for 'very true', 2 for 'true', 1 for 'sort of true', 0 for 'no strong preference'. You may choose only one response for each pair of statements.

Which of the statements in each pair is more true of you? How does this affect the way you study?

	Global styles			**Serialist styles**

When studying or working on a project, I prefer to . . .

1.	start off by gaining a broad overview	3 2 1 0 1 2 3	start off from interesting details
2.	have the whole subject mapped out in a diagram or description	3 2 1 0 1 2 3	find the logical sequence
3.	see or hear images and examples explained through things	3 2 1 0 1 2 3	have things laid out in a list
4.	use mind maps, 'picture' notes or a taped discussion	3 2 1 0 1 2 3	use headings and bullet points or a taped list of key points
5.	launch in at the deep end	3 2 1 0 1 2 3	plan things out carefully first
6.	use my intuition	3 2 1 0 1 2 3	adhere strictly to the facts
7.	use my imagination	3 2 1 0 1 2 3	reason things out
8.	search for connections between things	3 2 1 0 1 2 3	classify and categorise information
9.	search for similarities	3 2 1 0 1 2 3	search for differences
10.	draw things together	3 2 1 0 1 2 3	analyse the detail

Score for global styles _____   *Score for serialist styles* _____

Total score: [   ]

Interpreting your score

- **0–10** suggests you have no strong preferences for global or serialist performance styles
- **20–30** suggests you have very strong preferences about the way you work or study.
- A score of **20–30** for the 'global style' column suggests you have a strong preference for taking a holistic approach to work or study. This can be very useful for synthesising information, and making creative links. It is worth considering whether you need to bring more order and system to your activities. Search for possible weaknesses in managing clarity, detail, order and sequence in your work or writing.
- A score of **20–30** for the 'serialist style' column suggests you take a logical, analytical approach to study. This can be a very useful in ensuring clarity and structure in your work. It is worth considering whether you need to create opportunities for developing your imagination and intuition. It may help to experiment with searching out links and connections between ideas. Possible weaknesses may be in drawing together your ideas into a strong whole and in making connections between what you are studying and the bigger picture.
- Scores of **10–20** for either column suggest moderate strengths for that style of working. It may be useful to experiment with features of the opposite column.

6. Method

When you have something completely new to learn, how do you set about learning it?
Tick the boxes that are true of you.

I find it easier to learn through . . .

☐ listening   ☐ reading
☐ personalising the material   ☐ asking questions
☐ watching others   ☐ adapting the task to suit myself
☐ picturing it in my head   ☐ writing it out
☐ writing about it   ☐ making a chart
☐ turning it into a picture   ☐ colour-coding it
☐ turning it into headings   ☐ talking it through with others
☐ categorising and labelling it   ☐ linking it to what I know already
☐ day-dreaming about it   ☐ describing or explaining it to others
☐ talking it onto tape   ☐ thinking about it whilst I do housework or similar tasks

● Which of the above methods are you not using at present that might be of use to you?
● Are there other methods you could use that you are not using currently?

7. Honey and Mumford learning styles

Honey and Mumford (1982, 1992) developed a questionnaire that divided people into four main types. A broad outline of their learning types is given below. Which of the following are generally true of you (there may be more than one)? Which is the most true?

☐ **'Activist' learning style**. I prefer to work in intuitive, flexible and spontaneous ways, generating ideas and trying out new things. I usually have a lot to say and contribute. I like to learn from experience, such as through problem-solving, group-work, workshops, discussion, or team work.

☐ **'Reflector' learning style**. I like to watch and reflect, gathering data and taking time to consider all options and alternatives before making a decision. Lectures, project work and working alone suit me.

☐ **'Theorist' learning style**. I like to learn by going through things thoroughly and logically, step by step, with clear guidelines, and to feel I have learnt solidly before I have to apply what I know. I prefer to learn from books, problem-solving and discussion.

☐ **'Pragmatist' learning style**. I like to learn by 'trying things out' to see if they work, just getting on with it, getting to the point. I like to be practical and realistic. I prefer to learn on work-based projects and practical applications.

● Do you think you might benefit from choosing certain types of study module or programme in order to ensure the teaching and assessment match your preferred learning type?
● Could you organise your study or your work to suit your learning type?
● Do you think it is helpful to see yourself as a 'type' of learner? How does this impact upon your performance in different circumstances? What might be the disadvantages of identifying too closely with one method or style of learning?

8. Visual, auditory and kinaesthetic learning styles

Rate each of the following statements, depending on how true you think it is of you, by drawing a ring round the number.

Rating: *4 = yes, this is very true of me,   3 = yes, it is true of me,   2 = sort of true/ don't know*
1 = hardly ever true   0 = not true of me at all

1.	When I'm reading, I picture the scene in my head	4	3	2	1	0
2.	I have a good memory for conversation	4	3	2	1	0
3.	I will remember something better if I have seen it written down	4	3	2	1	0
4.	I remember things best if I get up and move about	4	3	2	1	0
5.	I use my hands a lot when I'm speaking	4	3	2	1	0
6.	I like to picture what I am learning	4	3	2	1	0
7.	I remember phone numbers by the movement I make to dial to them	4	3	2	1	0
8.	I repeat things out loud or over and over in my head to remember them	4	3	2	1	0
9.	I doodle whilst I am listening	4	3	2	1	0
10.	I add up numbers out loud	4	3	2	1	0
11.	I can't add up unless I can see the numbers written down	4	3	2	1	0
12.	I'm good at remembering the words to songs	4	3	2	1	0
13.	I prefer to watch something being done before I try it myself	4	3	2	1	0
14.	I like to ask a lot of questions in class	4	3	2	1	0
15.	I find it easy to remember where I last saw something	4	3	2	1	0
16.	I write out words to see if the spelling feels right	4	3	2	1	0
17.	I have a good eye for colour	4	3	2	1	0
18.	I'm good at sport	4	3	2	1	0
19.	I am able to learn things off by heart quite easily	4	3	2	1	0
20.	I have a good ear for music	4	3	2	1	0
21.	I'm good at practical things	4	3	2	1	0
22.	If somebody gives me a set of instructions, I can remember them quite easily	4	3	2	1	0
23.	I tend to move around a lot on my chair when working	4	3	2	1	0
24.	I tend to fiddle and play about with my hands a lot	4	3	2	1	0
25.	I prefer to have instructions written down so I can see them	4	3	2	1	0
26.	I like to learn by doing	4	3	2	1	0
27.	I visualise a spelling to see if I have got it right	4	3	2	1	0
28.	I run a film in my head of what I have to learn	4	3	2	1	0
29.	I prefer to learn through discussion	4	3	2	1	0
30.	I like to hear exactly what I have to do	4	3	2	1	0
31.	I like to 'just try it out' rather than following instructions	4	3	2	1	0
32.	I like to learn by doing practical things	4	3	2	1	0
33.	I remember a phone number by the way it sounds	4	3	2	1	0
34.	I like to learn from slides and pictures	4	3	2	1	0
35.	I sing and hum a lot	4	3	2	1	0
36.	I like the tutor to use overheads and write on the board	4	3	2	1	0

Scoring

Each statement that you rated above indicates a preference for either a visual, auditory or kinaesthetic way of learning and performing.

● Visual learners find it easier to learn if information is presented so they can see it, and where they use their eyes or visual imagination to learn.
● Auditory learners learn best by hearing and using their ears.
● Kinaesthetic learners tend to learn best where there is a physical sensation, such as movement, touch or a feeling.

Write down your scores for each statement and then add up your totals.

Visual scores	*Auditory scores*	*Kinaesthetic scores*
Statement 1:	Statement 2:	Statement 4:
Statement 3:	Statement 8:	Statement 5:
Statement 6:	Statement 10:	Statement 7:
Statement 11:	Statement 12:	Statement 9:
Statement 13:	Statement 14:	Statement 16:
Statement 15:	Statement 19:	Statement 18:
Statement 17:	Statement 20:	Statement 21:
Statement 25:	Statement 22:	Statement 23:
Statement 27:	Statement 29:	Statement 24:
Statement 28:	Statement 30:	Statement 26:
Statement 34:	Statement 33:	Statement 31:
Statement 36:	Statement 35:	Statement 32:

Total

Interpreting your score

No strong preference: If your scores for all three areas are similar, then you may not have a strong sensory preference for learning. If your scores are high (40–48 for each area), then you use all of your senses well to assist your learning. If scores are low (between 0 and 24), you may need to use your senses more consciously to assist your learning and experiment more with your learning.

A strong preference: The more marked the preference for one sense, the more you may need to ensure that you find ways of making good use of it, in order to make learning easier. Consider how you could incorporate into your study all the items listed above for that sense. Be creative. You might also like to consider whether you would gain from using the other senses more.

Learning S.H.A.P.E.

SHAPE stands for **S**tyle, **H**abits, **A**ttitudes, **P**references and **E**xperience.

There is not general agreement on what is a style, what a habit, what a preference. However, there is growing acceptance that we each learn in different ways and that awareness of one's own learning can make a significant difference to how one learns. By going through the learning styles questionnaires above, you should have a much clearer picture of yourself as a learner. In your reflective journal, jot down your responses to some of the following questions.

Style?

Some people believe that learning styles are like personality traits – that they are part of you and that you cannot really change them. If that is the case, you have to adapt your learning to fit your own style.

● Which of the approaches that you identified on the learning styles, habits and preferences questionnaire and the visual, auditory and kinaesthetic learning styles questionnaire do you feel are really unchangeable?
● If you had ten words to describe your own learning style, how would you describe it?
● How could you change the way you study in order to ensure that you make the best use of your own learning style and study preferences?

Habit?

How much do you think the style or preferences you identified could be the result of past habits?

● Are you over-attached to habits and patterns of study behaviour that do not really help you as an adult learner?
● If so, what would happen if you changed those habits?
● What opportunities would there be for developing your learning?
● What risks might there be?

Attitude?

How far do you think your learning is affected by the attitudes and beliefs that you bring to your own learning? For example:

● What are your beliefs about why you do or do not learn?
● What are your beliefs about what makes a good student?
● Do you believe you can study very successfully?
● Do you ever underperform because you worry about being successful or about failing?

Preferences?

How far do you think that your study characteristics are the result of personal preferences? Would you be able to change these preferences if you wanted to?

Experience?

● Could your current learning preferences be the result of your previous learning experiences? For example, were there particular experiences at school that have influenced the approach you take to study now?
● Who or what had the greatest influence on your learning?

Life qualities

The following quotation refers to a number of qualities that one person, Gordon H. Taggart, wished to develop in his life.

> I wish I were honest enough to admit all my shortcomings:
> – brilliant enough to accept flattery without it making me arrogant;
> – tall enough to tower above deceit;
> – strong enough to reassure love;
> – brave enough to welcome criticism;
> – compassionate enough to understand human frailties;
> – wise enough to recognise my mistakes;
> – humble enough to appreciate greatness;
> – staunch enough to stand by my friends;
> – human enough to be thankful of my neighbour
>
> Gordon H. Taggart

Reflection   Life qualities

- Which of the qualities identified by Taggart do you most value?
- Which do you make a conscious effort to develop?
- Which three of these qualities would be of most relevance in achieving your goals or vision?
- If you were asked to add another line to the quotation, what would you add that is relevant to your own values?

Closing comments

This chapter has provided structured opportunities to reflect upon the way your experiences contribute to your learning and current abilities. It invited you to engage in a wide range of activities to explore personal experiences, choices, strengths and expertise.

When we write and explain our life story with integrity, it may seem as though there could only be one possible way to tell it and that we have been true to the 'facts'. However, if you work through activities that explore your experiences every few years, you are very likely to find that your responses change. The main events may remain similar, but the way you write about them, the details you choose to emphasise, the way you interpret them over time, will change as your experience and attitudes change.

It is because the narrative and its interpretation change over time that we can take our story at any one time and look to see what it tells us about our approach to life. Some people have very extreme sets of life experiences, yet when they tell their stories, they emphasise the unexpected benefits or the people they met or the characteristics they developed as a result. Another person may have less challenging experiences and yet respond as if one of these has the power to control their life for ever.

As adult learners, we can adapt conditions to suit our personal needs. We can find ways of making effective use of our physical senses in order to better absorb and remember information. We can give thought to the assumptions we make about our learning and the restrictions we place upon ourselves. Whilst we cannot control all the circumstances that affect us, we do have the power to shape our thinking so that we learn more from our experiences. We can choose to have more power over our minds and to take control over our learning and performance.

Further reading

Beaver, D. (1998) *NLP for Lazy Learning* (Shaftesbury, Dorset, and Boston, Mass.: Element).

Cottrell, Stella (2003) *The Study Skills Handbook*, 2nd edn (Basingstoke: Palgrave Macmillan).

Dunn, R., Griggs, S., Olson, J., Beasley, M. and Gorman, B. (1995) 'A meta-analytic validation of the Dunn and Dunn model of learning style preferences'. *The Journal of Educational Research*, **88** (6), 353–62.

Honey, P. and Mumford, A. (1982 and 1992) *The Manual of Learning Styles Questionnaire* (Maidenhead, Berks: Peter Honey Publications).

Lawrence, G. (1995) *People Types and Tiger Stripes*, 3rd edn (Gainesville, FL: Centre for Applications of Psychological Type).

Chapter 3

Successful self-management

To conquer others is strong; to conquer oneself is mighty.

Lao-Tzu

Learning outcomes

This chapter offers opportunities to:

● identify tools and resources for successful self-management
● understand the importance of constructive attitudes to success in any field
● evaluate and develop your emotional intelligence
● identify factors that prevent you from achieving excellence.

Introduction

Self-management encompasses a very broad range of skills, qualities, attitudes and experience. It can include some or all of the following:

● being able to analyse your situation, identifying strengths, weaknesses, opportunities and threats;
● identifying resources and sources of support;
● managing your time;
● adopting attitudes that support your aims;
● taking a solution-focused approach to managing problems;
● managing your own emotions;
● coping when in distress;
● managing change, uncertainty and confusion.

These are usually demanded of students whilst at university or in their first jobs, and are addressed in this chapter. There are associated skills and strategies covered in other chapters. For example:

● being a self-starter (Chapter 4);
● being able to motivate yourself to finish what you start (Chapter 4);

● taking steps to improve your own performance (all chapters);
● being assertive (Chapter 5).

Intra-personal skills

'*Intra*-personal' refers to your own inner world, in contrast to '*inter*-personal', which refers to how you relate to other people. Intra-personal skills help us to manage our feelings, responses and actions, so that we are able to function at our best. Some branches of psychology have long recognised the importance of our emotional well-being to our capacity to perform well. You may have noticed this on occasions such as exams, if anxiety or personal matters prevented you from concentrating or remembering.

The world of emotions

The 'intra-personal' world has the most profound effect upon our responses, our thinking, our behaviour, our views of ourselves, our feelings and our achievement. It touches upon what is closest to our hearts and being. It is, especially, the arena of the emotions. When we work with emotions, we can expect to feel emotional at times. Most of us can find this quite challenging, and so there is a temptation to shy away from developing intra-personal skills. If we try to avoid any issue where emotions may be involved, it can mean we do not get to the heart of the issue, and so do not achieve all we could. On the other hand, when we understand more about ourselves, know our own triggers, and develop our emotional intelligence, we are more able to manage every situation we enter.

This chapter forms a brief introduction to a very wide-ranging subject. It does not go into detail about sensitive subjects. However, our life histories are very different and it is to be expected that some activities may raise a range of emotions for some people. If you feel you need to talk something through as a result of any activities, it is worth noting that student counselling services were set up to deal with all kinds of matters, small issues as well as major ones. You do not need to be in a crisis to see them. Services are confidential and they may also be able to find support for you away from the university if you prefer.

Activity: Focus

For this chapter, identify a personal goal or a situation that you wish to think about more deeply, in order to give focus to your responses.

SWOT analysis

A SWOT analysis is a useful, quick tool for taking stock of your situation. It is a simple way of analysing your level of readiness for a new task. It can take you to the core of an issue very quickly. SWOT stands for Strengths, Weaknesses, Opportunities, Threats.

Activity: SWOT Analysis

- For the focus you selected in the previous activity, use the resource sheet on p. 62 to jot down as many examples of strengths and weaknesses as you can under each heading. Include personal qualities, skills, experiences, knowledge, resources and support.
- Under 'Opportunities', jot down any opportunities that could arise from achieving this goal. Include short- and long-term benefits.
- Under 'Threats', jot down the things that seem threatening, worrying, very challenging, or which are causing you some anxiety.

The Activities in this book, and especially those in this chapter should help you to manage some of the 'threats'.

Emily prided herself on her emotional detachment.

SWOT Analysis Resource Sheet

Goal:

Strengths

Weaknesses

Opportunities

Threats

Personal resources

Very few of us have the ideal resources, but none of us is without any resources. This is especially true for students, as there is usually a wide range of services offered through the university and the local community. These sources of support are listed in various leaflets, books and directories.

Activity: Finding information

- Brainstorm types of information available to you about sources of support. Who could tell you about other sources of information?
- Make a list of all the sources of support available through the Student Union and Student Services that are likely to be useful to you.

Activity: Sources of support

In the boxes below, list the sources of support available to you for each item. Put a tick in the box by those that you need to pursue in the next few weeks.

Academic advice and guidance ☐

Financial ☐

Careers/finding a job ☐

Meeting people ☐

Finding somewhere to live ☐

Emotional questions, needs and support ☐

Health issues ☐

Other resource needs:

Follow this up

Make appointments to see the relevant people. Write these times in your diary. Before you attend appointments, ensure you have read any literature provided by these services, in case they need you to bring papers with you. Always bring your student card or student number.

Time management

Your time is one of your most valuable resources. How well do you use your time at present? Which of the following characteristics are typical of you?

Activity: Evaluating time management

For each item, identify which one response is most true for you, indicating this with a tick (✓).

Characteristic	Yes, a lot	Yes, sometimes	No	I don't know
I recognise the following characteristics as true of me:				
Being late	☐	☐	☐	☐
Not knowing where I am supposed to be	☐	☐	☐	☐
Missing appointments	☐	☐	☐	☐
Rushing at the end of a task	☐	☐	☐	☐
Missing deadlines	☐	☐	☐	☐
Taking too long to complete a task	☐	☐	☐	☐
Running out of time	☐	☐	☐	☐
Not knowing how long it takes me to complete a task	☐	☐	☐	☐
Dashing around all day	☐	☐	☐	☐
Forgetting what I have to do	☐	☐	☐	☐

- If your response to all of the above was 'NO' you seem to have very good time management. Is it perfect, or are there areas where you could improve further?
- If your response to some items was: 'I don't know', then you would seem to lack awareness about your time management. Speak to people who know you well and find out what they think about your time management.
- If your response to any of the above was 'Yes', which of the following factors contribute to your time-management difficulties?

Activity: Factors in time management

For each item, identify which one response is most true for you, indicating this with a tick (✓).

Factor	Very true	Sometimes true	Never true
1. I use small pockets of time in the day to sort out minor tasks	☐	☐	☐
2. I get down to work quickly; I am well motivated to start	☐	☐	☐
3. I have timed myself completing the different aspects of larger tasks	☐	☐	☐
4. I know when I have done enough rather than aiming at perfection	☐	☐	☐
5. I say 'NO' when I lack time	☐	☐	☐
6. I delegate work to others when I can	☐	☐	☐
7. I ask for help where possible	☐	☐	☐
8. I have a go rather than worrying too much about getting things wrong	☐	☐	☐
9. I have strategies for starting a task rather than wondering where to begin	☐	☐	☐
10. I keep an effective diary	☐	☐	☐
11. I look at my diary very often	☐	☐	☐
12. I plan my activities in a logical order	☐	☐	☐

Activity: Identify solutions

If you answered 'sometimes true' or 'never true' to any of the above time management factors, identify at least three you could improve.

- Some strategies for managing these time factors are given below. Which could you use to improve your time management?
- In your reflective journal, re-write these as positive 'I will...' statements. For example, 'I will keep an effective diary'
- Add specific details that make it more likely you will take action. For example, 'I will buy a diary today at the Student Shop after my Design lecture. I will carry it in my blue bag. I will check it every evening after dinner so that I can plan ahead for the next day.'

Managing time effectively

For each of the time management statements in the activity 'Factors in time management' (above), there are suggestions below about how to address that aspect.

1 Use small pockets of time in the day to sort out minor tasks

This is a key strategy for effective time management. Use time waiting in queues, on a bus or even waiting for the kettle to boil to recap on your learning, formulate lists, work out a problem, etc.

Keep a pencil and small notebook with detachable pages nearby to jot down your ideas. Make a mental note of the times in the day when you could multi-task in this way. This strategy also reduces the stress associated with queuing and tedious tasks.

2 Motivation to 'get going'

We saw in Chapter 1 how important motivation is to success. If you do not feel motivated, then be active in finding a source of motivation or inspiration. Focus on your long-term goals: check these are still important to you. Remind yourself of the benefits you expect. Write these where you can see them. Set short-term targets that you can manage, so that you get frequent tastes of success.

3 Time tasks

Time management requires you to know how long something takes. This is easier if you break a larger project down into smaller tasks. Often, one or two of these will take longer than you expect. It may be aspects of starting and finishing tasks that take longer than expected. Plan for all stages, and find out how much time you need to allocate for each stage.

4 Cost your time

Work out whether the amount of time you spend on each aspect of a task is 'cost-effective'. Usually the return (such as extra marks) decreases after a certain point. Academic work is hard to get perfect, as there isn't usually a single right answer. If you gain satisfaction from the additional study time, that is fine, as long as you have calculated what you are giving up in exchange.

5 Say 'no'

Identify what lies behind your difficulty in saying 'no'. It may be your beliefs, such as that 'a nice person' always helps out. If so, think what it means to be kind to yourself. Also, what are the negative consequences of always saying 'yes'? For example, does this give other people a chance to be kind or to take full responsibility? Alternatively, this might be a question of assertiveness or negotiation (see Chapter 5). There may be very long-standing or domestic issues which contribute to your difficulty in saying 'no'. If so, you should speak to a student counsellor.

6 Delegate to others

Identify what lies beneath a reluctance to delegate. For example, do you distrust others to do the job well? If so, what are the effects of this on your own time management, stress levels and personal efficiency? What would be the benefits to you and to others if you delegated more? How will others learn to do a job well if you do not delegate? Could you find a compromise where you share some tasks in the shorter term?

7 Ask for help

Recognise your own limits. Support services are set up because it is expected that people will need help. This is especially true for students. Asking friends and colleagues for help can contribute to their own personal development too. It can build their self-esteem and problem-solving skills. It gives them an opportunity to be helpful, which they may value.

8 and 9 Starting strategies

Use a basic starting strategy such as brainstorming or writing a list. Start with what you can do – and work from there. Often, a problem arises when we focus too much on what the end product should be rather than building from what we already know. Start small. Branch out. The ideas will come. If not, look for ideas in Chapters 4, 6 or 7.

10 and 11 Use a diary

A diary is an essential life tool. Some people prefer electronic organisers. Choose one that is light enough to carry around at all times. Check it at least three times a day. Develop the habit of writing everything in it to avoid double-booking. Enter all targets. Enter deadlines on the date of the deadline *and* the day you want to start work on that assignment.

Of all the donkeys, Geoffrey found it the hardest to say 'No'.

Student Day Planner

Early morning (to do before I leave home)

Time	Task	Place/Room	With	Bring/Say/ Do
8:00–9:00				
9:00–10:00				
10:00–11:00				
11:00–12:00				
12:00–1:00				
1:00–2:00				
2:00–3:00				
3:00–4:00				
4:00–5:00				
5:00–6:00				
Early evening				
Night				
Preparation for tomorrow (must do)				

12 Plan activities out in a logical order

Write a list of all the tasks you need to undertake during the day. Rewrite the list, grouping the activities by place. Allow sufficient time to move from one place to another. Write the locations in your diary.

Student Day Planner

The Student Day Planner (shown on p. 67) divides time into sections most commonly used by students. Block in all your lectures, seminars, tutorials, workshops, lab-sessions, and assignment deadlines for each term or semester and then copy it. This saves writing it out several times. Indicate the room, the lecturer, and any materials you have to bring with you, so the information is easy to find.

Things that get forgotten

- The time it takes to travel between appointments – mark that in.
- The time when work for a deadline should begin – rather than just the deadline itself.
- New locations. These may be hard to find. Plan to leave time for getting lost.
- Queuing time.
- Transport delays. These are not usually accepted as excuses unless they are very rare with unusual circumstances.
- Information technology going wrong; waiting to use a shared printer, etc.

Time management for academic work is covered in more detail in *The Study Skills Handbook* (Cottrell, 2003).

Attitudes

> *Up to a point, every man is what he thinks he is.*
>
> F. H. Bradley

What's in a thought?

No two people respond in the same way to the same event. One person may be angry and determined to take action if something goes wrong; a second may shrug and forget it; a third may feel it is 'yet another example of why there is no point trying'. Our thinking about an event influences our response to it and the outcome. Our thoughts shape our experience, affecting what we feel physically and emotionally, how we interpret events, how we respond in a crisis and how we direct our lives.

Taking responsibility

One of the first steps in managing a situation is taking responsibility for oneself as an active, thinking, creative agent within the process. It may well be the case that 'someone' should have acted better, or are even to blame for what happened. Taking responsibility does not mean excusing or taking the blame for somebody else's actions. It means moving beyond the 'blame' to find the most constructive outcome possible. The responsibility here is to yourself.

Often, the internal story that we create around events focuses on what went wrong and whose fault it was rather than on finding the best outcome. We run 'pre-recorded messages' about 'they' or 'it ', such as:

The Big Bad 'they'

- they make me . . .
- they should take the first step . . .
- they shouldn't put me in this position . . .
- they shouldn't set these deadlines . . .
- they should help me more . . .
- they started it . . .
- they design these so badly . . .

The Big Bad 'it'

- it is too difficult . . .
- it is too soon . . .
- it is too complex . . .
- it overwhelms me . . .
- 'it's doing my head in' . . .
- it won't work . . .
- it's a waste of time . . .
- it keeps doing this wrong . . .

📖 Reflection   The pre-recorded message

- Which 'it' do you tend to blame (if any?)
- Which 'they' do you tend to blame (if any?)
- What other responses do you make when things go wrong that avoid taking personal responsibility for a constructive outcome?

Constructive messages

We can create alternative messages that lead to more productive outcomes. For example:

- I can do this . . .
- It's OK. There is a way of dealing with this.
- We can find a solution.
- In the circumstances, the best step is . . .
- The first step is . . .
- I take responsibility for my part in this.
- I'll have a go.

If we repeat these often enough, these become new 'prerecorded messages' that will kick in automatically.

Activity: Change the message

- Write down five constructive responses you could use when things go wrong.
- Check that these enable you to take responsibility for yourself.
- Choose the *one* you like the most and write it where you will see it this week. Try it out and record what happens

Self-belief

Belief in oneself and one's own capabilities is essential. Low self-esteem creates stress, which makes the brain less efficient. It is also more likely to encourage a sense of defeat and a belief that there is 'no point'.

Self-confidence, a belief that one has the right to be and think and do what one wants, subject to reasonable limits and concern for others,

Reflection   Self-belief critical incident

In your reflective journal, jot down a list of things you have done, no matter how small, that you are pleased about or proud of. Then, choose one to think about in more detail. Jot down:

- What happened? What did you do or say?
- What were the consequences? How did you or others benefit from this situation?
- What personal characteristics are demonstrated in this incident?
- What can you find in this incident that should make you feel good about yourself?

Activity: Self-descriptions

- Brainstorm a list of 30 things that you like about yourself.

1. tall
2. handsome
3. flexible
4. manages change well...

- Go through your list, and underline all those that contain a positive description: 'I'm a reliable person', 'I am kind', 'I am helpful', etc.
- If there are less than 30 such positive phrases, add more to your list until there are 30. Don't underestimate yourself. If any phrases contain the words 'I try to...' or 'I am quite...', reword these so they are more definite and positive.

Which three descriptions of yourself do you like the best? What reasons have you for believing that these descriptions are accurate?

enhances performance. It motivates and drives you forward. It is also attractive to other people. This can bring more interest, resources and support, increasing the likelihood of success.

Self-permission

Sometimes, we are unable to move forward because we refuse to give ourselves 'permission'. It is as if we hear a pre-recorded message saying:

- 'I'm not allowed';
- 'I'm not good enough';
- 'I'm not worthy of the risk';
- 'I'm not deserving of the consequences';
- 'I'm not made for this sort of thing';
- 'I'm not strong enough to cope with failure';
- 'It's not me'.

This can be true of anybody, but it is especially the case if there were strong messages at school or in the family that encouraged low expectations.

Activity: permission

Take three minutes each to complete the following two lists. Write quickly, without analysing your responses as you write.

List 1
I am allowed to . . . (write as many things as you can think of).

List 2
I am not allowed to . . . (write as many things as you can think of).

Check back over your two lists and see if you can spot any themes.

● What sorts of things are you 'allowed' to do?
● What sorts of things are you 'not allowed' to do?
● Which list is longer? What might be the reason for that?
● Who says 'you are not allowed to . . .'? Is it really true that you do not have permission to achieve in these areas?

From this activity, you may recognise messages from a long time ago that are still echoing in the present. Many of the 'permissions' we refuse ourselves today began a long time ago. These do not have to remain as barriers to achievement. Take a look at your list and identify those on the 'I am not allowed list' that you could transfer to the 'I am allowed...' list. Write these down.

Taking a solution-focused approach

> *Whenever you are asked if you can do a job, tell 'em,*
> *Certainly I can! – and get busy and find out how to do it.*

> Theodore Roosevelt

Difficulty-focused thinking
Focusing on the difficulty usually produces negative responses: the problem can seem insoluble. It depletes your own and other people's emotional and physical energy, creating a sense of weariness, hopelessness or helplessness. The dominant message is that the problem is difficult, it will be hard work to find a solution, and solutions are unlikely. The difficulty-focused approach uses words and phrases such as:

● 'but . . .'
● 'I can't see how . . .'
● 'oh no!', 'not again!'
● 'it's hard to believe . . .'
● 'that won't work'
● 'I doubt it'.

At worst, difficulty-focused people tend to pick fault with every proposal, draw attention to flaws in the best possible solution, and discourage others from believing that there could be a sensible solution.

A solution-focused approach
A solution-focused approach describes the situation, identifies the points of difficulty, and moves quickly to a search for the best possible resolution. It uses words and phrases such as:

● 'yes, and we could also. . .'
● 'what if we. . . ?'
● 'are there other ways of looking at this?'

- 'let's brainstorm ideas . . .'
- 'let's look again at our options . . .'
- 'let's see if we have missed any options. . .'
- 'let's check whether we can make this work . . .'
- 'what could we adapt?'
- 'who else would know about this . . . ?'

The dominant message is that a solution of one kind or another will have to be found eventually, even if it is an interim one, so it is better to focus energies on finding the solution sooner rather than later. A solution-focused approach is often expected of those in managerial roles. As most graduates enter jobs with managerial responsibilities, it is worth developing this approach. If you have been surrounded by people who take a difficulty-focused approach, you might find this a useful challenge.

📖 **Reflection**   Solution-focus

- Do you tend to use the words and phrases associated with a 'difficulty-focused' approach or a 'solution-focused' approach?
- Which words and phrases are typical of you when faced with a complex situation?
- Do you tend to employ a solution-focused approach?
- What could you do to develop a more solution-focused attitude?

Ways of addressing a new challenge

Lazarus (1999) identifies two main strategies for approaching a difficulty: 'problem-focused coping' and 'emotion-focused' coping:

- problem-focused: looking outwards to the external, concrete problem and its circumstances;
- emotion-focused: looking inwards at personal attitudes and emotions that impact upon your individual reaction to the situation.

A solution-focused approach can use either approach, adopting a constructive and positive attitude for either. The solution-focused approach takes the position that there is a solution to every problem and that we have that solution within us. Sometimes, we arrive at the solution more easily if we talk to others or use a particular strategy. The 'solution' is the best constructive outcome that can be found for the situation in the circumstances. This may not be everything that we would like, but it directs energy in a positive way so that the best outcome possible is achieved.

A solution-focused approach requires very little, beyond an attitude of mind.

Changing your environment

A negative, blaming, 'can't be bothered' environment is not inspiring. A few people with such approaches can spread negativity very easily. They can even create a culture which is self-defeating. You can probably think of the people around you who create an aura of negativity. (Maybe you are that person?)

As adults, we can monitor the impact of our environment on our responses, taking note of what leaves us feeling encouraged and what does not. We can take action to create an environment around us that supports what we want to achieve.

It wasn't what Cuthbert said as much as the way he said it.

Identify positive inputs
- Identify the people around you who leave you feeling positive about your goals, direction or programme of study.
- What is it about them that seems to increase positive responses?
- What other things in the environment support your goal? Competition and constructive criticism can be included as positive inputs.

Jot down these factors, starting with 'I . . .', and identifying how you could increase the positive aspects of your environment. For example:

I appreciate the way Busola makes a point of saying she enjoys good seminars. I could identify the things I find positive about each seminar.

I find it useful that the library is open until 8:00 p.m. I could use it more in the evening.

Identify negative inputs
- Which people leave you feeling dejected, anxious, tired, despondent?
- What do you feel or do when you are in the presence of negative attitudes?

- What factors in your current environment could undermine or sabotage your goals?
- What can you do to reduce the impact of such factors upon you?

Emotional intelligence

Evaluating your emotional intelligence

The following activity enables you to evaluate your emotional intelligence. This is not a scientific test: emotions do not lend themselves easily to such testing. However, it gives you an opportunity to reflect upon your emotional life through a structured activity.

Activity: Evaluating your emotional intelligence

1. Emotional management (self)

For each item, identify which one response is most true for you, indicating this with a tick. ✓

Item	Always true	Usually true	Occasionally true	Not true	Don't know
1. I know which emotions I am experiencing	☐	☐	☐	☐	☐
2. I am aware of my emotions	☐	☐	☐	☐	☐
3. I allow myself to feel emotional	☐	☐	☐	☐	☐
4. I take notice of my emotions	☐	☐	☐	☐	☐
5. I can name the emotions I am feeling	☐	☐	☐	☐	☐
6. I tell other people what I am feeling	☐	☐	☐	☐	☐
7. I take responsibility for my own feelings	☐	☐	☐	☐	☐
8. I know what triggers different kinds of emotion in me	☐	☐	☐	☐	☐
9. I can respond without being overwhelmed by emotion	☐	☐	☐	☐	☐
10. I can express the right amount of feeling for the circumstances	☐	☐	☐	☐	☐
11. I can be assertive rather than aggressive or passive whilst feeling emotional	☐	☐	☐	☐	☐
12. I know when my feelings are not being expressed	☐	☐	☐	☐	☐
13. I make opportunities to express my feelings after an event, if needed	☐	☐	☐	☐	☐

Item	Always true	Usually true	Occasionally true	Not true	Don't know
14. I know the ways that my feelings affect my performance	☐	☐	☐	☐	☐
15. I regularly talk about my feelings to somebody I trust	☐	☐	☐	☐	☐
16. I reflect upon my feelings					
17. I allow myself to feel 'small' or vulnerable at times	☐	☐	☐	☐	☐
18. I cry if I need to					
19. I will allow myself to withdraw from a situation in order to experience my feelings, where feasible	☐	☐	☐	☐	☐
20. I am aware of how my feelings are affected by the people around me	☐	☐	☐	☐	☐

2. Emotional management (others)

For each item, identify which one response is most true for you, indicating this with a tick. ✓

Item	Always true	Usually true	Occasionally true	Not true	Don't know
1. I know which emotions other people are experiencing	☐	☐	☐	☐	☐
2. I am aware of other people's feelings	☐	☐	☐	☐	☐
3. I allow other people to feel their emotions	☐	☐	☐	☐	☐
4. I take notice of other people's emotions	☐	☐	☐	☐	☐
5. I can name the emotions other people are feeling	☐	☐	☐	☐	☐
6. I speak to other people about their feelings	☐	☐	☐	☐	☐
7. I take responsibility for my own feelings when other people are feeling emotional	☐	☐	☐	☐	☐
8. I know what triggers emotional responses in people I see regularly	☐	☐	☐	☐	☐
9. I am aware of my own responses to other people's emotions	☐	☐	☐	☐	☐
10. I allow others to express what they feel is right for the circumstances	☐	☐	☐	☐	☐

Item	Always true	Usually true	Occasionally true	Not true	Don't know
11. I can be assertive when other people are being aggressive, passive or emotional	☐	☐	☐	☐	☐
12. I am aware when other people are not expressing their feelings	☐	☐	☐	☐	☐
13. I make opportunities to enable other people to express their feelings	☐	☐	☐	☐	☐
14. I am aware of how I let other people's feelings affect my performance	☐	☐	☐	☐	☐
15. I regularly listen to someone I know well talking about their feelings	☐	☐	☐	☐	☐
16. I reflect upon the way feelings are experienced and expressed in groups	☐	☐	☐	☐	☐
17. I allow other people to feel 'small' or vulnerable	☐	☐	☐	☐	☐
18. I am comfortable when others cry if they need to	☐	☐	☐	☐	☐
19. I understand when other people withdraw from a situation in order to experience their feelings	☐	☐	☐	☐	☐
20. I am aware of how my feelings affect the people around me.	☐	☐	☐	☐	☐

3. Emotions in action

For each item, identify which one response is most true for you, indicating this with a tick.

Item	Always true	Usually true	Occasionally true	Not true	Don't know
1. I feel comfortable even when people disagree with me	☐	☐	☐	☐	☐
2. I can allow other people their own opinions	☐	☐	☐	☐	☐
3. I can feel angry without taking it out on others	☐	☐	☐	☐	☐
4. I can accept criticism without getting angry	☐	☐	☐	☐	☐
5. I can voice my own opinions	☐	☐	☐	☐	☐
6. I am able to remain positive even when the situation looks gloomy	☐	☐	☐	☐	☐

Item	Always true	Usually true	Occasionally true	Not true	Don't know
7. I can allow myself to be sad – and to experience the sadness without pushing it away	☐	☐	☐	☐	☐
8. I can make decisions and act upon them	☐	☐	☐	☐	☐
9. I can stop and assess a situation before I act or speak	☐	☐	☐	☐	☐
10. I feel comfortable working with people from very different backgrounds to mine	☐	☐	☐	☐	☐
11. I can enjoy diversity in the people around me	☐	☐	☐	☐	☐
12. I will speak out for what I believe is right	☐	☐	☐	☐	☐
13. I ask for help when I need it	☐	☐	☐	☐	☐
14. I can let myself feel emotions without taking a drink, cigarette, drug or comfort eating	☐	☐	☐	☐	☐
15. I am calm in a crisis	☐	☐	☐	☐	☐
16. I can identify when my behaviour is unreasonable – and stop it	☐	☐	☐	☐	☐
17. I can manage uncertainty without having to have an answer straight away	☐	☐	☐	☐	☐
18. I can manage my emotions under pressure	☐	☐	☐	☐	☐
19. I take responsibility for my own part in events	☐	☐	☐	☐	☐
20. I can admit a mistake and apologise.	☐	☐	☐	☐	☐

Scoring your responses

For each item on the above sets of questions, allocate to yourself the following scores: Always true (4); Usually true (3); Occasionally true (2); Not true (1); Don't know (0).

1. Emotional management (self): Score _____

2. Emotional management (others): Score _____

3. Emotions in action: Score _____

Total score: _____

Interpreting your scores

150–200 If your answers are accurate, this suggests that you have a sophisticated approach to emotional life. You seem capable of managing your own emotions as well as coping with the emotions of other people. You seem able to make the kinds of responses that accompany emotional intelligence. Your emotional intelligence should provide you with an asset in almost any situation.

100–149 This is a good score. If your evaluations are accurate, you have a very good foundation for developing your emotional intelligence further. Emotional intelligence is an asset in most situations so this is very much worth doing. Look at the responses which have high scores: what do these tell you about your strengths? Are there any themes evident in the questions that received lower scores? It is worth noting whether one of the three sections had a lower score than the others. Identify which of these is your priority for further self-development.

50–99 This is a reasonable score, especially if you entered university from school. However, it suggests that you have lots of room to develop your emotional management skills. If your evaluation is accurate, you would benefit from making emotional self-management a priority area. Identify which areas are your strengths. These are the assets you take into most situations. Look for themes in the lower scores. Which types of issues are most relevant to the achievement of your goals? Identify which of these is your priority for further self-development.

0–49 If your evaluation is accurate, you may have a real challenge on your hands. Remember that this is not a scientific test. There may be many areas of emotional intelligence in which you excel that are not covered by this activity. For example, some people are exceptional in crises – but there is only one question related to managing a crisis above. Other people are emotionally sophisticated with particular types of people, such as children, the elderly, sick people, etc. In addition, your evaluation may have been harsh. On the other hand, you may really feel that the emotional world is rather a tricky one. You may feel that people misunderstand you or your motives much of the time. You are not alone if you feel that. However, it is not necessarily a very comfortable position to be in. The good news is that emotional intelligence is an asset that can be developed. The student counselling service at the university will probably be able to give you confidential advice if you are at all concerned.

What is emotional intelligence?

'Emotional intelligence' is a term made current by Goleman (1995). It is slowly becoming recognised that it isn't simply what we do and what we think that affects our ability to cope, manage and succeed, but also how we manage our feelings.

Emotional intelligence involves:

- knowing the appropriate feelings for the circumstances;
- experiencing the appropriate feelings for the circumstances;
- expressing feelings appropriate to the circumstances;
- making opportunities to express feelings that cannot be expressed fully in the original circumstances.

This may sound easy. However, your reflections above may have indicated to you that emotions often get in the way of a rational interpretation of a situation. They tend to prevent us from working towards the best or most constructive solution to the issues. In general, people tend to over-express their feelings (excessive anger, passivity, distress and so forth) or to bottle up their feelings in order to cope. Different circumstances permit a different level of expression. We need to consider such matters as:

- What response will lead to the most constructive outcome?
- How will other people respond?
- What are other people's needs?

Reflection — Examples of emotional responses

Think of three situations where you had a strong emotional response. Choose three different types of communication (in a group, individually, face to face, telephone, email) or three types of situation (work, study, with friends, with strangers). For each situation, jot down thoughts in your reflective journal in response to the following questions.

● What happened?
● What did you feel?
● Which feelings did you express?
● What did you do at the time?
● What were the consequences?
● What did you do or feel within the next 48 hours?
● Did your responses enable you to gain the most constructive outcome possible from the situations?

Consider whether your responses seem to be different depending on the circumstances or people involved.

Where do the unexpressed feelings go?

Whilst it is important to know what we feel and to acknowledge our feelings, there are times when it is not appropriate to express all of what we feel. In the activity above, you will probably have identified some feelings you did not express at the time. Often, such feelings go unexpressed for a long time. Unfortunately, they do not usually just disappear. Where do they go?

There are numerous ways that unexpressed emotions make themselves felt. A few of these are given here. As you read through them, identify which responses seem to be most typical of your own. You would be a very remarkable person if you made none of the following responses.

Displacement

The emotion is ignored and sneaks out when not expected, usually when you experience a similar emotion later. For example, you say nothing when you are irritated several times

during a morning, and then snap or shout at somebody for something very minor later on in the day. Many people are not aware of what they are feeling yet their feelings may be all too evident to the people around them.

Ida knew for certain she had her anger under control.

Disproportion

This often goes hand in hand with displacement. When you express an emotion it should be proportionate to the situation. Disproportionate responses are noticeable when quite small things that do not seem to affect other people provoke a strong reaction in others. A small event may lead to tears, shouting, anger, violence, insults, or extreme distress.

If something has been building, unexpressed for a long time, it is usually advisable to speak to a counsellor. They can help you release the emotion in a manageable way.

Reflection — Displacing emotions

Think of a situation when your emotional reaction was very strong for the situation.

● What happened? What did you do or say?
● Which emotion was being displaced?
● What had originally provoked the emotion – was it something recent? Was it the result of a long-build up of emotion?
● What could you have done to prevent displacing the emotion onto the later situation?

Distorted thinking

Unexpressed emotions can eat away at people, leading to distorted thinking such as:

● Believing there is no solution or way out of a problem;

● Exaggerating how bad things are;

● Over-generalising: judging everything from one or few examples. For example: 'my first essay was bad so I know I shouldn't be at university';

● Exaggerating one's own role in events, so as to see oneself as very incompetent, bad, unkind or completely to blame for everything that went wrong. This is often a way of refusing to admit one's actual role (as it invites people it reassure you that you are not wholly to blame);

● 'All or nothing' thinking: 'If I can't have this then I don't want anything';

● 'Magical thinking': believing that one is jinxed, doomed, specially chosen, fated;

● Mistaking feelings for facts: 'I feel it is all terrible, so it must be';

● Focusing on the negatives: seeing only what went wrong, and judging a situation only by what was not perfect;

● Rationalising: finding a reason for doing what you want to do or for not doing what needs to be done.

📖 *Reflection*   Distorted thinking

We are all capable of distorted thinking from time to time.

● Which of the above methods do you use when you are not feeling good about yourself or your work?

● What kinds of situations prompt you to distorted thinking?

● What benefit does the distorted thinking give you in the short term? Bear in mind that if you didn't feel it was giving you something, you wouldn't do it.

● How does the distorted thinking stand in the way of achieving your goals? (It does!)

Managing personal distress

The ABC model for dealing with distress

Ellis (1994) and Dryden and Gordon (1993) outline the 'ABC model' for managing situations that cause distress. The ABC model helps to analyse the source of the distress. It separates the core of the issue from the beliefs and attitudes that then amplify the problem. This makes it easier to find a solution or way of coping, keeping the core issues in perspective. ABC stands for:

A = **Activating event**: What happened that led to the emotional distress?

B = **Beliefs**: What beliefs contribute to the emotional distress?

C = **Consequences**: e.g. anger, illness, inability to work, difficulty getting down to work or concentrating

The example below (p. 79) also adds a 'D':

D = **Dealing with it**: what action will you take to manage the situation?

Example ABC model for dealing with distress

A *Activating event*   The 'activating event' might be that a student, Gareth, has not read the course handbook. As a result, he did not realise that two essay deadlines fell on the same day. He asked for an extension, but was refused as it was not possible in the circumstances. Gareth must complete both essays in five days. If not, he will need to retake a module. The situation is not easy.

B *Beliefs*   Gareth can make a decision to work flat out to produce two essays, possibly accepting lower marks, or he can defer one of the modules and increase the possibility of higher marks for both in the long term. This would take a few months longer, but is feasible. However, Gareth argues that he is 'totally stupid' to have got into this situation and that this is typical of the mess he makes of his 'whole life'. He links the current problem with difficulties he experiences elsewhere so that the issue is no longer a missed deadline (which can be managed) but everything about his life. He does not believe he can write the essays as he has convinced himself that nothing he does will work.

C *Consequences*   The consequences are that Gareth's beliefs lock him into inaction. All of his energies are diverted into self-blame and hopelessness. He feels very small and is too embarrassed to talk to his friends. Instead of using his time to write the essays, he wastes time worrying or drinking, trying to push the problem away. Because he is stressed, he finds it difficult to concentrate. He can't study or make sense of what he reads. He misses his shift for his part time job, making his overall situation even worse – convincing him further that his 'life' is a problem.

D *Dealing with it*   What could you do if you found yourself in a similar situation? In this case, it is beliefs that are fuelling the distress and leading to unhelpful consequences. You could either focus on the problem so as to divert yourself from the beliefs, or change the beliefs.

If you focus on the problem, you can:

● Describe the activating event, reducing it to the basics. Acknowledge what went wrong and what has been learnt. Yes, Gareth should have read the handbook. However, he is unlikely to make this mistake again, and this could be a critical lesson from which he learns and gains in the longer term. He is far from being the only student to get into such a position.
● Consider what has to be done. List all your options. Find out what these are and write them down. Write the advantages of each option. Then consider the feasibility and consequences of each.
● Move as quickly as possible into 'problem-solving mode', using a problem-solving strategy (see Chapter 4). Brainstorm options for solving the core problem. Evaluate these and choose one.
● Make a decision - and then stick to it and accept the consequences. The consequences might not be ideal, but they can be the 'best possible' for the situation. They are not life-threatening or catastrophic in the larger picture.
● Develop an action plan and follow it.

To challenge unhelpful beliefs:

● Write down words that motivate you, such as: 'there is a solution' or 'I can do this'.
● List your negative thoughts (beliefs). Go through the list, undertaking a 'reality check'. Ask 'Is this belief going to help me find a solution?'
● Challenge all beliefs that start with 'I should have . . .' or 'I always . . .'.
● Challenge all beliefs that refer to any other situation except the current problem.
● Cross out, with a thick line, all beliefs that do not help achieve a solution to the current situation.
● Brainstorm constructive phrases or messages until you find at least one that seems both helpful and true to you. Underline that belief or idea three times. Put a line through all the others.
● Speak to a friend or counsellor to put the situation into perspective.

Managing change, confusion and uncertainty

Activity: Approaches to change

For each item, identify which one response is most true for you, indicating this with a tick.

Characteristic	Always true	Usually true	Occasionally true	Not true
1. I enjoy change	☐	☐	☐	☐
2. I look for the opportunities in new situations and circumstances	☐	☐	☐	☐
3. I feel comfortable meeting new people	☐	☐	☐	☐
4. I am confident about coping in new surroundings	☐	☐	☐	☐
5. I welcome new perspectives on an issue or problem	☐	☐	☐	☐
6. I ask people for feedback	☐	☐	☐	☐
7. I can change my plans at the last minute without feeling stressed	☐	☐	☐	☐
8. I can study reasonably well in a wide range of circumstances	☐	☐	☐	☐
9. I enjoy starting new subjects or projects	☐	☐	☐	☐
10. I will work early or late at short notice	☐	☐	☐	☐

Scoring your responses

For each item, allocate to yourself the following scores: Always true (3);   Usually true (2);
Occasionally true (1);   Not true (0)

Score _____

Reflecting on your score

24–30   This suggests you have a very strong and positive approach to change. What beneficial characteristics does this enable you to bring to study? How would this be of benefit in a work context? Do you look for change at the expense of continuity?

16–23   This suggests you have a positive approach to change. What beneficial characteristics does this enable you to bring to study? How would this be of benefit in a work context?

8–15   This suggests that you have an ambivalent approach to change. You can be positive about change. What benefits could you gain from developing a more positive approach?

0–7   Your score suggests a strong preference for continuity. You may need to be creative to find work and circumstances that enable you to maintain this level of continuity. It may be helpful to talk through your resistance to change with a counsellor. What disadvantages does your resistance to change bring you? Is there one area where you could develop greater flexibility?

The changing context

Technology and changes in the way that work is organised have revolutionised the way we work and study. For most of history, people knew from childhood what work they would do, their station in life, their relative income, the tools they would be using. Lives were mapped out often before a person was born, depending on their family circumstances. Even when education changed the level and range of opportunity, most people studied for a degree between the ages of 18 and 22, then entered the profession that they would stay with for the rest of their lives.

The dominant pattern for people in many countries now is that they can study towards almost any profession they choose. In Britain, you can return to any level of education at any age. Many people return to take a second or a higher degree. It is expected that a person will continue training in new skills throughout their lives. It is likely that you will have several or many jobs, probably in many different locations. The technical skills you learn today will be out of date very quickly. Factual information you acquire may also have a short shelf life. However, some skills you acquire now are likely to be of value throughout your life. These include:

● intra-personal skills and qualities (how you manage yourself and your attitudes)

● problem-solving skills (approaches to tasks)
● and inter-personal skills (how you relate to other people).

> **📖 Reflection**   Coping with change
>
> ● What kinds of change do you find easiest to accept and to cope with?
> ● What sorts of things do you prefer to stay constant or the 'same'?
> ● What kinds of change do you find difficult to cope with?

Dealing with uncertainty

The 'right answer'

University life and study can be very challenging to our way of seeing the world. Many would argue that it should be and that a university education should stretch students and make them re-evaluate their core beliefs and ways of thinking. The challenge can be difficult to manage at first. In the 1970s, Perry undertook research with students at Harvard and Ratcliffe colleges in the USA. He found that even outstanding students often expected to be given or led towards the 'right answers' by their tutors. How far is this true of you? Check your own responses using the following activity.

Activity: Is there a right answer?

This activity is likely to take at least half an hour and maybe much longer. There are three parts.

Part 1   Issues

On a piece of paper, jot down quickly your ideas about *three* of the following issues:

(a) It is ethical to clone human life.
(b) Students should be trained to develop their thinking skills as part of every programme.
(c) All adults should be required to contribute 50 hours a year to community or environmental work.
(d) To protect the environment, each person should have a restricted number of travel miles for holidays over their lifetime.
(e) Emotional intelligence should be part of the school curriculum.
(f) There should be a curfew on all people with a criminal record.
(g) Science requires creative thinking rather than logic.

(continued)

Activity: Is there a right answer? (continued)

Part 2   Approaches

Below is a list of approaches that students take when considering new problems or challenging issues (adapted from Perry, 1970.) For each of the issues you were asked to consider, decide which of the following positions best describes where you stand on the issue.

1. Absolute answer

I think this is a question of right and wrong or that the right answer to this issue is obvious. I know where I stand, I know my own opinion, and I don't think an alternative answer is acceptable. Recognised authorities such as my tutor, a book, the law or a professional body will be able to tell me what the right answer is on this.

2. Temporary unacceptable uncertainty

The right answer hasn't been found yet but needs to be. Professionals, academics or other authorities need to clarify what the right answer is in order to avoid confusion.

3. Acceptable uncertainty

Everyone has a right to his or her own opinion. All answers are equally acceptable. My answer is as good as anyone else's. Lecturers and experts do not have the answers.

4. Relativism

It's all relative. The 'right answer' would depend upon the circumstances. Another person may think differently from me and still be right, if their situation and experience is different. There are no right answers. There is no real way of deciding what is right for all situations.

5. Commitment to a considered viewpoint, taking responsibility for the decision

I understand and can appreciate other viewpoints on this issue, but I believe some answers or perspectives are better than others and that I need to make a personal decision on where I stand amongst conflicting opinions. I realise that making this choice of an answer may carry responsibilities and have implications for how I think, speak, and the choices I make.

6. On-going development

I am committed to this viewpoint, appreciate other viewpoints and realise that my decision carries personal responsibility. However, I also feel that this is something that I need to keep returning to, even if it means some uncertainty. The answer I have committed to is of great importance to who I am, to my values, and the kind of person I want to be.

Part 3: Interpreting your position

Perry explained the thinking that underlies each position. He ordered them into a hierarchy of responses (given below).

● Which position on his hierarchy is occupied by your answers? Are your answers generally in position 1, 2 or 3?
● In general, which of the nine stages described below do you think is most true of you?

Position 1: 'Right-answer positions' (Approaches 1 and 2 on the above activity)

1. Absolutist stage: there are right answers available. Things are either right or wrong. It is the teacher's job to provide the right answers.
2. Bad authority versus good authority: there are right answers but uncertainty is created unnecessarily by poor teachers or leaders. It is acceptable for right answers to be withheld when teachers want students to find the 'right' answer themselves.
3. Temporary uncertainty: there are right answers but it isn't clear what these are yet.

(continued)

Position 2: Relativism stages (Approaches 3 and 4 on the activity above)

4. Acceptable uncertainty: 'Everyone has a right to their own opinion', despite what teachers or leaders might think. For assignments, it is important to find out the lecturers' opinions.
5. 'All knowledge and value are contextual and relative.' For assignments, students should enquire: 'What is required of me in this context?'

Position 3: Commitment stages (Approaches 5 and 6 on the activity above)

6. Personal orientation: you feel it is necessary to make a commitment to certain viewpoints (out of a range of possibilities) with an understanding of, and tolerance for, other viewpoints.
7. You have made a commitment to certain viewpoints.
8. The implications of your commitment have been experienced and you realise the responsibilities this brings.
9. You regard your commitment to your views as 'an ongoing, unfolding activity' through which your lifestyle and identity are expressed.

📖 Reflections Uncertainty

- What are your expectations of your lecturers? Do you expect them to provide, or lead you towards, a 'right answer'?
- How comfortable do you feel with the idea that there may not be 'right answers' to questions that are important to you?
- How open you are to hearing opinions that contradict your own?

If this subject interests you, ask your tutors for literature that discusses the nature of 'truth' or 'fact' or 'right answers' in your subject area.

Changing position

Perry found that it can take years for students to feel comfortable at stages 7–9 of this hierarchy. You may find you are in very different positions on the hierarchy depending on the issue.

You do not have to agree that Perry's hierarchy applies to every question. However, the hierarchy can be a useful tool for evaluating the nature of your own responses to issues, and your readiness to accept uncertainty on that issue. You will know how comfortable or uncomfortable you feel about applying any particular stage to your own ideas. You may need a greater knowledge of all the issues and the consequences of taking a particular position in a wide range of circumstances in order to change position on the hierarchy.

It can be hard to feel comfortable at levels 4–9 on some issues unless your sense of self, your

beliefs or your values also change. There isn't a 'quick fix' to changing the way we think. However, being aware of how we are thinking and responding can help the process of development.

You can also use Perry's hierarchy to help you understand where other people are in their thinking. It is important to be sensitive to where people are situated: you cannot force people into a different set of beliefs.

Transitional learning and 'disequilibrium'

Issues discussed in higher education may not have 'right' answers. There may be several answers or it may depend on how particular evidence is assessed or there may be insufficient evidence to come to a firm conclusion. Some issues discussed at this level will directly challenge what you have learnt before, or seem to contradict views that you or people close to you hold as valuable. This can be unsettling or confusing.

📖 Reflection Confusion

- Do you feel that you are finding it harder to learn since entering university?
- Do you ever feel that you are more confused about what an issue involves when you find out more about it?
- Do you feel you are going backwards the more you learn?
- How does this make you feel? Do you think you are really 'going backwards'?

'Equilibration'

Saven-Baden (2000) uses the term 'transitional learning' to refer to 'shifts' that occur when students' frames of references, or 'life world' are challenged by their learning, especially as the result of critical reflection. You may feel this at certain times when you move onto a higher level of learning. Saven-Baden decribes this state as: 'characterised by frustration and confusion, and a loss of sense of self'.

This suggests that we can interpret some confusion as a healthy sign. It indicates that we are pushing ourselves, our learning, our knowledge, our skills beyond their former level. In other words, we are not stagnating. Piaget (1975) regarded this process of 'equilibration' as essential to our development. Equilibration occurs in three stages:

1. Equilibrium: first there is a state of satisfaction with our current ways of thinking and doing.

2. Disequilibrium: then we gain a sense of growing dissatisfaction and an awareness of the limitations of our existing ways of thinking and doing. This is the stage where confusion and worry can set in.

3. A more stable equilibrium: finally, if we persist in our enquiries, we can move to a more sophisticated way of thinking that overcomes the limitations of our previous thinking and performance.

Siegler (1991) cites the example of a child who thinks that only animals are living things. When she hears plants referred to as being 'alive', she becomes uncertain of what 'alive' means. This uncertainty, although temporarily uncomfortable, is a necessary stage in opening up to a new understanding of the world. Dissatisfaction begins an internal questioning which then opens us up to exploring new options.

For students to progress to more sophisticated ways of thinking, they need to be receptive to disequilibrium and to be able to manage or 'contain' short-term confusion. Otherwise, they may cling to the 'security' of their former equilibrium.

> ### 📖 *Reflection*   Coping with disequilibrium
>
> - Think back to a time when you felt you would never learn something – but did. What was it that was difficult to learn?
> - How did you manage to work through the 'confusion' or disheartened stage to the stage where you had achieved your goal?
> - What was it like to be successful in the end?
> - How well do you feel you can manage the 'disequilibrium stage' as a student? What kind of support would help?

Holding the uncertainty

When we feel uncertain or confused, we lose our sense of equilibrium. Naturally, this makes us want to find our 'balance' again. The temptation is to act too quickly, rushing in to find a solution so that we feel better. Often, this leads to hasty action which limits our possibilities.

Although it may feel uncomfortable, it is important to learn to experience the feelings of discomfort and to 'sit with them' for a while, whilst we find out more about the situation. We need to:

- acknowledge the feeling of discomfort or anxiety;
- allow ourselves to wait before rushing into action;

- find help and support if we need it. Talking to somebody can help;
- find out more about the idea or situation that challenges us;
- aim to understand what it is that we find so challenging – and look for potential opportunities;
- consider our options, preferably within a problem-solving strategy;
- act when we have weighed up the options.

Not everyone appreciated Gary's capacity to sit with uncertainty until he had weighed up all options carefully.

📖 *Reflection*   Managing uncertainty

In your reflective journal, jot down your responses to the following questions.

- What kinds of uncertainty have you been faced with recently?
- What was your response?
- In retrospect, do you think you could have managed this uncertainty differently or more constructively?
- Did you look for any support in managing this uncertainty? If not, what stopped you?
- What could you do to improve the way you manage uncertainty?

Motivators and inhibitors to excellence

For both study and work, we are subject to influences that either enhance performance, or else inhibit our progress. Dilts et al. (1990) offer a useful framework for exploring factors that can inhibit or promote learning. This section adapts Dilts's model, using eight levels to analyse performance. We are usually affected at one or more of these levels, which prevent us from achieving excellence.

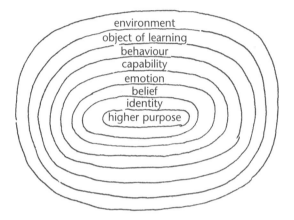

Levels of inhibition and motivation (adapted from Dilts et al., 1990).

Improving performance

1. Environmental (where? when? with whom?)

The over-arching context in which learning takes place has a profound effect upon learning. This could be the wider social, cultural or ideological context or the immediate physical environment such as the lighting or background distractions. If your primary difficulty in improving performance is primarily environmental, this may be evident in the way you speak:

'I can't learn *here, now*, with *them*, on *this* course, at *this university*, with *that lecturer*, from *this book* . . .'

If this sounds like you, what can you do to change the environment to suit your needs?

2. The object of learning: content (what?)

If you find something difficult, it can help to change way the task is worded:

- rephrase instructions;
- put things into your own words;
- imagine you are explaining the issue to someone much younger;
- look for real-life examples that are similar;
- draw the problem out as a chart, diagram or picture.   .

If your primary difficulty lies in the subject matter, this may be evident in comments such as:

- 'I can't learn *that*';
- '*it* doesn't make sense';
- '*what's it* supposed to be about?';
- '*it's* nonsense to me.'
- '*it's* boring.' '*It's* irrelevant.'

3. Behaviours (what do we do?)

You may feel you want one thing, but behave as if you wanted something else. For example, students usually want to get a good grade for their work. However, they may not read or think or talk enough around the subject to develop deep understanding and expertise. This may be a question of priorities (too many conflicting demands on their time) or poor induction into the culture of higher education (not realising that this is what students are expected to do.) Inhibition at this level is expressed in speech that emphasises 'doing words':

- 'I can't *learn* or *do* that';
- '*writing* essays is too difficult';
- 'It takes me too long *to do* that'.

4. Capability (how?)

If your prime difficulty is at the capability level, you are likely to put the emphasis on words and phrases expressing ability:

- 'I'm *not able* to learn that'.
- 'I *don't know how* to learn that'.

If this sounds like you, then consider why you are not able to do what you wish:

- it could be lack of practice;
- it could be because you have not spent long enough building up a good foundation

knowledge and appropriate thinking skills: see Chapter 6 on the way the brain develops to support new learning;

- you may need to improve study skills;
- you may be in the 'transitional stage' referred to above (p. 84);
- you may work better at a different pace: many people find university programmes are very rushed;
- you may benefit from additional support and guidance.

Give yourself time to approach each task. Break bigger tasks into smaller, manageable targets. Find or set up a support group or action set (see Chapter 5).

5. Emotional (affect)

If the primary difficulty lies at an emotional level, you may emphasise words that refer to emotions: 'I *feel* I'll never learn this.' 'This *irritates, annoys, angers, upsets* me.' Alternatively, you may express emotions through tears or your behaviour. The emotion may be related simply to difficulties with current study. However, there is very often a link to earlier learning which was distressing in some way.

On the other hand, positive emotions can have a beneficial effect upon learning. Positive feelings about oneself, the learning context, the course, and potential outcomes can produce much higher motivation.

6. Beliefs and values (why?)

Our belief systems exercise a strong hold over our learning. We use beliefs as a basis for action. Beliefs about self-worth and individual potential are especially powerful: some students have a deeply held belief that they 'not supposed to be' at university. Have you ever felt that you 'are not good enough', or 'people like me cannot do well at university'? Do you feel the subject you are studying is really worthwhile? If your primary difficulty lies on the belief level, this may be apparent in speech such as:

- 'I'm not likely to star at this subject';
- 'This is a soft option: I need to focus my attention on the other modules';
- 'It's only a discussion group so I don't need to turn up.'

There may also be a conflict between values and behaviours: 'Music is what is important to me, that's what I'd like to study, but I need a job at the end of this so, here I am, taking Business Studies.'

You can work through some of the activities earlier in this chapter and Chapter 1. Challenge negative thinking. Speak to someone who can give you useful and constructive advice about how to achieve your aims. Consider where the negative beliefs originated. Bear in mind that it can take time to change something as fundamental as our beliefs.

7. Identity (who?)

Some students, when they encounter difficulties, experience this at the identity level. They decide that they are 'the kind of person who can't learn'. They emphasise the 'I' in descriptions of their difficulties: '*I* can't learn it . . .' or even 'People *like me* can't . . .'. Do you identify with being:

● a 'bad student';
● a 'lost cause';
● 'mediocre' or 'average';
● 'the clown in the group';
● 'the one who sits at the back;'
● 'not a scientist';
● a similar negative identity?

If so, where did this identity come from?

Our sense of identity is very powerful, so if the primary difficulty is at the identity level, it is a good idea to address this as a priority.

8. Higher purpose or mission

'Higher purpose' refers to overall direction and motivation that drives a person. This might be the good that you hope will stem from completing your degree: to help others, be a role model, gain more independence, enter a profession that matters to you, etc. Usually, higher purpose is associated with wanting good for others, with creativity and artistic endeavour or with spirituality. If study is associated with a higher purpose, you are more likely to be well-motivated and to persevere through difficulties.

📖 *Reflection*   Identify your primary level for improvement

● Which of the previous levels do you think is most significant in its effects upon your learning and performance?
● Which levels have positive effects upon your studies or performance?
● To which levels do you most need to pay attention? What action will you take to address this?

This chapter covers a great deal of ground. As with any issues that relate to intra-personal matters, it is not a chapter to race through and feel you have 'got it'.

Many of the exercises in this chapter can be repeated with specific issues or questions in mind. You will also find that the responses you give on a day when you wake up feeling confident and happy are very different from those you give on days when you feel more vulnerable. This is to be expected. The issues covered in this chapter provide useful material for further exploration through your reflective journal.

This chapter offered a basic introduction to some of the issues associated with personal self-management. The activities and strategies here may be all you will need for the issues that face you as a student and in your first graduate jobs. The chapter offers tools for analysing a situation quickly, for identifying resources, for managing your time, and for exploring your own mind-set. It offers strategies for developing a solution-focused, positive thinking style that can be applied in any circumstance, and not simply for study. It also offers you tools for beginning to analyse and understand emotional intelligence.

As a student, you are especially likely to experience times of uncertainty. A stimulating, higher-level education should be challenging. You should feel stretched. You should feel that occasionally the ground is moving beneath your feet. Confusion and uncertainty are characteristics of moving from 'novice' to more expert or sophisticated levels of thinking. If you know this, then you should be able to cope with that uncertainty without feeling something is very wrong.

Your intra-personal life is a rich source of information for you. It is one of the most important and valuable subjects you can ever study: you cannot know enough about the 'inner life' of your mind. The knowledge you gain about yourself and how you can best manage your own attitudes and thought processes will enable you to optimise your performance in any walk of life.

Further reading

Cottrell, Stella (2003) *The Study Skills Handbook*, 2nd edn (Basingstoke: Palgrave Macmillan).

Covey, S. R. (1999) *The Seven Habits of Highly Effective People: Restoring the Character Ethic* (London: Simon and Schuster).

Fennell, M. (1999) *Overcoming Low Self-esteem: A Self-Help Guide Using Cognitive Behavioural Techniques* (London: Robinson).

Goleman, D. (1995) *Emotional Intelligence* (London: Bloomsbury).

Heron, J. (1992) *Feeling and Personhood* (London: Sage Publications).

Neenan, M. and Dryden, W. (2002) *Life Coaching: A Cognitive–Behavioural Approach* (New York: Brunner-Routledge).

Chapter 4

Successful problem-solving and task management

A problem well stated is a problem half solved.

Charles F. Kettering

Learning outcomes

This chapter offers you opportunities to:

● understand what is meant by problem-solving
● develop techniques and approaches associated with successful problem-solving
● develop the confidence to take on tasks, problems and projects
● become a 'good self-starter'
● understand the processes involved in basic project management
● audit your own 'competitiveness'.

Introduction

Problem-solving is highly valued by employers. They want graduates to 'hit the ground running', able to apply skills to new situations and deal with new tasks with minimum supervision. Almost every activity, task or problem will draw on the following set of processes and skills:

1. Strategy: tactics and an overall plan.
2. Techniques: methods to use.
3. People skills: working with others in appropriate ways to achieve the goal.
4. Self-management: managing your time, personal issues, feelings and performance.
5. Creativity: finding ideas that contribute towards a solution.

People who are very good at problem-solving usually bring people skills, self-management and creativity to the task. These three factors are so important that they each have chapters dedicated to them. This chapter introduces some basic problem-solving and task-management techniques.

Tasks and problems

'Task' covers a wide range of circumstances. In this chapter, 'task' is used flexibly to refer to any activity or part of a larger project. The term 'problem' is also used flexibly. It can be:

● any question that calls for an answer;
● a puzzle waiting to be solved;
● a situation requiring a response;
● a challenge to be met.

It is important to separate the idea of 'problem-solving' from that of 'difficulty' or 'trouble'. Problem-solving is not necessarily difficult, although it can be applied to difficult situations. Any situation that presents a challenge or an opportunity for a new approach can be treated as a formal 'problem' that requires a solution.

Activity: Selecting a focus

In order to provide a focus for this chapter, identify one problem, task, assignment or personal goal that is relevant to you. Refer to this as you work through each of the sections below.

For each of the following statements, rate your confidence on a score of 4 to zero.

Rating: *Very confident = 4   Confident = 3   Quite confident = 2   Not very confident = 1*
Not confident at all/Don't know = 0

I am confident in:	Rating	See pp.
1. using basic approaches to problem-solving		91–3
2. knowing what is meant by 'elaborating' a problem		93
3. applying a similarity approach to problem-solving		93–4
4. applying a strategy to problem-solving		95
5. applying a multiple-solution approach to problem-solving		96
6. evaluating multiple solutions		98
7. setting criteria to evaluate a solution		99
8. identifying priorities		99
9. setting targets		100–3
10. drawing up an action plan		102
11. organising project time		103–4
12. my ability to get down to work on a task		105
13. my ability to be a good self-starter		106
14. my ability to stick with a task until it is completed		106
15. my ability to finish off a task		107
16. my understanding of what is meant by a 'project'		107–8
17. my understanding of the difference between student essays and student projects		108
managing a project		108–10
19. using performance indicators		110
20. using soft criteria to evaluate my performance		111
21. using benchmarks		111
22. my understanding of personal 'competitiveness'		112
23. my ability to lead a project		143–5
24. making best use of the strengths of project team members 121–6		121–6
25. my ability to find creative solutions to problems		158

Score _____

Interpreting your score

If your self-ratings were accurate, you have a score for your overall problem-solving skills. This is a rough indicator of how confident you are about these skills, which may, of course, be different from your actual ability. A score over 40 is reasonable, a score over 55 is quite good, a score over 70 is very good, and a score over 85 is excellent. However, you should interpret how good your score is depending on:

● how long you have been on the programme;
● how much experience you have had in project work;
● how much guidance you have already received in project work.

Compare your score now with the score you give yourself when you have completed the chapter or when you have undertaken some project work.

Basic approaches to problem solving

Basic approaches

Your list probably included some or all of the following:

Talking to others

You would probably want to ask other people for ideas, their experience, what they know about the persons and places involved. People are a key resource in problem-solving. This is why successful companies value 'people skills'. Finding out what you need to know from others, or 'informal learning', is the dominant form of professional development for most American companies (Rossett and Sheldon, 2001).

Lists

Many people organise their lives by lists. They are quick and easy tools to use and excellent starting points for any problem.

Finding out information

You may have included approaches such as browsing the Internet, checking catalogues and looking in books. Researching information, weighing it up and selecting what you need are all useful to problem-solving.

Calculating

Many problems include a number component, such as working out the budget and finances. Some problems are solved more easily by using a mathematical formula. You may have used calculations to work out how much time there would be for different aspects of each of the two essays, or how to meet the budget for the meal or holiday.

Item	£
glass	39
paint	24
glue	12
timber	53

Following the rules

Sometimes it is easier to follow procedures laid down for the activity. Mixing chemicals for a particular purpose requires very precise measurements of specific chemicals, for example. If you are not used to cooking, following a recipe step by step will be helpful. When you become more familiar with the process, you will know how and when to adapt rules in order to achieve the results you want.

Trial and error

You may prefer to jump in at the deep end, trying out various ideas until you hit the right one. This works well for some people, but is a very labour-intensive way of working unless there really are no options. You may find you are good at 'trial and error' for some areas (such as cooking) and less so in others (gardening). Sometimes this is regarded as intuition, but may be the result of expertise built up over time.

Visualising

You may have pictured the problem in your 'mind's eye', checking off all the places where you might go on such a holiday or what the meal might be like. You may also have visualised each of the different activities, seeing yourself performing each. Successful sportspeople tend to use visualising techniques to see the exact details of how they will achieve victory. This can be applied to most areas of life.

Charting

You may have used a chart, flow diagram or other graphic device to draw out the problem, so that you could work it out visually.

Calling upon a similar experience

You may have thought about recent meals that you have cooked and whether you could adapt these to suit a child or the person with the allergy. If you have already completed an essay, you may have run through the different processes, working out how much time you would need for each process, based on your experience. You might even have been able to work out some ways of saving time in order to meet the deadlines.

Many problems are relatively simple like these. We can use different problem-solving strategies at once, moving back and forward between them as necessary. For example, to organise yourself to meet essay deadlines, you might:

- ring an academic adviser or tutor to ask for advice
- negotiate with other people to arrange for cover for your work shift or cooking rota
- draw on a similar essay you completed for a previous programme
- calculate the time available for all the things you have to do
- chart the time available to you in your diary
- visualise where you left your notes
- draw a network or outline pattern of all the ideas you have on the essay
- research further information
- go for a walk to clear your mind
- Etc.

Seven key steps to task management

1. Clarify the task: know exactly what you need to do and why.
2. Start where the energy is . . . all other things being equal.
3. Start much earlier that you think is necessary. This gives you more room for manoeuvre.
4. Think several steps ahead: plan out all the steps required to take you to the end point.
5. Always look for several solutions . . . it is easier than looking for THE one answer.
6. Give yourself tight time limits within early deadlines . . . otherwise tasks tend to expand to fill *all* the time available.
7. Find out the background to the project. Not only are you more likely to meet the project aims, things are also more interesting from the position of an 'expert'.

Problem-solving on the back of an envelope

Simplify

If you feel daunted by all the things there are to consider in working with a problem, begin by simplifying the problem down to essential features. For example, you might be able to summarise your strategy in ten steps on the back of an envelope.

```
Basic problem-solving
  1. Define the problem      What is the real issue?
  2. Desired outcome          What do I want?
  3. Options                  What outcomes are possible?
  4. Feasibility             What is the best option
                              I am likely to achieve?
  5. Feelings                 If I follow through on
                              this option: how will I feel?
  6. Decision                 What is my decision?
  7. Steps                    What must I do, when,
                              with whom, where?
  8. Obstacles                What might get in the way?
                              How will I deal with these?
  9. Action                   Do it!
  10. Evaluation              Did it work?
```

Find the natural sequence

You may find that the problem raises issues in a different order. For example, although the 'core question' is usually the essential question, you may find that you are only able to answer that once you have addressed some of the other issues. It may be that the real problem is working with the obstacles, or managing other people's feelings if they cannot have what they want.

You will probably have to move backward and forward between these questions until you reach the decision-making and action stages. It is worth noticing how many of the ten stages above refer to thinking about the problem before any action is taken.

Problem elaboration

Research shows that people who spend more time at the beginning working out what a task really involves, perform much better. For example, successful mathematics students spend much longer reflecting on what category of mathematical problems they have been set. They look for similarities with problems they have worked on before. They consider various approaches and weigh these up before beginning calculations to solve the problem.

Less successful students tend to launch in too quickly without defining clearly what the problem entails and what needs to be done.

The early planning stage is sometimes referred to as 'problem elaboration'. Elaboration involves analysing a task from all perspectives and defining what the task really involves. The similarity approach outlines one way of doing this.

The 'similarity approach' to problem-solving

Butterworth (1992) argues that if we see how one situation is similar to another, we are better able to cope with that situation. If we cannot see those parallels, then we may believe ourselves incapable of dealing with situations that are well within our actual competence. This suggests that it is worth giving time and thought to what we have achieved in any one situation and considering its applicability to other situations.

The key features of this approach are:

1. Clarify the core questions

State the core questions as simply as possible. Remove unnecessary wording so as to pare the problem down to the essential features. This makes it easier to see whether this problem is similar to one with which you are already familiar.

2. Identify an analogous problem

● What are the core features or components of the problem? What skills, methods or techniques are needed?
● What similarities are there between problems or activities have you undertaken before and the current task?
● How can previous problems help you to think through what is needed for this problem?
● How can you make use of your previous experience and skills to solve this problem?

3. Identify the limitations of the analogy

List the differences between the current problem and previous tasks. The situations will not be identical so the same strategy may not work for the current problem. Identifying the difference is as important as identifying the similarity.

4. Establish significance

● Weigh up the significance of the similarities and differences.
● How will you adapt your strategy to take account of these differences?
● What else do you need to know or to do?

The best way to test out the similarity approach is to put it into action for an issue that is important to you. Work through the activity below, identifying which aspects you find work best for you.

Activity: Solve that problem!

Use the problem you identified in the activity on p. 89 as your 'target problem' for this activity. Either in your journal or on a piece of paper, write answers to as many of the following questions as you can, referring to the target problem.

Orientation (prepare)

1. Define the task. What exactly is the target problem? Can you describe the problem in different words so that it is clearer what needs to be done? What do you want to be different? What is your goal?

2. Identify a situation or problem at which you are more successful. Select one that is as similar as possible to your target problem. Call this the 'area of expertise'.

3. In what ways is the target problem similar to the area of expertise?

4. For the area of expertise, jot down a list of all the things you do to solve the problem or perform the activity. (See p. 46.)

   ● What skills do you use?
   ● Which processes do you use?
   ● What kind of an approach do you take?
   ● What are the steps involved in achieving an end product?

5. In what ways can you apply the skills, processes and methods used in your area of expertise to the target problem?

6. What else could you do?

7. What makes the target problem different from the area of expertise? How will your strategy need to be different in order to fit the target problem?

8. Do you need any additional information, data or assistance? If so, what will you do to gain this?

Strategy (plan)

9. Decide on a course of action.

10. Draw up your action plan, identifying your mini-goals or targets as well as deadlines for these. Your action plan might be elaborate, or it may just be a list. It depends on how complex the problem is – and what suits you. (An outline is provided on p. 102.)

Action (do)

11. Do it! Keep a record of what happens, and check that you are on target.

Evaluation (evaluate)

12. How well did the strategy work for you? What needed to be different for a more successful outcome?

📖 **Reflect**

● How useful was your previous experience in finding and implementing a solution for this problem?
● What did you do well?
● What could you have done better?

The ROSA-E strategy

The approach taken above followed a set format to help analyse the problem. This is the ROSA-E strategy, shown in the diagram below. This is a cycle that can be applied to the overall project and also for tasks within a project. Reflection is at the core of the cycle, and is applied to all processes.

Orientation

The cycle begins with orientation, which includes problem evaluation and good advance planning. The orientation stage is like starting out on a journey. When starting a journey, solving a problem or managing a task, you need to begin with some basic questions. You need to know where you are going – your direction. However, the reason for the journey is likely to be more important than the journey itself: what are you hoping to achieve? What is the central purpose? What needs to be done? What do you hope to see at the end of the journey? You need to know your starting point – and to make sure you have the necessary resources to achieve your goals.

ROSA-E Problem-solving strategy

Strategy

Identify an approach or methodology to achieve your goals. For academic purposes, there are usually methods appropriate to your own subject. Your tutor will give you guidance on this.

Actions, targets, deadlines
- Identify specific actions: what exactly must you do?

- what are the main steps or stages?
- set targets and time-scales for each stage;
- set SMART-F targets (see p. 100);
- how will you meet these targets?
- draw these up into an action plan (see p. 102).

Priorities
- Identify priorities: what are all the things you need to do?
- What is essential? What can be left?

Monitoring points
- Set specific times for monitoring your progress as you go along. Write these into your action plan.

At the end of the strategy stage, you should feel that you have planned effectively, having thought through all possible angles. You should be clear about what action now needs to be taken.

Action

This is the 'doing' stage'. Work through your action plan, observing your targets. This is the first real test of your planning and strategy.

Monitor your performance
Consider how well you are progressing towards your goals. What have you achieved? What remains to be done?

Review your progress
- Do you need to revise your overall strategy?
- Are you meeting targets and deadlines? If not, do you need to revise these?
- Are you maintaining your motivation? If not, what can you do to improve this?
- Are you working within your budget and resources? If not, what action must you take?

Keep records
- Consider how you can demonstrate that you have worked to a strategy, reflected on your progress and revised your plan to increase your effectiveness. Gathering evidence as you go along will help you to do this.
- Keep a record of what you do.

Evaluation

Evaluation is easier if clear targets have been set, and usually is measured in terms of those targets. However, it is useful to evaluate the overall strategy and to step back to look at the 'bigger picture'.

Achievement

Did you:

- Achieve your targets?
- Meet the deadlines for the overall project?
- Achieve the overall goal?
- Keep to budget?
- Maintain good working relationships?
- Learn anything?

Strategy effectiveness

For each aspect of the cycle (reflection, orientation, planning and action):

- What worked well?
- What could be improved?
- What evidence is there of your performance, reflection and achievement?

The 'multiple solution approach' to problem-solving

You are more likely to arrive at the best option if you consider many solutions. The 'multiple solution approach' puts emphasis on generating several different solutions to the same problem.

Propose an initial solution

This may be through using the similarity approach described above. This does not need to be a perfect solution as it is only one of many that you will consider. Jot down:

- the ways in which this already meets the needs of the situation;
- weak points in the proposal or aspects that need to be considered further.

Brainstorm further ideas

- Jot down, quickly, as many ideas as possible. For this stage, put words such as 'realistic' and 'sensible' aside for a moment: release your imagination.

- Brainstorm solutions to the 'weak points' of the first solution you proposed.

Identify 'seed' ideas

For every idea, look for the seed of one positive aspect. The idea itself may be maverick ('relocate to the moon'; 'win the lottery'; 'kidnap the professor') but it may hint at a workable solution. For example:

- 'Relocating to the moon'. The idea of relocation might be useful. Would a change of room or building help? Have all options been considered?
- 'Winning the lottery'. There may be other sources of money. Would it be useful to look for financial backing from a local business or charity?
- 'Kidnapping the professor'. Would a tutor, student or local employer offer advice or mentorship?

Evaluate solutions

Weigh up factors for and against each solution, considering such criteria as:

- Cost: can it be afforded?
- Time: can it be completed in the time available?
- Expertise: is the necessary expertise available?
- Suitability: does it suit the circumstances and people involved?
- Value: which solution provides a good solution with the least effort and cost?
- Risk: will it work? What are the risks?
- Goal: which best meets the project objectives?

Synthesise the best

- Select two or three solutions to consider in more detail.
- Identify the best aspects of each solution.

- Identify ways of synthesising the best features of each solution.
- Check whether the best features of each still work well when brought together into one strategy.

Identify the essential criteria

- Which criteria must be met (time, cost, design, etc.)?
- List these in order of priority. Which are the most important criteria to meet?
- Which solution do you want to go with? Does this meet the criteria you identified as priorities? If not, what can you change or do to ensure that those priorities are met?

Decision making

- Select one solution that best meets essential criteria.
- Fine-tune this option to meet the essential criteria.

Resource sheet

The resource sheet on the following page can be used to weigh up each solution.

Activity: Solve that problem again!

Return to the problem you identified earlier in the chapter as your 'focus'. In your journal, follow through the strategy below, referring to the comments in the previous paragraphs.

Orientation (prepare)
1. Define the task. What exactly is the problem? What do you want to be different? What is your goal?

2. Propose an initial solution. Identify the ways it does and does not solve the problem.

3. Identify the essential criteria that must be met by any solution for your problem.

Strategy (plan)
4. Brainstorm as many other solutions as you can.

5. Identify the good ideas hidden within each solution.

6. Select two or three solutions to consider in more detail.

7. Evaluate each solution according to criteria relevant to you (cost, time, etc.).

8. Synthesise the best ideas from all the solutions.

9. Decide on a solution that best fits the priorities and adapt it to meet the criteria.

Action (do)
10. Carry out your plan.

Evaluation (evaluate)
11. What worked and what could be improved?

📖 Reflect

- How useful was your initial solution in contributing to the final solution?
- How did your solution evolve by working through a multiple solution approach?

Evaluating Multiple Solutions

Problem (*state briefly*):

Criteria that must be met (in order of importance):

1.

2.

3.

4.

Aspect	Solution no.
Details of this proposed solution	
Strengths of this solution	
Gaps and weaknesses	
Seed ideas: interesting aspects of this solution	
Time considerations:	
Costs: good, bad, resolvable?	
How far does the solution meet key criterion 1?	
How far does the solution meet key criterion 2?	
How far does the solution meet key criterion 3?	
How far does the solution meet key criterion 4?	
Parts to keep and build into the final solution	

Problem-solving techniques

This section introduces some common problem-solving techniques difficulties. These include:

- setting goals;
- setting criteria to evaluate a solution;
- identifying priorities;
- setting targets and drawing up an action plan;
- planning project time;
- getting down to it;
- becoming a good 'self-starter';
- sticking with a task;
- completing a task.

Setting goals

Setting goals is an important part of the orientation stage of your strategy. When considering your goal:

- visualise what it would be like to achieve it (see pp. 21–2, Chapter 1);
- identify how you will know when you have achieved it: what will be different?
- evaluate whether it is realistic;
- identify what you will have to sacrifice in order to achieve it. Is it worth it?
- think about your beliefs and values. Is it 'you'?

Setting criteria to evaluate a solution

Although evaluation takes place at the end of a task or project, you need to consider, at the beginning, the criteria by which you will evaluate success. Develop criteria that give you what you want but which are achievable.

Dream solution
Begin with the ideal. As Chapter 1 emphasises, it is important to work towards a 'vision'. However, use the vision to inform what you want, using it as a guide rather than a strait-jacket.

Realistic option
What would you accept as a reasonably good outcome that is both motivating and

achievable? What are the main features of this option?

Identify relevant criteria for a solution
For each problem, consider the relative importance of issues such as:

- maximum cost;
- value for money;
- total time in hours (absolute maximum);
- desired finish date;
- meeting deadlines;
- quality issues;
- design features;
- specific expertise needed;
- levels of permissible risk;
- meeting assignment criteria;
- meeting clients' criteria;
- particular details to be included;
- health and safety issues;
- equal opportunities issues;
- legal considerations;
- other issues.

Identify priorities amongst the criteria
When you have a complete list, write these down in the order that is most important.

- Which criteria are essential and must be met?
- Which criteria are relatively flexible?
- Which criteria are very flexible?

Select only a few essential criteria and be prepared to be flexible on the others. The more essential criteria you set, the more difficult it will be to find a solution.

Identifying priorities

One common reason for not getting under way with a problem or project is that there are too many things competing for your attention. Emotions such as fear of not getting everything done, or guilt at letting someone down, make it hard to separate out what can be left and what must be addressed straight away.

To help set priorities, Neenan and Dryden (2002) suggest dividing tasks into one of four categories:

1. Urgent and important
2. Not urgent but important

3. Urgent but not important
4. Not urgent and not important

You may find it helpful to colour-code these using the resource sheet on p. 101 so that you can see urgent items most easily. For example:

1. **Red – Category 1: urgent and important**
   Deadlines, crises, tasks timed for today, tasks which must come first in a sequence.

2. **Yellow – Category 2: not urgent but important**
   Category 2 activities enable you to plan ahead. These should be addressed before they become urgent. Prioritise between these according to when they must take place in a sequence, or the consequences of leaving them for too long.

3. **Orange – Category 3: Urgent but not important**
   If possible, leave these until category 1 tasks are completed. Category 3 items may not need to be undertaken at all, but can attract our attention unduly because they are 'urgent'. Emails are a good example of this. What other examples are typical of your own week?

4. **Blue – Category 4: not urgent and not important**
   These are often good time-wasting activities. They can make us feel like we are busy, so that we do not get down to what is really needed. Reading junk mail, sorting out old papers, cleaning out cupboards may fall into this category.

SMART-F target setting

Most tasks benefit from clear, achievable targets. SMART targets make it easier to see what must be done and then to evaluate success. SMART-F targets build in reasonable flexibility, so you can plan for unexpected contingencies. SMART-F stands for:

Activity: Identify priorities

For the problem you are addressing at present:

● Brainstorm a list all the things you need to do.
● Divide the items on your list into the four categories on the priority sheet on p. 101. Write the things that are most important and urgent in the top left-hand box. Use the top left of that box for the most urgent items.
● Use the bottom right of the page for the least important items.

When you have completed the priority sheet, use it to guide you in organising tasks into a logical order:

● Reorganise your original list of priorities into the order you will now complete tasks.
● Set targets for each priority (see 'SMART-F targets' below).

● *Specific*: 'I will complete the first section of my essay by this evening.'
● *Measurable*: 'I will produce the first three draft pages of my essay by this evening.'
● *Achievable:* 'This should be achievable because I have completed the research, organised my notes, and already produced the outline plan.'
● *Realistic*: 'I should be able to write three pages as I have written up to ten pages in a day before, and have done the preparatory work.'
● *Time-bound*: ' I will finish by 8:30 p.m.'
● *Flexible*: 'I could continue until 10:30 p.m. if necessary. If I find I have additional research to do for those pages, I can slot that in tomorrow between 9:00 and 11.00 a.m.'

Targets should provide clear guidelines for action and be built into an action plan (see p. 102). However, they are not written in stone: they should be monitored and reviewed as the project proceeds so that it can be completed on time.

Priority Sheet

Divide your list of tasks into the four categories below. Then set targets for each priority (see 'identifying priorities' on pp. 99–100).

1. **RED**
   Urgent and important

2. **YELLOW**
   Not urgent but important

3. **ORANGE**
   Urgent but not important

4. **BLUE**
   Not urgent and not important

Action Plan

Goal:

Completion date:

Target	Milestones (steps to be taken)	By date	By whom	Evidence that milestone is completed	Done (✓)
	1				
	2				
	3				
	4				
	1				
	2				
	3				
	4				
	5				
	1				
	2				
	3				
	4				
	5				
	1				
	2				
	3				

Evaluate each of the following targets and tick where appropriate. Which of these are well-formed targets? How far is each a SMART-F target? Look for key weaknesses in each.

Target	Specific	Measurable	Achievable	Realistic	Time-bound	Flexible
1. Everyone will like me.						
2. No mistakes in this essay.						
3. Give up smoking.						
4. Accomplish something by 6:00 p.m. tonight.						
5. Write a 250–300-word introduction by 3:00 p.m. today. (Essay to be handed in at 6:00 p.m. in two days' time.)						
6. Write a 1000-word report within the next 24 hours.						
7. Attend more lectures from October onwards.						
8. Increase my marks by 5% for all assignments during this semester.						
9. Find a 3-month work placement in a retail industry before the start of next semester.						
10. Gain a work placement in the BBC by September.						

In your jounal, jot down any weaknesses you can identify in these targets. When you have completed your evaluation, check your responses with those on p. 114.

Planning project time

Project schedules

Good time management may require you to use several time-management tools simultaneously:

- action plans: set targets and deadlines for each step. Action plans are organised according to theme.
- schedules: organise all tasks and steps in the order they must be completed. For large projects, there is software available to organise the work schedule;
- diaries: organise tasks more closely within a week or day.

Example of a work schedule

Item	Jan 1	Jan 2	Jan 3	Jan 4	Jan 5	Jan 6	Jan 7	Jan 8	Jan 9	Jan 10	Jan 11	Jan 12	Jan 13	Jan 14
Group meetings	X			X	X		X		X	X		X	X	X
Elaborate the problem	X	X	X	X										
Allocate group tasks and roles	X													
Allocate research tasks		X		X	X				X	X				
Finalise strategy				X										
Research			X	X	X	X	X	X	X	X				
Discuss research progress				X			X		X					
Analyse and discuss data									X	X	X			
Allocate writing tasks				X					X					
First draft to group											X			
Responses to first draft													X	
Etc.														

Project diary

The time slots on the project schedule are very broad. Several days are allocated for some aspects of the project. So that every project team member knows what they are doing, the project diary organises time in detail on a daily basis. For your projects, you may find it helpful to map out in diary form more specific aspects of each task, indicating when each task will finish. An example of a project diary entry is given below.

Projects often go wrong because there is no flexibility to the time schedule, or no 'slack' time, built in. Final deadlines are usually strict, leaving little scope for changes at the last minute. It is useful, therefore, to schedule the early stages of a project very closely, in order to increase the incentive to work efficiently. Set interim deadlines so that there are early achievements and so you can check if the project is running to schedule. This will make it easier to meet the final deadlines.

Example of a project diary

Tuesday 2nd January

9:00–10:00	Jane buys coach tickets.
11:00–12:00	Jane and Miko attend the primary school to discuss project with headteacher.
10:00–12:00	Paul undertakes literature search.
12:00	Jane and Miko catch the coach back to college.
12:00–2:00	Paul and Raphaela look for articles on similar projects.
2:30	Whole team meets to discuss findings.
4:00–6:00	Elaborate the problem and define the area of research.

Getting down to it!

Do you delay beginning an activity because:

- you get easily distracted into irrelevant activities?
- the time isn't right?
- you need more experience?
- you work better at the last moment?
- tomorrow is better?
- you worry that the outcome won't be right?
- you think something will go wrong?
- everything else is more important?

If so, procrastination prevents you from following through on an action plan.

As the project deadline looms, Michael finds it ever more essential to ensure that his pencils are lined up parallel to the Greenwich Meridian.

Procrastination can be a chronic condition (Sapadin, 1997). If you always struggle to start a task, you may need professional help. However, if the problem is less serious, some of the following steps can help.

Identify the core issue
- Acknowledge that you are procrastinating.
- What sort of things are you better at getting down to?
- What kinds of activity do you keep putting off?

- Identify what characterises the things you put off: are there any themes?
- Do you procrastinate more over some tasks than others? Are some times worse than others?

Check your motivation, vision and targets
- Check your motivation. Give yourself more rewards for each stage you complete.
- Check your 'vision' (see Chapter 1). It may not be motivating you sufficiently. Link tasks more closely to your long-term vision.
- Break goals and targets into small chunks that could be completed in a short burst.

Identify the hindrance zone
- Identify what feelings (boredom, fear, irritation, anger, frustration) you associate with the activity. Can you commit yourself to putting up with the discomfort of these feelings until the task is done? What would help you tolerate these until the task is completed?
- Give yourself more encouraging messages about the task.
- Find a different way of describing the activity so that it becomes more interesting for you.
- Combine the task with something you enjoy, such as listening to music.
- Stay away from anyone who encourages your procrastination.
- Identify the level of inhibition (p. 85).

Commandeer support
- Arrange to do tasks in pairs or a group. It is harder to avoid a task if others are involved.
- Ask a friend to check on you. Give them permission to tell you to get started.
- Join an action set (see p. 126).

Create unavoidable reminders
- Write yourself 20 'post-its'™ giving yourself instructions to get started on a particular task today. Put these on surfaces where you cannot avoid them
- Write 20 'post-its'™ detailing what you will gain by completing the project.
- Write more precise details of what you have to do into your diary.

Becoming a good 'self-starter'

Many job specifications ask for 'good self-starters'. Some people are naturally motivated to launch into a project with minimum assistance. However, the characteristics of a good self-starter can be acquired by most people. Self-starters tend to be:

- highly motivated; they create a clear vision of the task and set themselves specific goals;
- have strategies for 'getting going';
- open to the possibility of success;
- solution-focused: they will search out information that will bring about a solution;
- organised: they develop a strategy and they use their time well;
- self-confident: they trust they can manage the task reasonably well.
- good at finding support and asking for help when they need it;
- good at people skills (this is necessary as, when starting a new task, they usually need information and assistance);
- aware of their own limitations: this is essential – a good self-starter will be open about what they do not know and what they cannot do. They either develop the skills themselves or find someone who can help.

Such characteristics are usually acquired in the process of other tasks, such as team working, leading groups, managing smaller projects, and working up to larger projects. However, each

time you undertake any assignment, you can practise techniques that are relevant to being a good self-starter.

Sticking with a task

The characteristics of successful people, noted in Chapter 1, included a willingness to 'do what it takes', even if this means working very long hours, and developing patience. Edison, who is quoted in the activity below, is remembered today for inventions that contributed to the development of film and the light bulb. Edison is also famous for his adage that genius owes only 5 per cent to inspiration and 95 per cent to perspiration!

Completing a task

The following characteristics are usually needed to take tasks through to completion on a consistent basis:

● enthusiasm
● ability to see or conceptualise the 'end product'
● perseverance
● patience
● self-belief: belief that you can do it
● being willing to give the task sufficient time
● being prepared to practice
● being prepared to keep thinking of different solutions
● accepting constructive criticism
● searching out a point of interest
● keeping the goal and benefits in mind
● pride in a job well done.

📖 *Reflection*   Finishing off

● Which of the above characteristics are your strongest?
● What examples can you give of where you used those characteristics?
● Which do you need to develop further?
● Do you have other qualities that help you to take a task through to completion?

● Think of five things you could do to develop your 'finishing' skills.
● How and when will you apply these to meet your current goals?

If you find it very difficult to develop these characteristics, you may find it helpful to speak to a student counsellor.

Projects

What is a project?

A project is:
'A temporary endeavour undertaken to create a unique product or service.'

Project management is:
'The application of knowledge, skills, tools and techniques to project activities to meet project requirements.'

(Project Management Institute, 2000)

Characteristics of a project

Projects are characterised by:

● *A goal*   There is a purpose, a desired outcome.
● *A discrete focus*   The activity is 'set apart' in some way. It is not part of the usual course of day-to-day events.
● *Magnitude*   Projects are associated with setting aside time to focus on something special, important or that needs to be completed. It suggests a mustering of effort and resources.
● *Time limits*   Projects must be completed within a set time-frame. It should be clear when a project is complete. As the definition above indicates, a project is a temporary event.
● *Management*   Projects are managed, organised and planned events, leading to an outcome within a time-frame.
● *Individuality*   The nature of a project is that it is a one-off event, leading to something unique.

Scale of the project

The characteristics of a project could apply to activities of any scale. An essay, for example, has:

● *A goal*   to address the essay title; to gain a good grade.
● *Discrete focus*   each essay is a separate assignment.
● *Magnitude*   essay writing requires a 'mustering' of time and resources.
● *Time limits*   deadlines are set for assignments.
● *Management*   essay writing involves multiple processes of elaborating the question, research, information management, selection, organising ideas, drafting, editing, fine-tuning, proof-reading. These have to be orchestrated to achieve the final goal.
● *Individuality:*   although all students on a programme may be given the same assignment title, each student is expected to provide an individual answer.

Writing essays can develop some of the skills needed for project work.

Student projects

However, essays are usually distinguished from student 'projects'. For example:

● *Goal:* the purpose of a student project is to develop a more in-depth study than would be expected in an essay. The desired outcomes are usually both the results of the project itself and the development of the competences necessary to manage a project.
● *Discrete focus:* projects are usually one-off pieces of work, related to the overall programme but covering ground decided by the student.
● *Magnitude:* projects usually have greater word limits, but the magnitude is in the level of personal responsibility involved.
● *Individuality:* as you have more control over the content and processes, it is typical for student projects to be more individual and varied than student essays.
● *Time limits:* the time allocations for projects tend to be greater than for essays
● *Management:* projects are usually more complex than essays, requiring more management of the various processes.

Employers' interests in student project skills

Employers are interested in:

● skills and qualities associated with project management;
● experience of undertaking projects;
● the scale of the largest project that you have taken part in;
● the scale of the largest problem you have managed alone.

The scale of projects can be differentiated by such factors as:

● how many people were involved;
● the time scale – how long it was planned to last and how long it did last;
● who 'commissioned it' – whether it was yourself, a tutor, an employer, an agency;
● the size of the budget;
● how many beneficiaries there were (who benefited?);
● the significance of the outcomes. What was the impact of the project?

Student projects do not always give opportunities to develop all these skills or to work on a grand scale, but some work placements do. The student union and voluntary work are also good sources for gaining such experience.

Successful project management

The skills identified on p. 90 are applicable to most projects as well as to general task management. The following items also contribute to project success.

Problem-solving

Problem-solving techniques can be applied to successfully to projects.

Elaboration

Problem-elaboration is especially important to project work as the wrong strategy wastes time and other resources. Heerkens (2002) warns against 'solution jumping': 'the tendency of people to talk about what to do before analysing the situation adequately, trying to develop a solution before thoroughly understanding a problem'.

Piloting the methods

Have a trial run or 'pilot' to test out your methods and materials on a small scale before embarking on the full-scale project. Identify what needs to be changed. This is easier to do after a pilot rather than when the project is well underway.

'Doing what it takes'

Make a commitment to achieve specific goals. You can decide that you will give 'whatever it takes' to make a relationship work, to get good grades for your course-work, to get to grips with a subject you do not understand, to get a job in a specific field, or to launch a business.

'Doing what it takes' may mean that the majority of your time, energies, thinking and even finances go towards the achievement of the goal. This is not necessarily a healthy approach. However, that might be the difference between fully achieving a goal and accepting a compromise. It is a personal decision how far you want to accept a reasonable compromise.

Because projects work to set deadlines and focus on new areas, they tend to demand more time and thought than is usually anticipated. The project leader, in particular, is likely to spend every waking moment on the project if it falls behind deadlines, or if new solutions are required.

'Doing what it takes' is difficult to apply to more than one goal at a time.

📖 Reflection   Commitment

- How far do you think you are generally someone who is willing to 'do what it takes' to gets something done?
- What kinds of activity are more likely to prompt you to put in the most effort and commitment?
- What conditions encourage you to increase your level of commitment?
- What are your limits?

Clarity

Good problem elaboration and planning should mean that it is clear what needs to be done, by whom, where and when. When the plan is clear, the team can work more effectively. Confusion leads to additional work, puts deadlines at risk, puts the team under stress, and can put up the costs.

Decision making

When projects are under-way, you may have to make decisions at speed. This is easier if you have already considered different solutions and planned for contingencies. Keep

the main goal in sight and know which compromises are possible. You will also have to weigh up the relative importance of key criteria such as:

- costs;
- deadlines;
- effects on other people;
- the availability of expertise;
- aspects of quality;
- which changes will be acceptable to the client or commissioning agent (or tutor).

Know the project 'inside out'

To make decisions under pressure, you need to know the project 'inside out'. You need a keen sense of what the 'client' (maybe the tutor in your case) will consider acceptable. Spend time finding out the background to the project. For example, why is it considered important? Are there ethical or political considerations which should be taken into account? What are the most similar projects that have been initiated in the past – and what were the outcomes of these? This information can help you with your own planning and decision making.

Keep the vision in mind

Whilst it is important to keep to deadlines and budgets, it is easy to lose sight of the main purpose of a project. A good leader will keep the team focused on the end-point as well as on interim targets.

The leader is the one who climbs the tallest tree, surveys the entire situation and yells "Wrong jungle!" But how do the busy, efficient producers and managers often respond? "Shut up! We're making progress."   (Covey, 1999).

The whole team must be clear about the background to the project and understand the vision of the person who commissioned it (you, your tutor, a client). This makes each team member feel more involved. It also means that each person is better informed to make interim decisions in line with the overall 'vision'. All project decisions should be guided by the overall goal, not by the requirements of short-term targets.

Team work

Most projects in the workplace are team efforts. If the team does not pull together, the project becomes a 'sick' project: people are unhappy and less willing to put in the extra effort needed to bring the project to completion. Successful managers ascribe their achievements to good team-work and to trusting their team.

Team work requires the ability both to be a good team member, and to be able to take the lead where relevant. This calls for a range of people skills. Hallows (1997), argues: 'Hard though it may be to admit, the people side of projects is more important than the technical side.' Because of the importance of people skills, a specific chapter has been dedicated to this (Chapter 5).

Performance indicators (PI)

How do you know whether what you are doing is successful? 'Performance indicators' are one way of monitoring and evaluating your performance. They 'indicate' where you are doing well or need to improve. Performance indicators should be 'measurable' so that you can compare performance either over time or against the performance of other people. Some examples are:

- 95 per cent of targets to be achieved by the deadline.
- The project to be completed within 5 per cent of the project budget.
- 75 per cent of the participants to indicate in a feedback questionnaire that they are 'very content' with the outcome.

- A mark of 60 per cent or more to be achieved for every assignment.
- Attendance levels to achieve at least 95 per cent.
- Punctuality to be at least 95 per cent.

Meeting the criteria

Performance indicators should be closely linked to the criteria for success identified earlier in the project (see p. 99). They are unlikely to be exactly the same because some criteria may not be measurable. You may meet the criteria of a project without feeling that you performed well in all respects. Your individual or team performance may be different from the criteria for individual projects.

Activity: Meeting the criteria

When you have completed a current project, return to the criteria you set near the beginning of the project (see p. 99). Consider:

- Did you meet the essential criteria (the 'bottom line') that you set?
- Were these criteria realistic?
- What criteria do you think could have been better, if any?

Work with performance indicators

Performance indicators you could use for study or project work include:

- how often you meet deadlines for assignments;
- the number and percentage of the times that you complete a particular action successfully;
- how long it takes to perform a specific activity;
- how often you reach your targets;
- feedback received from others;
- how many of the milestones you set for yourself were achieved;
- how much it cost compared to budget;
- percentage improvement over previous performance;
- grades and marks.

Soft criteria

Some project criteria cannot easily include a number or 'measurable' component. For example, it is hard to quantify:

● creativity;
● innovation;
● ethical approaches;
● sensitivity;
● flexibility;
● emotional intelligence;
● how well you manage a difficult situation;
● responsiveness;
● assertiveness.

Soft criteria require you to develop skills in being an objective evaluator of your own performance. You have to develop a 'feel' for whether something is going well or not. Wherever possible, this should still be evaluated against specific criteria and performance indicators to get a rounded picture of how you are doing. Compare your personal evaluations with feedback from others.

Benchmarks

A benchmark is a point of comparison. For example, a sportsperson might benchmark their speed or accuracy against the records of people at the top of their own sport. A programme on TV might benchmark itself against audience ratings for other programmes. Organisations and projects use benchmarks to measure their performance against other companies or projects.

Good benchmarks compare like with like. For example, if your project involves writing an information leaflet for the public, the benchmarks would need to relate to another project that aimed at producing a similar number of leaflets in a similar time-scale on a similar kind of issue. The performance indicators for such a project might include some of the following:

● how much it costs to produce each leaflet;
● how many readers, when asked, rated the leaflet as useful;
● the percentage of readers who, when asked, rated the leaflet as useful;
● an independent mark (by an independent assessor or tutor);
● a measure of how far the leaflet changed opinion or behaviour.

A good benchmark enables you to evaluate your own outcomes against those of a comparable project or set of benchmarks.

For example, you may find that you wanted to achieve a 90 per cent return for a questionnaire and yet received only 35 per cent. This might feel like failure as it is far short of the target. If you compare this to similar questionnaires in comparable circumstances, you may find that a typical (or benchmark) response is only 20 per cent. This would mean that your target was unrealistic but your performance for the questionnaire was good.

The drawback with benchmarks is that if all similar projects are mediocre, the benchmark will be low. You may need to set targets that ensure you exceed the benchmark in order for your project to be successful.

Competitiveness

Competitiveness is a concept used to promote and evaluate good practice in business and industry. A high percentage of business projects fail very early on. Employers are being encouraged to think about their businesses or spheres of work in terms of 'competitiveness'. Depending on the business, this will include such factors as:

- skills and experience of staff;
- use of performance indicators;
- using feedback from other people;
- improvements in quality and efficiency;
- awareness of developments in the field;

- thinking and planning ahead of the competition.

As people are the most important resource of any project, the quality of the personnel is a key factor in the competitiveness and success of a business or project. When you apply for work, employers may be considering how you could contribute to the overall competitiveness of their business or project.

The activity on p. 113 is a personal 'competitiveness audit'. It will give you a score out of a hundred – or your 'percentage competitiveness'. This is only a rough estimate. However, it gives you an indication of how you may be viewed in competition with other people. If you score well, you can be more confident about what you have to offer in job interviews. If your score isn't high, you have an indicator of where you can focus your energies next in order to develop your skills and extend your experience.

Closing comments

Problem-solving is essentially a way of getting things done, and therefore can be applied to a very wide range of circumstances. If you develop the skills associated with problem-solving, you will have a good starting place for taking on any task.

This chapter has looked at the skills and processes that contribute to successful problem-solving and task management. It addresses some of the generic skills that contribute to the success of any kind of 'project' such as writing an assignment, conducting a student project, undertaking projects at work, or taking on an undertaking in your personal life. This includes such processes as defining the task, elaborating the problem, setting priorities, developing an appropriate strategy, setting SMART-F targets, developing an action plan, monitoring performance against targets and indicators, and taking a task to completion. These processes are key to almost any project in any environment.

Problem-solving and task management tend to push us beyond our previous limits. At university, for example, assignments become increasingly more challenging as we move from one year or level to the next. At work, the problems and projects facing graduates will tend to contain new aspects that colleagues will not have covered before. A good problem-solving strategy, along with developed people skills, will enable you to take on such new tasks with greater confidence.

Competitiveness Audit

Rate each statement according to how typical it is of you.

Rating: *Very typical = 4;   Typical = 3;   Quite typical = 2;   Hardly ever the case = 1;*
Never true/Don't know = 0

		Score
1.	I am aware of my skills, personal qualities and expertise	
2.	I know how to apply these strengths to new situations	
3.	I take active steps to learn new skills and expertise	
4.	I ask for help when I need it	
5.	I have a clear vision of what I want to achieve	
6.	I set myself challenging targets	
7.	I am keen to receive feedback on my performance	
8.	I pay attention to feedback I receive and use it to improve my performance	
9.	I am usually keen to better my past performance	
10.	I take steps to discover and meet my personal development needs	
11.	I know how to measure my performance	
12.	I can set clear priorities	
13.	I am good at planning ahead	
14.	I pay attention to small details	
15.	I can see quick ways of doing things, without impairing quality	
16.	I can get going on a new task without much direction	
17.	I can make decisions quickly about what needs to be done	
18.	I am good at managing money and keeping to budget	
19.	I am good at meeting deadlines	
20.	I can co-ordinate my work with that of other people	
21.	I can manage responsibility	
22.	I can take orders from other people	
23.	I am good at finding solutions to problems	
24.	I can adapt and be flexible according to what is needed	
25.	I am prepared to 'do what it takes' to get a job done	

Your 'competitiveness' score   Total out of 100_____

Further reading

Davidson, J. (2000) *The Ten-Minute Guide to Project Management* (Indianapolis: Alpha). (A basic introduction to project management.)

Heerkens, G. R. (2002) *Project Management* (New York: McGraw-Hill). (A readable introduction that also covers the 'softer' aspects of project management, such as personal qualities.)

Mingus, N. (2002) *Teach Yourself Project Management in 24 Hours* (Indianapolis: Alpha). (An advanced text.)

Feedback on activity: 'Evaluating targets' on p. 103

- Target 1: This is too vague, has no time limits and is unlikely to be achievable or measurable. It isn't realistic.
- Target 2: This is unlikely to be achievable or measurable as it is hard to define a 'mistake' with respect to an essay. Very few essays are perfect. This is not a realistic target.
- Target 3. This may be realistic and achievable for the person. Success could be measured. No time-scales have been set so the target is not SMART.
- Target 4: This has a clear time-scale and is likely to be achievable and realistic. However, it so vague that it is meaningless.
- Target 5: this is specific, measurable, and time-bound. It is likely to be realistic and achievable, and if not, there is sufficient time before the hand-in date to adjust the deadline.
- Target 6. This is specific, measurable and time-bound. You would need to know more about the writer and the circumstances to see if the target was achievable and realistic and sufficiently flexible.
- Target 7. 'More' is too vague. 'From October' sets an initial time-scale but does not indicate how long this will continue.
- Target 8. This is specific and measurable. A 5 per cent improvement is likely to be achievable and reasonable, unless the mark was already very high. Setting a target for *all* assignments is challenging: it does not contain much flexibility. This target would need to be accompanied by other targets which specify more clearly how the improved mark will be achieved.
- Target 9: This target is likely to be a SMART-F target.
- Target 10. This is too precise and allows for little flexibility in choice of work placement. It is not likely to be realistic or achievable.

Chapter 5

People skills

The most important single ingredient in the formula of success is knowing how to get along with people.

Theodore Roosevelt

Learning outcomes

This chapter offers you opportunities to develop skills in:

- building a good rapport with others
- being a better team member
- setting up an 'action set'
- giving and receiving constructive criticism
- assertiveness
- dealing with difficult people
- negotiation
- leadership

Introduction

'People skills' are a combination of good inter-personal skills (being able to work well with others) and intra-personal skills (being able to manage one's own attitudes and emotions). 'People skills' are now critical to success in a wide range of careers. They are as important to the modern economy as are knowledge, information and technical skills.

This has been a much neglected part of the curriculum in the past, perhaps because there was less demand for subtle understandings of inter-personal relationships. However, changes in the kind of work we do, in technology, in tele-communications, in social structure, and the global economy have altered the way we interact. There are now much higher expectations for good interpersonal and communication skills.

In particular, compared to previous generations, we are more likely to meet and work with an extremely diverse range of people, often in global contexts. In the past, most people grew up and worked within a very confined world, with a narrow set of social rules. It was clear what behaviour was expected of you down to the finest detail of your personal life. People knew almost from birth what they should say, to whom and when. They tended to meet people from a very small geographical area, often only their own village or part of town. Horizons were very narrow.

Today, most of the old social codes are disappearing. The context is infinitely more varied than in the past, the range of options in any one situation is much greater. This requires much higher levels of sophistication in our attitudes to others, in how we manage our personal beliefs and values in social settings, and how we respond to diversity. We have much more personal responsibility for developing good social relations, making relationships work and forming judgements about the appropriate behaviour in any setting. We all, too, have greater individual legal responsibility for our decisions and actions.

'People skills' is a vast and rapidly developing area. This chapter looks at some key aspects of developing people skills from the perspective of a student or new graduate.

Activity: Self-evaluation – How good are your people skills now?

Make two copies of this table. Complete one now and one later in your programme. Rate each of the following statements as follows:

Rating: *Stongly agree = 3;   Agree = 2;   Sort of agree = 1;   Disagree/ don't know/no opportunities = 0*

	Score
1. I have worked with a wide range of people of different ages and backgrounds	
2. I am told that I am very good at working with others	
3. I feel very confident about talking to people I do not know well	
4. I am comfortable about leaving silences whilst other people gather their thoughts	
5. I can start a conversation easily	
6. I find people extremely interesting	
7. I am aware of my body language and its effects upon others	
8. I can be very helpful and polite to people I hate or despise	
9. I can see the good points in most of the people I meet during a week	
10. I can listen well without interrupting somebody who talks a lot	
11. I am very good at developing trust between myself and others	
12. When I am in a group, I can easily tell the strengths of each person	
13. When I am in a team, I can tell easily who will be the best for each job	
14. I work very well as a member of a team	
15. I am clear about the particular strengths I bring to the group or team	
16. I am able to be very supportive of other people	
17. I am very good at resolving difficulties that arise in group or team work	
18. I know what support I need from others	
19. I am able to ask for what I need	
20. I am assertive	
21. I can deal well with difficult people	
22. I am able to accept, publicly, responsibility for my own part in interactions that go wrong	
23. I am skilled at offering constructive criticism to others	
24. I am able to take negative criticism well	
25. I am able to accept praise well	
26. I negotiate well with other people	
27. I know how to arrive at a good compromise	
28. I am clear what direction I need from people in leadership roles	
29. I feel very comfortable about taking the lead in activities	
30. I am very aware of what other people need	
Add up your score **Total**	

Interpreting your score

70–90 This is an excellent score. If your ratings were accurate, you are able to manage very well your relationships with other people. This suggests an invaluable set of people skills. Consider how you could develop these further. How can you use these skills in the career areas that interest you?

40–69 This is a good score. If your ratings were accurate, this suggests your people skills are already well developed. Look for themes in the statements to which you gave lower ratings. Which areas could be further improved?

20–39 If your ratings were accurate, this suggests you have developed some people skills as well as an awareness of where you lack strengths currently. Look for themes in the statements to which you gave lower ratings. Taking your programme needs and career interests into consideration, which is your next priority for development?

0–19 If your ratings were accurate, this suggests that you have identified that people skills are not currently a strength for you. Check with people who know you well whether you have rated yourself too harshly. It is also important that you identify which people skills are most critical for meeting the requirements of your programme and career interests. Consider speaking to the careers service or your tutors to identify areas of priority for future development. This score also suggests that you might have difficulties in relationships generally. That can be stressful. If so, student counselling services can offer useful ideas about how to make your interactions with others run more smoothly.

📖 *Reflection*   People skill needs

Which people skills are needed for:

● the careers areas that interest you;
● meeting the requirements of your programme;
● your personal needs and interests?

● If you are unsure, speak to the Careers Service at the university and to your tutors.
● What are your priorities for developing your people skills?

Developing rapport

Forming a good rapport is the cornerstone of relationships with other people. Rapport requires such behaviours as:

● 'making a connection'
● taking a genuine interest in the other person
● skilful listening
● developing mutual trust and cooperation

Making a connection

Making a connection requires only a little effort. From this, the basis of good trust or even life-long friendships can develop. The minimum requirements are two or three very basic gestures that show good will:

● making eye contact;
● giving a genuine smile;
● being helpful when asked;
● giving a friendly greeting;
● showing basic consideration for the other person;
● using a friendly, polite manner;
● making a comment or asking a question that shows interest without being intrusive;
● being consistent in either friendly or distant behaviour.

These may seem small and obvious. However, think about the contact you have with people you find difficult. Which of the above gestures were missing either at your first encounter or on a regular basis? Which of these gestures do you value? A forced smile, an abrupt response, an

---

unpleasant tone in the voice, and such small details can set relationships off on a wrong footing – making hard work of any future connections.

Taking a genuine interest

Generally, we appreciate people with similar values and beliefs to our own, who do not challenge our own view of the world or our material interests. 'Difference' can be unsettling. It suggests there might be more than one way of doing or being. Our survival mechanisms do not like this idea: it suggests someone else might be 'right' and our way 'wrong'. We are not usually comfortable with such ideas. Our minds tend to throw us lifelines such as 'that's boring', 'he's a fool', 'that's rubbish!' very early, before we are even aware it is happening, so that we do not have to really consider what we are feeling.

As we develop people skills, we are better able to accept a wider range of differences in other people. We learn to find the point of interest in difference and the value of diversity. We cease to see the world in terms of 'right' and 'wrong', but as a rich spectrum.

The benefits of finding the point of interest in other people are that:

● we find the world around us to be more interesting;
● boredom disappears and our life experience is richer;
● we feel more comfortable, emotionally, when with strangers;
● people are able to feel more comfortable around us;
● we have a better understanding of the world around us and of the motivations of others;
● we are better able to manage any situation that involves other people.

Activity: Balloon game

In your journal or a notebook, give one page to each of the following (ten pages in all).

The characters
First, write the name of one person on the top of each page, so that you have the names of:

● two people that you really know, like and admire;
● two people that you know vaguely and have no strong feelings about;
● two people that you think are just not like you at all and that you do not like much;
● two that you know well and really dislike or despise;
● two people that you do not know at all (you may invent names for them if you do not know them).

The motivation
Now, imagine you are in a television challenge. You are aloft in a balloon with these ten people. You will receive a prize of your choice (up to £5 million) if you can bring all ten people back to earth. Otherwise, you will be fined your income for a year. If you fail, they get a prize instead.

The challenge
However, you are only allowed to transport back any person if you can convince the audience that each person is really worth saving. You will need to show that you know about the person and can say things about them that bring out their best features.

For each person, use their name page to brainstorm responses to the following:

● what I like, value, admire, find interesting already about this person;
● what I dislike about this person at present;
● what this person contributes to the world that is different or valuable;
● questions I could ask to find out more;
● anything I could do to develop a better understanding of this person.

Skilful listening

Good listening skills are invaluable to forming a rapport with others. Most people react very strongly to feeling they are 'not heard' or that 'someone really listened'. This is especially true where people feel vulnerable (if they are new to a group, distressed, angry, have received bad news, etc.).

'Listening' is something we take for granted. However, skilful listening is about more than 'hearing the words'. It involves understanding the message, the situation and other people.

Good listening skills enable other people to feel at ease, to trust the listener, and to express more easily what they really wish to communicate.

There is an art to being able to discover what another person is trying to communicate, and this can take many years to perfect. However, the following are good starting places.

Body language
Demonstrate clearly that you are listening, using appropriate body language. Usually this means slightly exaggerating what you would normally do anyway. For example, ensure you make eye contact, without staring.

Use body language that shows you are listening: lean forward a little, tilt your head slightly to the side, nod occasionally to show you are taking in what is being said. Many people do this naturally when they are really listening but some do not.

Let them finish
Let people complete the point they are making without interruption. Wait for a pause or an intake of breath before you start to respond. Make any necessary interruptions with consideration for the other person – even if you feel they have not been considering your needs. If you really must interrupt, because of time constraints, for example, apologise for interrupting. State the reason for the interruption politely. Make some reference, however brief, to what has been said before you change the subject or rush away.

Listen for the underlying message
The 'underlying message' may be different from the actual words used. What does the person really mean? What do they really want you to hear or to know? Are they saying one thing but communicating something different? For example, they may say 'I'm fine!' but look or sound very angry or distressed. Just note these differences. If it feels right to say so, you may point out the message that you are receiving: 'You sound very upset.' or 'You look very angry.'

Check for meaning
People may not be skilled at communicating what they want you to hear. Alternatively, you

may mishear or misread the situation. The only way to be sure of the message being communicated is to feed it back to the person and check their response. Summarise what you think you have heard. Usually, this is best in brief phrases, prompts or questions when the other person is pausing for breath. Do this in ways that suggest you are trying to understand:

- 'They said you have to fill in the form today?'
- 'And that wasn't what you wanted?'
- 'So you don't want to go ahead any more?'

Clarify details
- Ask questions to clarify points and show your interest.
- If something isn't clear, point out that you haven't quite understood. Ask the other person to explain it again or in a different way.
- Be specific about the exact points you do not understand. Your confusion may arise because the other person is not fully clear about the issue either. Your questions may help them to clarify their thinking.

Leave silences
Some people find silence awkward and it can be tempting to keep talking in order to avoid silences. However, silence fulfils important functions:

- it gives a clear signal that you have finished speaking;
- it gives opportunities for other people to contribute;
- it allows time for reflection;
- it gives people time to develop their ideas;
- it allows people time to manage their feelings and emotions;
- it can enable non-verbal communication to take place, which is often more powerful than speaking.

📖 **Reflection**   Listening skills

- In your reflective journal, note down which of these listening skills you find easiest.
- Which do you find most difficult?
- Which could you develop further?
- Can you think of recent examples where you used any of these skills?

Developing mutual trust

📖 **Reflection**   Developing trust

- Who do you really trust with your secrets?
- Who do you really trust with your money?
- Who do you trust to tell you the truth about themselves?
- Who do you trust to tell you the truth about yourself?

In each case, what has led to the development of that trust?

Your responses to the above activity probably elicited an awareness that trust develops out of acquaintance. It also takes time. It can be easily broken. It can take time to repair once broken. You cannot force trust onto people; the harder you try, the more suspicious people may become. You really do 'earn it' through the proof of your actions.

It is difficult to establish good working relationships if these are not founded on trust. Co-operation with others, sharing ideas, revealing personal information, negotiating compromises, commissioning work, offering contracts, and numerous other everyday activities are all facilitated by the development of mutual trust.

📖 **Reflection**   Losing trust in others

In your reflective journal, think of an occasion when you lost your trust in somebody.

- What happened?
- What did this feel like?
- What were the consequences?
- How has this affected your behaviour towards that person?
- What would that person have to do to regain your trust?
- Which kinds of behaviour break trust?

In your reflective journal,

- Think of an occasion when you did something to undermine other people's trust in you.
- What happened?
- What did this feel like?
- What were the consequences?
- How has this affected the relationship between you and that person?
- What was (or is) needed to restore that person's trust in you?
- What did you learn about trust from this experience ?

Brainstorm:

- What kinds of behaviour develop people's trust?
- What kinds of things could you do to develop your abilities in gaining other people's trust in you?

Team work

Learning in groups reaps greater benefits than attending formal lectures or presentations. It gives students more scope to express themselves, to establish effective relationships with tutors and others in the group, and to develop a range of skills such as team working.

Skills and Enterprise Network, 2001

'Finding and keeping a good team' is amongst chief executives' most highly rated ingredients of success (Taylor and Humphrey, 2002). Despite the importance of team work to working life, few people have developed outstanding team skills. Team players are usually well-appreciated by both employers and colleagues. On the other hand, our natural self-interest in our own needs, moods, beliefs, wants and feelings can make it very easy for us to sabotage the teams or groups that we find ourselves in.

You can build trust if you:

Are clear what you can and cannot do

Do what you say you will do

Avoid making promises you can't keep

Keep confidential information confidential

Are consistent in your behaviour from one day to the next

Are dependable and fulfil your responsibilities; turn up on time

Sabotaging the team

Activity: Sabotaging a team

In your reflective journal, take two pages.

- On the first page, brainstorm a list of things people could do to sabotage a group. How could they make the group an unpleasant, unproductive, irritating experience? When you have finished compare it with the list given below.
- On the second page, make a list of what people can do to make groups work. Compare your list with the one under 'Creating a good team' below.
- Which of those behaviours do you demonstrate? Be honest. What could you do to improve your own contribution to groups and teams?

You may have come up with a long list of items. Typical responses include:

- not bothering to get to know some of the team members;
- dominating the group;

- not contributing enough;
- leaving one or two people to do all the work;
- speaking badly about some team members;
- trying to split the team into 'goodies' and 'baddies';
- not taking responsibility for tasks that need to be done;
- being late or not turning up at all;
- putting your own needs before those of the team;
- not listening to other people's ideas;
- not using the strengths and qualities of each person to best effect;
- messing about;
- not caring what happens to others on the team;
- not being able to take criticism.

Creating a good team

A good team will show the following characteristics:

Works as one
- It has a shared vision. It knows what it wants to achieve;
- puts the desired team outcome first: individual interests take a secondary place;
- is clear about targets and priorities – and agrees these together;
- shares information;
- can make decisions.

Works to strengths
- It has members with different qualities, who can make different contributions;
- takes time to discover the experience, skills and interests of all and how it can make best use of these;

- shares expertise. A team that is together for some time is strengthened if individuals share their knowledge and skills.

Includes everyone
- It makes efforts to ensure that nobody feels left out or undervalued;
- gives room to individuals. Teamwork does not mean that everybody has to be and think the same. On the contrary, variety and difference can be a source of strength. There are different ways of being a good team player.

Respects its members
- It respects everyone's time by: being punctual for meetings, completing individual targets on time, being aware of how one person's own work affects other people's achievements, monitoring personal contributions to meetings so that time is not wasted in long anecdotes and tangents;
- respects the opinions of the team and uses strategies to enable all team members to give their views: feeding in at the beginning of meetings, giving each member equal time to speak on an issue, inviting people who have not spoken yet to contribute their views.

What I can contribute to the team?

The skills and qualities you contribute to a team will develop through experience. However, if you are not used to teamwork, you will feel more confident at the beginning if you think of what you are already able to contribute. The following activity helps you identify some things you could contribute to team-work at present.

Activity: Contributing to a team

For each way of contributing to teams (listed below) tick as many boxes as apply to you.

Contribution	Willing to do	Have experience of	An area of strength	Want to develop
Hearing other people's views, ideas and opinions				
Listening to others				
Weighing up options				
Making decisions, based on the facts				
Finding ways of working effectively				
Looking for solutions				
Administrative skills				
Working out priorities				
Speaking my mind				
Specialist skills that can be useful				
Seeing when the discussion has gone off track, and pulling it back on target				
Working hard				
Keeping going when it gets tough				
Seeing when people are left out				
Drawing in other people				
Logical thinking				
Numbers and statistics				
Charts and drawings				
Researching information				
Writing up findings				
Organising events				
Networking				
Time-keeping				
Other things:				
(1)				
(2)				
(3)				
(4)				

Other people's views of my short-comings as a team member

Activity: Weaknesses in team performance

How well do you perform in teams at present? Use the following statements to evaluate your performance and to guide your reflection.

Tick as relevant ✓

☐ I talk too much

☐ I turn up late

☐ I interrupt others

☐ I take up too much of the discussion space

☐ I let other people carry the team

☐ I always think I am in the right

☐ I act as if I were the team leader

☐ I like everything to stick exactly to the agenda

☐ I keep going off at tangents

☐ I get caught up in the details and lose the big picture

☐ I have lots of ideas, but many of them are not relevant

☐ I get too emotional

☐ I don't keep to the deadlines

Other things:

☐ (1)

☐ (2)

☐ (3)

Activity: Turn short-comings into strengths

● How realistic is the above view of yourself?
● Would you have the confidence to discuss this with someone else and be able to cope with their responses?
● What targets can you set yourself to improve your performance for one of those areas?
● What, if any, are the positive aspects to your 'short-comings'? What do these suggest about your potential strengths (such as flexibility, caring for others, willingness to accept responsibility, confidence in speaking your mind) that could be adapted to the benefit of the team?
● Take at least one short-coming and look for the way this could be adapted or converted into a strength. For example, if you are poor at attendance, how could you make up for non-attendance in other ways?

Belbin team types

Belbin and the Cambridge Industrial Training Research Unit made a dramatic discovery about teams. In an experiment that was repeated many times with different participants, it was found that teams made up entirely of the best business brains were far less successful than those with very mixed memberships. Belbin (1996) went on to outline different kinds of roles that people could occupy in a team, depending on their personal characteristics. The activity on p. 125 summarises some of the characteristics associated with each Belbin type.

● With which types do you identify?
● With which one type do you identify the most?
● Which three other types would you most appreciate having in your team?

Belbin type	Positive characteristics	Potential short-comings	Tick all that apply to you. Draw *** by the most typical	The three 'types' I would most want on my team (tick)
Implementer	Steady, reliable, sensible, gets things done. Well-disciplined, organised approach.	May not welcome change and new ideas. Expects too much from others.		
Co-ordinator	Focused, looks for consensus, tries to involve everyone. Delegates work; chairs meetings well. Can accept and reject the ideas of others.	Doesn't shine intellectually; may be seen as manipulative. Passes their own work onto others.		
Shaper	Outgoing, high-energy, no-nonsense, blunt; speaks their mind; ready to overcome obstacles; gets things moving.	Impatient, irritable, insensitive to others' feelings; may say the wrong thing at the wrong time.		
Plant	Creative, lateral thinker, generates ideas, enjoys looking for solutions, inventive. Good at holding the 'big picture'.	Inflated sense of their own 'genius'; ignores targets and details; in their own dream-world; does not communicate ideas well to others.		
Resource investigator	Curious, interested, out-going. Likes exploration, information, meeting new people, challenge, trying out new gadgets.	Short interest or attention span; invests and then moves onto something else; may pilfer other people's ideas.		
Monitor–evaluator	Considers all angles; unemotional; takes on many perspectives; good at weighing up the evidence and making a judgement; good at decision making.	Rigid in ideas and in their love of 'logic'; not open to creative or lateral thinking; over-critical. Not good at generating novel ideas.		
Team-worker	Observant; listens and responds well; smooths over conflict; diplomatic; good social skills; sensitive to others; puts the team first.	Can be swayed by all views; easily influenced; prevaricates; finds it hard to come to a decision.		

Belbin type	Positive characteristics	Potential short-comings	Tick all that apply to you. Draw *** by the most typical	The three 'types' I would most want on my team (tick)
Completer-finisher	Good attention to detail; conscientious; responsible; reliable; delivers to target; fine-tunes their final effort.	Bad at delegating and trusting others; picks fault; over-perfectionist.		
Specialist	Single-minded, dedicated, offers skills that are hard to find; gets on with the task; self-motivating.	Not interested in the big picture; doesn't mix with the team; narrow horizons.		

The best mix?

Belbin found some combinations work well. In particular, a group seems to work well if there is:

- a co-ordinator type – to chair the group
- a good 'plant' – an imaginative person with the right kind of creative skills for the project
- a monitor–evaluator who can spot and weigh up good and bad ideas
- a spread of other types. In particular, an implementer or completer-finisher is useful. A balance of types is valuable: extrovert and introvert, those who generate ideas and those who can assess them, those who bring in change and those who maintain some continuity.

What kind of balance is there in the team of four (including yourself) that you selected in the activity above.

What strengths would a team like that demonstrate? What would its weaknesses be?

If you wish to complete a full Belbin self-perception inventory, ask for a copy at your University Careers Service.

Action sets

'Action sets' (McGill and Beaty, 1992) are a particular kind of team. They are semi-formal groups which offer opportunities to gain input and alternatives from others and receive structured support.

Action sets, as the name suggests, focus on getting things done. Unlike most groups, however, the aim is to help each person to find a solution to a problem or difficulty of their own choice. The group brainstorms ideas and discusses solutions within a tight time-frame, and at the next meeting checks to see what action was undertaken. The group itself does not carry out the action: it merely proposes and monitors action, at the invitation of each member.

Advantages of action sets

The advantages of action sets are:

- the rules are easy to follow;
- all members are equal;
- they provide supportive contexts: usually, you choose to be in an action set;
- you have a place where you can take a difficult issue and work it through;
- they are very focused;
- they offer a range of perspectives on a problem you choose to bring;
- they generate ideas and solutions;
- they require rapid decision making, and so assist decision-making skills for all members;
- they give practice in arriving at a solution in a very short time;

- they offer an additional source of motivation: reporting back to the group at the next meeting encourages you to take action;
- members get to know each other well and know what works for each member.

You may find it useful to select an action set according to Belbin types. If so, bear in mind the aims of the group. What types of person are likely to work best together for the kinds of problems that arise from your programme? Would it help to include someone who is not on the programme?

The limits of action sets

Action sets are not usually:

- emotional support groups
- discussion groups: talk is very circumscribed
- social groups
- project groups: they do not 'do' the work needed to solve an individual's problem outside of the meeting.

Guidelines for the meeting of an action set

 Ideally, leave at least 15 minutes for each member. If you have only an hour a week for such meetings, a set of four people is probably best. If you have 2 hours, a group of six is probably the optimum size. An even number will work best. The timing below assumes 6 people in a 2-hour slot. With a 15-minute break, that gives each person 17 minutes each.

For each person:

Stage 1 (3 minutes)
- Each person has a set time to discuss the area they wish to improve. Time is limited so each person needs to get to the point quickly.
- Whilst that person is speaking, the group listens without interrupting.
- One person keeps the time.
- Once the time is up, the person must stop speaking immediately.

Stage 2 (2 minutes)
The group may ask one or two questions, briefly, to clarify the situation.

Stage 3 (3 minutes)
The person whose issue is being considered listens without speaking whilst the rest of the group brainstorms possible solutions and ways of thinking about the problem. Again, a limited time is allowed.

Stage 4 (4 minutes)
The person and the group have a set time to clarify and discuss options together briefly.

Stage 5 (2 minutes)
The person whose issue is being discussed has a set time to state which actions they will undertake before the next meeting. All members write down what has been agreed, and monitor this at the next meeting.

Stage 6 (3 minutes)
In the following session, each person reports back on actions they have taken. The group encourages successes and improvements. If the person has not followed through on what was agreed, this may be used as their focus for the session. Feedback must be timetabled into the time allocated to each person.

Running the action set

Ideally, action sets are meetings of peers where everybody takes equal responsibility. Tasks are rotated or allocated to individual strengths:

- organising the room;
- phoning members to remind them of the next meeting and of agreed actions;
- time-keeping in meetings;
- keeping the group strictly to the right stage and item under discussion;
- maintaining a supportive atmosphere;
- ensuring everyone contributes;
- ensuring everybody gets equal time;
- ensuring different people go first or last each time.

Roles

You may find action sets work better if you allocate roles to the team. Useful roles to include are:

- **A Co-ordinator or Implementer:** to ensure the group sticks to task, keeps to time, and that everyone gets equal time. Each stage must be very strictly timed.

- **A Plant or a Shaper or Resource Investigator**: who may bring a different way of looking at things.
- **A Team-worker**: to enhance the social skills of the group.
- **A Monitor-evaluator or Completer-finisher**: to assist the group to move on and to choose between options.

Constructive Criticism

📖 ***Reflection***   Constructive Criticism

In your reflective notebook, jot down some ideas about what you think is meant by 'constructive criticism'.

Criticism does not mean pointing out 'what is wrong'. Technically, criticism draws out what is good, bad and satisfactory. Constructive criticism goes further: it offers a clear and practicable 'next step forward' and is expressed in a positive way. It leads towards improvement. For constructive criticism to be effective, it has to be expressed in a way that is easy to 'hear' and understand.

Making constructive criticism and giving feedback

The aim of feedback is to help other people to see how they could improve their performance or gain a new perspective on their work. The focus of criticism is the other person, their needs or the requirements of the task. It is not about showing how clever you are at 'picking holes' in what other people do or say.

Constructive criticism is phrased so that it offers truthful but skilful feedback with ideas on how to improve or to progress. It is very easy to hurt people's feelings through unskilful feedback, and nothing is gained by this.

Good feedback involves:

- waiting until invited for your opinion;
- recognising effort;
- being well informed: ensure you know the circumstances, intentions and requirements before offering feedback;

- being clear and truthful but not blunt or hurtful;
- indicating what the other person has got right – so they continue to do this in the future;
- indicating what has already improved;
- indicating a small number of achievable goals for improvement;
- giving concrete examples of what is required:
  'I think this would look even better if . . .'
  'I like this. Have you thought about . . .'
  'The first half was good. The second half would benefit from . . .'

It should:

- be formulated positively – as something which can be done to improve performance, rather than what is wrong;
- take the person forward – it is not simply a vague directive to do something differently;
- be realistic – the suggestion can actually be put into practice by the recipient;
- be selective – it addresses priorities rather than every aspect of performance;
- be offered kindly – delivered in a voice and manner that make it easier to accept.

📖 ***Reflection***   Offering constructive criticism

Think of a recent occasion when you offered feedback to someone about their work or study. Jot down:

- What were the circumstances?
- What did you do or say?
- Which of the above characteristics did you include or omit?
- What else could you have said or done to improve your feedback?

Poor feedback includes:

- too much comment and criticism. This is off-putting. People stop listening and may get distressed;
- negative feedback. People ignore this if they feel their efforts are not recognised;
- vague feedback such as 'Unclear' or 'More detail needed'. State exactly what is unclear or which details are needed;
- demoralising comments such as 'this is nonsense'; 'gobbledegook!'; 'could do better';

● illegible feedback. People usually do not bother to decipher illegible writing unless they think it says something very positive about them.

Constructive questions and responses

Use constructive questions to discover why the person made the choices or took the steps they did – and to explore their next step forward. For example:

● 'What did you think worked well?'
● 'Is there anything you would do differently next time?'
● 'What was your inspiration for this?'
● 'Did you find this worked?'
● 'That is an unusual approach. I am interested in why you did it this way?'
● 'Have you had any ideas about where we could apply this?'

Jane was starting to realise that her helpful advice was not universally appreciated.

Receiving criticism

Accept criticism gracefully, however it is given. Not everybody is skilled at giving criticism.

● Consider all criticism carefully, even if it sounds unacceptable.
● Look for the elements of truth in what is said. This is sometimes easier after you have had some time to reflect.
● Hear both the positive and the negative aspects. Many people hear only negative feedback.

● Check you have understood what is being said. It is easy to mishear, especially if it didn't sound positive.
● Acknowledge the feedback. It was probably not easy for the other person to give it.
● Say thank-you.
● Reflect upon the meaning of what you have heard. What steps could you take to improve your performance?

📖 **Reflection**   Receiving criticism

Think of a recent occasion when somebody offered you feedback or criticism about your work or performance.
In your reflective notebook, jot down:

● What were the circumstances?
● What did they do or say?
● How did you respond? What else could you have done to make best use of the criticism?
● What does this experience tell you about giving and receiving criticism well?

Being assertive

What is assertiveness?

Assertiveness means standing up for yourself without demonstrating anger. Assertive people look for solutions that suit both parties, respecting the rights of both.

📖 **Reflection**   Characteristics of assertive people

What picture comes to mind when you think of an assertive person? Jot down your thoughts in your reflective journal.

Assertiveness is about:

● respecting your own and other people's rights;
● respecting your own and others' needs;
● being clear and straightforward with other people;
● taking more control over your own life and taking responsibility for changing what you do not like.

Rights

Palmer and Dryden (1995) offer a list of rights associated with assertiveness. These include the right to:

- say 'no';
- make mistakes;
- consider your needs important;
- express your feelings in an appropriate way without violating anybody else's rights;
- take responsibility for your actions;
- respect yourself;
- set your own priorities;
- be assertive without feeling guilty.

You could include others such as the right to:

- do well in life;
- ask for what you need to know;
- be taken into consideration in decisions that affect you;
- fairness and justice;
- personal safety;
- love;
- think;
- be free of insult and discriminatory behaviour on the grounds of race, colour, nationality, sex, sexual orientation, disability, parentage, work history or personal beliefs;
- your opinions.

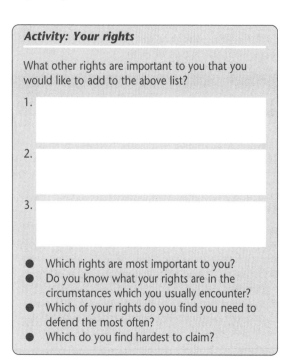

Activity: Your rights

What other rights are important to you that you would like to add to the above list?

1.

2.

3.

- Which rights are most important to you?
- Do you know what your rights are in the circumstances which you usually encounter?
- Which of your rights do you find you need to defend the most often?
- Which do you find hardest to claim?

Respecting your own and others' rights and needs

'Rights' are not universal nor equally applied. They are not all 'human rights' by international agreement and may not apply in all countries or conditions. People in prison cannot set all their own priorities, for example. Some rights are protected by law; others are commonly held beliefs about human rights. You may have to decide what rights are reasonable or legal for your own circumstances.

An individual's interests have to be weighed against the rights of other people and the nature of the circumstances. We are not generally comfortable with the idea that a surgeon might have 'the right to make mistakes' on a regular basis. Having the right to an opinion means you have the right to hold the opinion, but not necessarily to subject other people to insult or harm as a result.

Assertiveness is not about insisting on your own interests, irrespective of the consequences to yourself and others or without consideration of the circumstances. When you are assertive, you ensure that:

- you look at the whole picture, but you put yourself in that picture;
- you know your own opinions;
- you are able to identify your own needs and interests;
- you weigh up, realistically, whether it is appropriate to stand up for your rights and interests in the situation. Sometimes it is too dangerous or risky to assert our rights unless we can ensure safety and support.

Being clear and straightforward with other people

When we state our needs in a calm, clear, straightforward manner, then we are showing respect both to ourselves and to others. When other people know where you stand, they can then choose to respond in an appropriate way. You gain a clearer picture of their position.

Assertiveness is not:

- **Being aggressive**   Assertiveness does not include: rage, shouting, forcing other people to do what you want, physical force or threats of force, aggressive body language, intimidating others. You have the right to feel angry, or to shout in private, but not to express these to others in ways that might make them feel coerced into doing what you want.

- **Being manipulative**   Assertiveness does not include: using psychological games to manoeuvre people into doing what you want. For example, it does not involve shaming people, trying to make them feel guilty or anxious, reminding them of debts, playing upon people's doubts and fears.

- **Being passive**   Assertiveness does not include: being silent about your own needs and interests; being a 'martyr'; letting other people have what they want whilst you go without; staying quiet when you want to speak out; effacing yourself so that you are not seen, heard or considered. This behaviour can be very irritating to others – and means they have to take responsibility for your needs.

- **Being passive aggressive**   Assertiveness does not include: appearing to be passive whilst being clear that you are angry. Passive aggressive behaviour is very distressing to other people, and confuses situations so they are harder to resolve. It includes behaviour such as saying 'I don't mind', 'do what you want', 'whatever!' whilst using angry facial expressions, body language or tone of voice. Angry silences, walking out of the room, making a noise to block out what another person is saying, not turning up to appointments and generally not co-operating, are ways of expressing passive aggression.

Taking control over your life

When we use assertiveness techniques, we take responsibility for our actions in order to increase our control over an aspect of our life.

Assertiveness techniques

> ### Activity: Assertive techniques
>
> Consider the assertiveness techniques below in relation to your 'recurring situation'.

1. Identify blocks to assertiveness

What has been preventing you from using assertive techniques up to now?

☐ Not being aware of the differences between aggression, passivity, manipulation and assertiveness

☐ It wasn't part of my family or cultural background

☐ Fear of other people's responses

☐ Fear of failure

☐ Blaming myself for the situation

☐ Not wanting to hurt other people's feelings

☐ I wanted a quiet life

☐ My current methods may not be fair but I get what I want

2. Put yourself in the picture

This means that you:

● look at the 'big picture'. Identify all the interests of all the parties, including your own;

● ensure you are in the picture. If you are more likely to respond in a passive way, you may not feel you have a right to be considered;

● consider whether you really should be at the centre, near the centre or on the periphery of the picture. Passive people can believe it is polite or kind or good manners to put themselves on the margins. If this happens all the time, it is likely to be irritating to others, as they will always be put into the position of being the more selfish, greedy, inconsiderate person, which is not pleasant. Aggressive people may always find reasons to be at the centre.

3. Make 'I' statements

People who find it hard to be assertive can find it difficult to make 'I' statements such as:

● 'I want . . .'
● 'I need . . .'
● 'I am responsible for . . .'

'Put yourself in the picture'

Sometimes this is very noticeable because they refer to their own needs in very general terms:

- 'Everybody needs . . .'
- 'We all need . . .'
- 'It is important to . . .'
- 'You have to . . .'
- 'One has to . . .'

Activity: Making 'I' statements

Make 'I' statements for the 'recurring situation' you selected on p. 131.

Aspect	'I' Statement
What do you want?	I want ...
What do you need?	I need...
How do you feel?	I feel...
What rights are involved?	I have the right to...
What are your responsibilities?	I am responsible for...
My behaviours	I will (do).....

In your reflective journal, jot down your responses to the following:

- How easy was this activity for you?
- What kind of speech do you use in order to avoid using 'I' statements?
- Which statement was the most difficult to make?
- When will you use these 'I' statements?

---

4. Choose the moment

Ensure that:

- *The time is right.*   This does not mean waiting for a perfect moment that may never arrive. It means choosing the best time available. Make an agreed time with the person or ensure that at a meeting time is put aside to discuss the matter. Be clear how long you need.

- *You have the person's full attention.*   Ask for this if necessary. Choose a moment when they are able to give you attention. Avoid competing with television, radio or loud music.

5. State the issue and the desired change

Take responsibility for letting the person know what you find unacceptable or difficult about their behaviour. Do so in a manner that is calm, and does not sound blaming. Describe behaviours rather than the person. Say what the behaviour is, and acknowledge responsibility for your own part in the event and for your own feelings and responses. Make it clear what you want.

Example 1

'I feel hurt when you do not respond when I speak to you in the mornings. I would like you to say "hello".'

Rather than:

'You are so rude in the mornings. You make me feel ignored and angry and it affects my whole day'.

Example 2

'I need the price lists by 4:00 p.m. If you send them after 4:00, it is difficult to get our updates in the post.'

Rather than:

'You know the post goes out at 4:00. I don't know how you expect us all to get everything done when you can't be bothered to get the lists to us in time. It's your fault I was so upset last night – you really stress us out.'

6. Use positive language structures

When you make 'I' statements, use positive language structures. Positive language structures avoid the use of 'no', or 'not'. They are also clear, to the point and say exactly what you will do. Avoid words such as 'try', which suggests hard work or failure. Avoid modifiers such as 'some', 'maybe', 'sort of', 'quite'.

Positive language structure	Avoid
● I will ask for a lift.	I'll try and see if I can get a lift.
● I am entitled to this money.	I really think I should have what is due to me.
● I want these comments to stop.	I think it would be better if there were a little less of these comments.
● I will complete the race.	I intend to make a good shot at completing the race.
● Can I have help lifting this, please?	I can't lift this on my own! You could help!
● I need to say something.	I'm never given a chance to say what I need.
● I feel angry and upset.	I am trying not to get angry here!

7. Ask the other person's opinion

When you have stated what the issue is for you, check whether there could be a different interpretation. Ask the person how they see the situation and what they think about it. Show that you have a genuine interest in hearing their point of view. Let them give their interpretation without interrupting them.

8. Acknowledge the feelings

It is very common to see people arguing, even hissing through gritted teeth, 'I am not angry! I am not angry!' when it is clear to others that they are. This can make a situation difficult to resolve because the truth isn't being acknowledged.

It isn't always pleasant or easy to talk about feelings, but it is usually useful. Even if you do not voice your feelings, make sure that you at least know what they are. Otherwise, other people will know more about you than you do yourself.

● Check what you are feeling.
● Acknowledge to yourself how you are feeling.
● Make an 'I' statement about this: 'I feel...'
● Take care not to spill out the emotion on the people around you. You have a right to feel angry, for example, but not to coerce others with your feelings.
● Be prepared to hear how other people feel and consider what that means. You might not like hearing what they say, but they have the right to express how they feel too.

9. Suggest and invite solutions

Being assertive means looking for a solution that suits both sides as far as possible. Make constructive suggestions for a way forward.

Point out the advantages to both parties. Ask the person for their suggestions and be prepared to negotiate (see p. 138).

10. Clarify what has been agreed

Check you both agree the details of what is agreed. This will avoid disputes later. Writing down the agreement strengthens the commitment. Read what the other person has written and check you agree with the details. Keep a copy.

📖 Reflection   Assertiveness

In your reflective journal, jot your responses to the following questions:

● What could you gain by being more assertive?
● What difficulties are there for you in putting assertiveness techniques into action?
● How will you address these?
● Which of the above techniques could you use?

If you are not used to being assertive, it will take time to change your habits and thinking. You can build your confidence by using some 'practice runs', either with a trusted friend or with a student counsellor. Keep a record of times when you are assertive so that you can monitor your progress.

Dealing with difficult people

On becoming a monster

Any of us can be a difficult person some of the time. Most of us have 'pet hates': situations and people that we do not manage skilfully and which seem to make us unreasonable. When we are confronted by a 'difficult person', empathy can be a useful starting place. It is worth considering that this person might, like us, be very reasonable if the circumstances were different.

> ### 📖 *Reflection*   Being difficult
>
> In your reflective journal jot down one occasion when you acted unreasonably or 'out of character', – when you found yourself shouting at somebody, complaining unnecessarily, making a difficult situation worse, or blowing something out of proportion.
>
> - What was it about the circumstances that led you to behave like that?
> - What can you learn from your own experience that might help you to understand when other people seem to be unnecessarily difficult?
> - Jot down a list of all the circumstances that can turn you into 'monster'. Are these things that might be typical of the day of a 'difficult person' you know?

Is it just me?

If you experience the same person as difficult on several occasions, you might conclude that the person is just plain awkward. That may be the case, but there may be ways that you can ease your own relations with that person, so that your day runs more smoothly. Consider:

- Do other people find this person difficult?
- Who seems to manage situations with this person best? What do they do?
- What is it about the difficult person that provokes a response in you?
- What is about the person that makes you find it difficult to give calm and measured responses?
- What do you do that contributes to making the situation more difficult than it need be? What could you do to improve the situation?

> ### 📖 *Reflection*   Dealing with difficult people
>
> Think of one occasion with a 'difficult person' that you consider had a significant impact upon you. Jot down a brief outline of what happened.
>
> - How did you feel at the time?
> - How were you affected afterwards? For example, was it hard to settle down to work, enjoy your evening, sleep, feel calm?
> - How many times did you narrate the episode to others? How much time did this take up? What would you have done with that time otherwise?
> - In retrospect, how might you have responded differently, either during the event or afterwards, so the experience affected you less?
> - What do you have to gain by changing the interaction you have with this person?

The effect on me?

Difficult people can have a profound effect upon the people around them. They can become the source of constant conversation and a good source of gossip. Dealing with them, talking about them, going back over what happened, planning what you will say or do on the next occasion, all take up time and energy. That time could have been spent more fruitfully. Although it may be important to plan how to cope with a difficult person, it is just as important to ensure that the person does not become an excuse for time wasting, and for diverting energies from other problems.

Whatever the difficult person may have done, you have a personal responsibility to yourself to manage the effects upon yourself.

Managing the situation

Identify the behaviour
The golden rule for interacting with people is to separate the behaviour from the person. This is easy to say but much more difficult in practice. When thinking about the person, make a conscious effort to focus on their actions. For example: 'That irritates me' rather than 'She irritates me'. This distinction will then come more easily to you when you are with the person.

Isolate the source of irritation
For the 'difficult person' you identified above, jot down all their behaviours that really irritate or concern you. For example, do they:

● interrupt you all the time?
● refuse to let you express your point of view?
● interrupt your study or work?
● arrive late for each seminar or meeting?
● take up all the discussion time with their opinions?
● other things?

Look for positive interpretations of their behaviour
Look for characteristics about the person that you can genuinely appreciate. Look for a positive aspect to their unwanted behaviour, such as a desire to please, a willingness to contribute, a sense of humour.

Consider their needs
Usually behaviour has an intention – even if it is inappropriate to the context. Sometimes people simply go about getting what they need in a misguided way. The people you find difficult will be acting the way they do in order to achieve something. This might be to:

● gain attention;
● be noticed;
● be respected;
● feel that people think they are clever;
● be heard;
● draw attention away from something else;
● make friends?

Consider how you (or the group) could give that person some of what they need. This may make them less demanding, and easier to cope with.

Acknowledge the other person
People behave unreasonably when their needs are not met. Listen to what they are communicating, and let them know you have heard. For example;

Their situation	*Your response*
● They are distressed	'I can see/hear that you are upset.'
● They are angry	'I can see/hear you are angry.'
● They want attention	'That is a good idea.' 'That's an interesting point.'

Identify what they want
● Ask the person what they want.
● Repeat this back to them so they know you have listened and heard them correctly.
● Consider whether the request is feasible.
● Let them know what is feasible.
● Stay calm and repeat this if the offer is refused.

Acknowledge your own feelings
● Identify your own feelings. This will give you more control over your own responses. Are you angry? distressed? unhappy? raging? guilty? irritated?
● Check how well you are managing your emotions? Do you need to calm down?
● State your feelings clearly and simply so that the other person knows how you feel.

State indisputable facts
Rather than get into an entangled argument, focus on statements of fact:

● 'They are closing the doors. We have to go now.'

- 'This is a seminar. The issue cannot be resolved now.'
- 'We haven't got the receipts here. We can look at this again once we have them.'

Keep it clear and simple
- Keep it simple. Unless it is really necessary, avoid arguing about points of detail.
- State what needs to be done.
- Keep to the present situation: avoid going over past events.

State what you want
Consider what would be a reasonable outcome for you from the situation. State this calmly, simply and clearly. Avoid unnecessary details or commentary. You may need to repeat what you want several times if the person is shouting or in full flow.

- 'I want to leave this until we all feel calmer.'
- 'I want you to stop ringing me after 9 p.m.'
- 'I want to have more time for group discussion.'
- 'I want to hear what other people have to say.'
- 'I want a refund.'

Offer positive solutions
- Maintain a positive focus. Look for an acceptable solution.
- Offer a way out of a stalemate.
- State the advantages of the proposed solution.
- Be prepared to negotiate a reasonable compromise or to find a 'bridge' – even if you feel the other person should be taking the initiative.
- Invite all parties to write down the agreed solution so that it is clear and on record.

Clarify tasks
If people are difficult team members, they may not be clear or happy about what is expected of them.

- Involve them in key decisions.
- Negotiate and clarify targets.
- Ensure their role offers sufficient challenge and interest.

Look for the 'bottled up' emotions

Even if somebody is being difficult, they probably think they are very reasonable. At that stage, there is probably very little you can say to change their mind. When we are emotional, we are not open to logical reasoning. Be prepared to let your perspective wait until the person is calmer.

The probability is that the person has built up emotions such as anger, frustration, rage or fear over a very long time. If this has not been acknowledged, they may be 'dumping' this emotion on other people without realising it. This will be evident in disproportionate responses to small things.

If the emotions are dumped on you: this is not fair, and you should not put up with it.

The angry person probably cannot see what they are doing. It is unlikely to be helpful to discuss this at the time unless:

- you know the person very well;
- you have a relationship which permits discussing personal matters (as the source of the emotion may be very personal);
- you have agreed to set time aside for this;
- you are both very calm.

Don't 'pass the parcel'
It is very tempting to respond to emotional 'dumping' by unloading all your own emotions. This may even feel good at the time. However, it is not a skilful way of dealing with the person or the situation, and makes it even harder to resolve differences over the longer term. To avoid unloading your emotions on others:

- Check which emotions you are most likely to unload onto others.
- What are the triggers for this response?
- What kinds of 'emotional dumping' do you seem to invite most from other people (their anger? guilt? shame? anxiety? fear?).
- Plan a coping strategy so that you are not drawn into this sort of interaction.

Negotiating

Negotiation covers a wide spectrum. It can cover everyday situations, such as how much of the food budget goes on beer, chocolate or vegetables. It is an important part of group work, and most types of work include at least an element of negotiation with customers, clients or third parties.

Good negotiators exercise a broad and very subtle set of skills and qualities. These include:

● decision-making
● reading the situation and the 'opposition'
● persuasiveness and communication skills
● assertiveness
● dealing with difficult people.

Decision making

When negotiating, you may have to make decisions very quickly. It is important to be well prepared before you arrive, and to have thought through the issues and the questions you will face so that you are clear about your own position.

The stakes

What is really at stake? What is the ultimate aim? This should inform the negotiation process. The ultimate aim may not be achievable now: world peace, a harmonious group atmosphere, or a successful group project will not be established by solving a single argument or making a single deal. However, the negotiation should aim to take you closer to the ultimate aim. If it takes you a small way forward, then something has been achieved. If it takes you a long way forward, then you have less to do in future negotiations.

The ideal outcome

Consider the ideal outcome for you. What would this look like? What would be the benefits? Form a clear picture of this so that it motivates you to negotiate strongly.

The bottom line

Consider your 'bottom line': what is the minimum you will accept? This is usually less than we really want. Negotiation usually

involves two sides with competing interests. Each side will have to concede something if an agreement is to be reached. Be clear what you want from the situation. Consider:

The ideal solution   What would be your ideal solution? A clear vision can strengthen your bargaining position.

A good acceptable outcome What would this look like? What would be the benefits of this for you? What parts of your 'ideal outcome' are you prepared to relinquish?

The next best option   This may mean giving up more of the 'dream option'.

The likely outcome   Be realistic. What is likely to happen? Is this acceptable? You may gain a better deal, but if you do not, how will you come to terms with the likely outcome?

The minimum offer   What is your bottom line? What aspects are you prepared to negotiate, and what are your upper or lower limits for these? Practise saying these in a calm, clear way so that you sound firm and convincing when you come to argue your case. Write these down and take them with you so you do not concede on essentials.

Know when to concede

It is not always easy to strike the perfect balance between holding out for the best possible option, and knowing when to concede in order to gain something from the negotiation. You will need to weigh up:

● *Deadlines*   How much time you have in order to hold out for the best option.
● *Costs*   What might you lose if you take a long time to come to an agreement? How long can you hold out for what you want?
● *Risks*   What will happen if you hold out and

do not get what you want? Will you still be able to manage the situation (or your life)?
- *Competition* Is anybody else likely to make a better offer and put you out of the bargaining?
- *The history* In similar situations, or with this person or team, what usually tends to happen? What is likely to be agreed? What are the points that they are unlikely to concede?

All too late, George realised he hadn't included negotiation skills in his personal development plan.

Flexibility
From what has been described above, it should be evident that negotiation requires you to weigh up many possibilities, to assess the situation, and be able to accept one of a number of outcomes, depending upon the circumstances. One option is to be inflexible, and to insist on the best possible option. You may be successful, but you are more likely to leave with nothing. This usually means you have to start again on a new set of negotiations, so you need to weigh up the costs of a 'Nothing' option very carefully.

Reading the situation and the 'opposition'
Investigate the background
Find out as much as you can about the other person or team and their needs, interests and motivations. This puts you in a stronger position to negotiate.

Clarify mutual positions
Invite both sides to discuss their objectives and the possible options. This will enable you to see where there is room for manoeuvre. There will be a range of items that are not negotiable. It can take a lot of energy to try to alter the 'non-negotiables'. Ensure you are clear what the other side will or will not accept. If you can live with these requirements, then leave them out of the discussion, and focus on what can be negotiated.

Body language
The Institute of Management draws attention to the significance of body language as a means of communication – and the importance of understanding its impact in the workplace. Ribbens and Thompson (2001) argue that up to 90 per cent of communication may be non-verbal. Look for signs that suggest the other party is feeling defensive. People are less likely to negotiate to your advantage if they feel they need to 'defend' their own position. Look for:

- signs of distress (fidgeting; agitated movements; rocking; eyes looking downwards; moving hands over the face; pacing);
- a closed stance (arms and legs crossed; pursed lips; hands tightly clasped, the body leaning forward in a defensive position);
- obstructiveness (avoiding eye contact; shaking the head; refusal to engage in communication);
- anxiety about speaking (moving hands across the mouth; biting the lips);
- unwillingness to listen (sitting forward with hands moving over the ears; moving to interrupt; drumming fingers on the table).

Persuasiveness and good communication skills
Create an open relaxed atmosphere
If people look, sound or feel defensive, as described above, it helps to put them more at their ease so that they open up to your ideas. You can improve the situation if you:

- avoid 'hard sell' approaches;
- focus on their agenda for a while, as this is familiar terrain for them;
- ask for a break so you can interact more informally for a few minutes;

- mirror their body language for a few minutes and gradually introduce more relaxed postures (arms in relaxed positions, legs uncrossed, sitting back in the chair, using calm movements of the head or hands);
- smile;
- think through the situation from their point of view: you are more likely to act in a way they can accept if you are genuinely thinking about their position.

Speak to their vision

Let them know you have been listening to what they said. Keep referring to their objectives and interests, identifying how your proposal goes some way towards achieving these. Spell out the advantages. It is important that the other parties see that their goals can be met through the solution you propose. If not, they are unlikely to agree.

Show willingness to compromise

Let the other party know that you are willing to make concessions. Do not identify your own 'bottom line' straight away, as you will have no room to negotiate. Be clear about your 'ideal' scenario, so they can see clearly where you are prepared to negotiate: people do not like to feel that they are the only ones making concessions. Watch their response to your offer to see whether it is one they look comfortable with, or whether more persuasion is needed.

Keep the lines of communication open

Stay calm, even if you are not getting what you want. Do not 'burn your bridges' by walking out or giving ultimatums. Leave possibilities for further dialogue. If necessary, brainstorm more options together, take breaks and reconsider your options, start again from the beginning, or look for different combinations of options.

Activity: Changing a recurring situation

For this activity, identify a recurring situation where you could apply skills in assertiveness and negotiation. This may be the same situation that you used for other activities in the chapter. Write your responses in the boxes.

The situation. Give brief details of the context and what usually happens.	
What do you do? What kind of behaviour do you use?	
What are the effects of this behaviour?	
How do you feel about the situation? 'I feel . . .'	
A constructive way of thinking about this situation is . . .	

Identify your goal. 'The change I want to bring about is . . .'	
What are your rights? 'I am entitled to . . .'	
What are the rights of the other party or other people in this situation? 'They are entitled to . . .'	
What are your responsibilities in this situation? 'It is my responsibility to . . .'	
What are the responsibilities of other people? 'They are responsible for . . .'	
What will be the right time and place? How will you ensure you have their full attention?	
What other 'I' statements could you make?	
Your recommendations for a solution are . . .	
The minimum you will accept is . . .	
What support can you get from others (such as practice runs, somebody to encourage you)?	
Other comments	

Activity: Monitoring effectiveness in negotiating skills and assertiveness

	Situation	What I did (include details of how you applied an assertiveness technique)	Positive outcomes for myself	The effect upon other people	Further action needed
1					
2					
3					
4					
5					

Leadership

The role of leader

Leaders provide the vision. They motivate others. Leaders need to have a clear internal model of their role. This is likely to be strongly influenced by other roles that they fill in life, by their values, and by the sources of inspiration that they call upon. You will have an internal model in your head, now, of what you think a leader is or should be. For example, some people might describe a leader by using one or more of the following metaphors. A leader is:

- an architect, designing and constructing a project;
- a sales-manager, selling a vision;
- a social worker, intervening to improve the lot of others;
- a general, commanding an army;
- an actor, playing to an audience.
- a diplomat, pouring oil on troubled waters;
- an artist, with a particular vision.

Leadership from the position of the led

Reflection   Leadership

- What metaphor of your own best describes your view of a good leader? What does this metaphor tell you about your feelings towards leaders and leadership?
- Does your view of leaders and leadership encourage you to be a leader or avoid this? What metaphor would inspire and encourage you more to be a leader? Does that metaphor apply to any roles that you already fill?
- How do you feel a team would respond to a leader who fitted the metaphor you have selected?
- Which metaphors for leadership would best encourage active, motivated, self-reliant team-members?

Characteristics of an effective leader

Inspire others

A good leader will ensure that the vision is kept in view, and does not become lost amongst a forest of targets, deadlines, and problems

Heerkens, 2002

A leader develops the vision and exudes a realistic confidence in that vision. They must also communicate it well to others, ensuring that everybody else can see what the benefits of achieving that vision would be.

A good leader can see ways that the overall goal can contribute to individual and personal goals. Typically, the vision of successful leaders is for the project or the team, rather than for their personal goals (Taylor and Humphrey, 2002).

Activity: Your advice to the leaders?

- If you want some ideas on how to motivate and lead others, give consideration to what it is like to be 'led'. What kind of behaviour, communication or strategy would motivate you to 'go the extra mile' that is often needed for successful project completion?
- Jot down a list of behaviours that you would associate with an effective team leader.
- Use your insights to formulate a list of 'Advice' points for team leaders.

When you have completed your list, compare it with the 'characteristics of an effective leader' given above.

Create a sense of commitment

Team members are more likely to contribute if they feel committed to the project. An effective team leader:

● offers a clear and motivating 'vision';
● ensures that the whole team is clear about the purpose and aims of the project;
● identifies the significance or relevance of a successful outcome to the project;
● clarifies how the work of each member is significant to the overall project;
● leads by example.

Develop the strategy

One of the main tasks of the team or project leader is to develop the strategy. This will orchestrate the efforts and resources of the team towards the goal. A strategy may be simple or complex.

Encourage contributions from others

Team members are more likely to contribute if they feel valued. An effective team leader:

● notices people's contributions;
● thanks people for their contributions;
● makes it clear to the whole team where everyone fits in – and draws attention to achievements that are less visible;
● clarifies how the achievements of individuals contribute to the benefit of the overall project;
● Treats all of the team with fairness, courtesy and consideration.

Demonstrate the value of all team members

Team members are more likely to contribute if they feel their opinions are valued. An effective team leader:

● creates opportunities to ask the team for their opinions and encourages them to help evolve a solution;
● creates opportunities for the team to contribute to the planning and setting of targets;
● demonstrates how suggestions and comments from the team have been considered and adopted;
● allows individuals opportunities to develop their own plans for achieving targets.

Clarify expectations

Team members are more likely to contribute if they know what is expected of them. An effective team leader:

● negotiates clear targets for each person;
● clarifies how each person's work connects to the work of others;
● negotiates clear ground rules for group behaviours;
● makes it clear what a successful outcome would be for each person;
● ensures that feelings of uncertainty are kept to a minimum.

Ensure the team works

Leaders ensure that the team works well, knowing what different people can contribute. Good leaders ensure their team is functioning smoothly, and intervene when it is not. They act as full members of their teams, and are readily available if things become difficult. (See 'Team work', above)

- For what aspect of team work would you find it easiest to take a lead?
- When or where do you do that now?
- If you lack experience in leading groups or sessions, what opportunities could you create to gain that experience?

Take responsibility

Leaders are the most prominent members of the team. They take the lion's share of the glory when things go well. They must also be prepared to take responsibility if things do not go well. This can be quite a daunting thought. However, taking responsibility for our actions is important in most contexts.

Demonstrate excellent 'people' skills

Leaders need to communicate well. Without good inter-personal skills, it would be almost impossible to bring a set of people to share a vision, pull together, commit to a project, meet deadlines and resolve their differences. Leaders may also have an ambassadorial function, speaking and negotiating on behalf of the team.

Consider a situation where you had responsibility for the outcomes. If possible, select an occasion when it was difficult to take responsibility but where you did so.

- What happened?
- What was your role?
- What did it feel like to take responsibility then?
- What have you learnt from the experience that will be useful to you in other circumstances?

Activity: Updated self-evaluation

Complete a new self-evaluation of your people skills (see p. 116).

Compare this with the initial self-evaluation you undertook. What differences do you notice?

- What are your current priorities for developing your people skills?
- What opportunities could you create to develop your people skills further?

Closing comments

Increasing numbers of graduate and non-graduate jobs will include a managerial function, with responsibility for managing other people and their relationships with each other. There are much higher expectations of most employees now for managing other people, whether colleagues, customers or clients.

On the other hand, academic work is often organised to emphasise individual effort and achievement. There are a number of reasons for this, including the need to secure academic standards and to ensure every student is performing well on an individual basis. However, many programmes now include group work, team work and work placements to ensure students have real opportunities to develop their people skills.

Whether inter-personal skills are provided through the curriculum or not, it is a good idea to search out opportunities to develop them. Careers Services, the Students' Union, Schools Liaison Offices at the university and voluntary agencies can provide such opportunities.

Inter-personal skills require, above all, good self-management. This chapter should be read alongside Chapter 3. Emotional intelligence is a key factor in being able to manage oneself in interactions with others and to understand the needs and requirements of other people. Some universities run additional programmes such as basic counselling skills and assertiveness to develop people skills.

Effective people skills are invaluable in all aspects of life, study and work. They provide the oil that enables your interactions with others to run smoothly. When you develop good people skills, you can see ahead to where difficulties may emerge, take steps to minimise these, and increase the harmony in everyday social interactions. This reduces stress, saves time and improves conditions for everybody. Everybody is happier – which is why people skills are becoming so valued.

Further reading

Belbin, M. R. (1996) *Team Roles at Work* (London: Butterworth-Heinemann). (For more about using Belbin types for team work.)

Benson, J. F. (1987) *Working More Creatively with Groups* (London: Tavistock). (Useful for dipping into; contains many ideas about making groups work effectively.)

Cottrell, Stella (2003) *The Study Skills Handbook*, 2nd edn (Basingstoke: Palgrave Macmillan), Chapter 5. (An introduction to the skills of working with others, specifically in university contexts.)

Kozubska, J. (1997) *The 7 Keys of Charisma: The Secrets of Those Who Have It* (London: Kogan Page). (Particularly useful for those considering management, media and high-profile jobs.)

Luft, J. (1984) *Group Processes: An Introduction to Group Dynamics* (Mayfield, CA: Mountain View). (For more advanced reading about group dynamics.)

McGill, I. and Beaty, L. (1992) *Action Learning: A Practitioner's Guide* (London: Kogan Page). Chapters 2, 5 and 9. (For more detail specifically about action sets.)

Ribbens, G. and Thompson, R. (2001) *Understanding Body Language* (Abingdon: Gower). (Looks at body language in a range of everyday work settings.)

Taylor, R. and Humphrey, J. (2002) *Fast Track to the Top: Skills for Career Success* (London: Kogan Page). (The skills associated with successful chief executives, including inter-personal skills.)

Chapter 6

Thinking outside the box

All acts performed in the world begin in the imagination.

Barbara Grizzuti Harrison

Learning outcomes

This chapter offers opportunities to:

- understand how your brain works so you can use it more effectively
- develop your natural ability to learn new things
- develop confidence in your creativity
- use strategies to generate ideas
- use creative approaches to thinking.

Introduction

Born to learn

Learning is a natural process. Our brains are set up to learn – they consist of approximately a hundred billion neurons, which are linked in elaborate networks. These neural networks enable us to:

- transmit information from one part of the brain to another;
- form associations between new information and what we already know;
- make sense of what we experience;
- encode information for memory.

We can envisage our brains as billions of trees laid out in all directions, and whose roots and branches are all in contact. For any one activity, several billion contacts may be made between those branches and roots – and this happens in milliseconds. A thought is like a bolt of lightning illuminating a vast forest of connections.

Our brains are also very flexible. They allow us to learn in innumerable ways, through:

- listening
- imitation
- taking small steps
- practice
- watching others
- day-dreaming
- taking an inspired leap
- linking different problems

and so on.

Learning can be easy. The most complex things our brains will ever have to learn were accomplished when we did not even know what 'learning' was, before the age of five. This chapter will look at how you can make best use of your brain's amazing capacities. The earlier part of the chapter looks at some characteristics of your brain, so that you can use its natural tendencies to best effect.

Inspiration is most difficult when we think in rigid, logical ways. This chapter looks at ways of stimulating the idea-generating capacities of the brain – which may mean thinking and acting in ways that are not typical of your usual study or work habits. To begin, do the activity below.

Activity: The 'box'

In your reflective journal, jot down your response to the following question:

- What is the use of a shoebox?

We will return to this later in the chapter.

Limiting intelligence

Are cleverness and creativity the same thing? If you did well at school, does that mean you are automatically a creative thinker? De Bono (1994) argues that clever people are often hampered by their apparent intelligence in two keys ways:

1. They are very good at arguing and are usually better at defending their position. As they are more likely to win the argument, they are more likely to think they have the best solution. You may know people like this. If you think you are 'right', there is no reason to listen to other people or to look for a better solution.

    As a result, many intelligent people are trapped in poor ideas because they can defend them so well.

    (De Bono, 1994)

2. It is easier, quicker, and more dramatic to prove somebody else wrong than to devise constructive solutions. Negative criticism adds to your visible 'superiority' . Being constructive can take longer and can make other people look good rather than yourself. However, negative criticism doesn't promote creative thinking.

Our views of what is 'intelligent' can prevent us from developing our minds to their full potential. If we hold negative thoughts about our own intelligence, for example, those thoughts can also limit our ability to perform well (Cottrell, 2003). People who feel they are 'not very bright' or 'not very creative' probably will fulfil that estimation of themselves. On the other hand, positive thinking and constructive mental activity develop the mind. Creativity is like a muscle: it gets stronger the more you exercise it.

📖 *Reflection*   Limiting creativity

Note in your reflective journal:

- any ways that you currently put limits on your capacity to think;
- any ways you prevent yourself from achieving your full potential as a creative, imaginative person.

Activity: Self-evaluation of creative thinking skills

Make two copies of this table. Complete one now and one when you have completed the chapter or later in your programme. Rate each statement as follows:

Rating: Very often = 4;   Often = 3;   Sometimes/it depends = 2;   Hardly ever = 1;   Never/don't know = 0

	Score
1. I experiment with many ideas before I make a decision	
2. When I am working on a project, I discuss 'work in progress' with others	
3. I like to find out a lot about things I do not understand	
4. I have a wide range of interests	
5. I enjoy talking to a wide range of people	
6. I take a different route home at least once a week	
7. I set myself new challenges, regularly, so I feel 'stretched'	
8. I like the challenge of difficult problems	
9. I actively look for patterns and trends	
10. I actively look for similarities between things	
11. I actively look for connections between things	
12. I enjoy looking for the reasons that underlie patterns and trends	
13. I like to think up new ways of doing things	
14. I try to break my routine	
15. I actively look for new sources of inspiration	
16. I try things out even if I am no good at them	
17. If I get something wrong, I look to see what I could have done better	
18. I like to imagine different ways of doing things	
19. I take calculated risks	
20. Even if I am good at something, I look for better ways of doing it	
21. I have strategies for generating ideas when I need to	
22. I look for solutions even when it looks as if something is impossible	
23. I look for more than one perspective on an issue	
24. I like to play about with different ideas	
25. I spend time thinking about how I think	

Add up your score   Total _____

Interpreting your creative thinking score

You now have an approximate score for creative thinking. This is not an exact science, but it gives you an idea of how confident you are about your own creativity. It also gives you an insight into how you could develop your creative thinking skills further.

75–100   This is an excellent score. If your ratings were accurate, you already use the kinds of strategies that contribute to creative thinking. This suggests an invaluable approach to problem-solving and to life in general. Consider how you could develop these further, especially in relation to your programme and to the career areas that interest you. It is also worth checking whether your logical, analytical skills are as well developed as your creative thinking skills. It is important to develop both kinds of thinking.

50–74   This is a good score. If your ratings were accurate, this suggests your creative thinking skills are already well developed. Look for themes in the statements to which you gave lower ratings. What else could you do to develop your thinking skills? This chapter may give you some ideas.

25–49   If your ratings were accurate, this suggests that you have started to develop creative thinking skills. There is probably a lot more you could do to build these further. It is worth spending time considering what prevents you from developing your creativity at present. It is important not to try too hard at creative thinking: it may be that you worry too much about doing things the right way. Experiment with a more relaxed approach and make sure you leave plenty of time to try out new approaches as well as your usual methods. It can take time to build confidence in new approaches.

0–24   If your ratings were accurate, this suggests that you have identified that creative thinking skills are not currently a major area of strength for you. Check with people who know you well whether you have rated yourself too harshly. Identify what kinds of thinking skills are most critical for meeting the requirements of your programme and career interests. Read through the comments for the score 25–49 above. These may also apply to you. Most importantly, do not be discouraged. This is not a scientific test – and creative thinking skills can be developed.

A dozen really useful things to know about your brain

- The brain loves complexity and change;
- the more you learn, the easier it is to learn;
- it uses short cuts;
- it loves organisation and patterns;
- it is naturally playful;
- it works when you are not looking;
- you can send it on errands;
- it likes to be fed;
- you can take it for a walk;
- it won't work well when it is upset or does not feel safe;
- it works well when it is excited;
- it likes to be refreshed.

The brain likes complexity and change

The mind loves complexity. Even babies get bored with simple patterns; they look at complex images for much longer. Choirs prefer more difficult tunes: these are harder to learn but retain their interest when rehearsed and delivered many times. Throughout history, people have been fascinated by riddles, puzzles, codes, mazes and labyrinths. In many ages, art has been heavily allegorical or symbolic, so that an apparently simple picture could be decoded or interpreted, item by item, to read out a hidden message.

📖 *Reflection*   Complexity

- What kinds of complex, skilled, multi-layered or multi-sequenced activities do you enjoy?
- What kinds of complicated tasks do you avoid?
- What makes you seek out and enjoy one kind of complexity and avoid others?

Our brain can cope with very complex problems. It sets up connections between our new experiences and what we already know. It develops increasingly elaborate networks as we become more expert in an area. However, it can't do this all at once.

What we are *able* to learn is partly the result of what we have *already* learnt.

The more you learn, the easier the next thing is to learn

When we encounter new situations, we draw upon and develop our existing knowledge. We then organise this into internal models called 'schema'.

If we have been on one picnic, for example, we do not know how typical that is of any other picnic. When we have been on ten picnics, we have an elaborated idea of a picnic. We know the variations that are possible, we can anticipate what to expect at future picnics, plan for such occasions, and develop criteria to evaluate whether they are 'good' or 'bad' picnics depending on our experience. At this stage, we have a well-developed schema.

As we go through the day, this process is going on all the time. According to Piaget (1952), our experiences reinforce or alter what we already know.

If we expose the brain to varied and complex problems at a reasonable pace, it will usually develop the neural networks we need. It isn't how many neurons or brain cells we have that makes us capable of tasks, but the number of connections between them. We develop these connections through engagement with the environment, with activity, with stimulation.

If we try to be experts when we are still novices at a task, the brain may not have developed the right connections to solve the problems we encounter. It can leave us feeling that we are incapable of the task. This can seem like failure and encourage us to give up when we may simply need more practice. The longer we perform or practice an activity, the more we build up the mental connections that we need to do it well. There really is sense in the old saying, 'If at first you don't succeed, try, try, try again.'

We often find that the things we found hardest to do, and had to practice the most, are those for which we develop the best overall and long-term understanding.

📖 *Reflection*   Stimulating your brain

- What kinds of new challenges do you give your brain to keep it 'stretched' and stimulated?
- For what kinds of activity do you tend to stick with the task, increasing your chances of succeeding in the long run?
- What kinds of activities do you 'give up on' early?

The brain uses short cuts

The brain likes short cuts. Professional magicians know this and trick the eye by encouraging such 'short-cuts'.

If the brain thinks it knows what it is seeing, it stops looking for explanations. It matches what it thinks it is experiencing with the 'schema' or mental models it has already built up. If it finds a good enough match, it uses the stored information to make sense of the new experience. If not, it uses the new experience to adapt the mental models.

The brain likes organisation and patterns

The brain organises information in many different ways. A colour, a scent or a few bars of music can evoke very detailed memories. Similarly, we can generate information quickly on the basis of the first letter of a word, the end of the word, words that mean the same thing, or any number of other similarities or differences. It is easier to remember information if we:

● organise it into groups, clusters or categories;
● organise it into hierarchies;
● make links between pieces of information.

If we find links between one kind of activity and another, we are better able to perform the second activity. Looking for patterns or similarities enables us to transfer 'expertise' from one area to solve new problems (see Chapter 2).

Most of the time the brain's short cuts are useful. We often refer to these as 'generalisations'. Generalisations help us to make sense of what is going on from one moment to the next, without having to start from scratch each time. We are able to tell what are 'typical' experiences, what are variations and what is new. If we can see a connection between something we are good at and the problem in hand, then we may offer the brain a short cut to solving the problem (see Chapter 2).

We can also feed messages to the brain that encourage it to take short cuts. 'I have tried and cannot do this' is one such message. Alternatively, we could choose to feed it encouraging messages such as: 'There is a way to solve this', or 'let's look at this again' or 'This is interesting', and the brain will respond differently.

Expert chess players

Experts are experts because of the power of the brain in recognising patterns. Expert chess players can recall how all the pieces were arranged on a chessboard even if given only five seconds to view it. This is not because they have superior memories. Expert chess players see the whole configuration as one meaningful whole. They see it as one 'chunk'. They can only do this if they recognise the pattern as one that they have seen and used before. In effect, they are remembering only one pattern, which is easy.

Novice players have to remember the positions of up to 32 items – but the short-term memory struggles with more than 5–7 items. Novices have to work harder in order to remember more items – and are less likely to get the answer right. However, expert chess players are no better than remembering the layout of the pieces than anyone else if they haven't seen the pattern before (Chase and Simon, 1973). The effect of spending time practising, seeing and learning significant patterns over and over again, is very evident here.

Significant patterns

Although the brain can get used to any pattern, it works more effectively if the pattern you look for has an underlying meaning. The brain likes significance and meaning. For example, it is easier to remember a set of names if they all belong to members of your family. Similarly, if expert technicians are asked to reconstruct a circuit board, they will do so on the basis of what each part does – its function or significance to the working of the board. Novices will try to assemble the board according to how it looks (Egan and Schwartz, 1979). This approach is superficial and recall is less effective. You can test this for yourself with the activity below.

Activity: Memory for patterns (1)

- Write down the start time.
- Time how long it takes you to learn the following sequence, in order. You can learn this in any way you like, as long as you end up being able to recite it or write it without looking.

O h n s t d o w t e u o r h

- Put the sequence and all copies where you cannot see them. Now write it down.
- Check for accuracy.
- If you have not got it right, keep going until you do. Then write down the time again.
- Write down how long it took you, altogether, to learn the sequence perfectly.

- When you have finished. Time yourself learning the second sequence, found on p. 168.

You probably found it took less time to remember the second sequence, even though you may never have seen this written down before. This is because you are familiar with the chunks of meaning (the words) and a single bigger chunk (the meaning of the sentence). The knowledge of experts for any task is divided into meaningful chunks, similar to words and sentences.

As you become more expert in any subject, you will start to construct the 'meaningful chunks' of the subject, so that you can 'read it off' as quickly as you did the second sequence in the activity on p. 168.

Activity: Subject chunks

Sometimes working from two or three books, seeing how the material is arranged in each, can help to develop a sense of how the information can be organised into different sets of meaningful chunks. You may find some texts organise information in ways that are easier for you to understand.

- Look at three different books for a topic you find difficult.
- Write down the headings and sub-headings used by each.
- Browse the material written under each.
- Which book organises the information in the way that suits you best?

If you work with material in this way, you may also find that seeing the same information from several different angles helps to build up your overall picture of the subject.

The brain is naturally playful

The brain makes odd, unusual and unexpected connections. This enables us to make jokes and puns, to invent, to find solutions. Children use play as their main tool for learning. They act out adult roles. They play with the world around them, and experiment in order to find out more about it. As adults, we may be self-conscious about using 'play' in order to develop our thinking. When we allow it to be playful, the brain can provide the answers we need.

However, the brain often presents information to us in unexpected ways. It may disguise the answers in riddles or give us clues to decipher. It encourages us to 'play' with information.

Our brain may spot a dinner fork on the table, make a connection with garden tools, and send us a signal about gardens. In the past, we may have associated gardening with hard work, and the brain has spotted the fork as a reminder to us to work on an essay. Sometimes we can catch hold of this odd train of connections, which is meaningful only to the person concerned. More often, the links are hidden. When the brain plays with us in this way, we can, if we play with the 'clues' it sends us, find the solutions to problems that are teasing us.

The brain works when you are not looking

The brain is working on our behalf all of the time. Most of what we do and learn, we do without even realising it. The brain does not respond well to being forced. For example, if a word or idea is 'on the tip of your tongue' you can try for hours to remember but without success. However, a few hours later, when you are focusing on something else, the answer will seem to 'pop into your head' from nowhere.

You can use the brain to work for you by focusing on a problem, analysing it as far as you can, generating as many solutions as possible – and then leaving it for a while. When you stop analysing and labouring over the problem, allowing the mind to relax, the brain will continue to work on the problem for you.

Indeed, if you change environment, and return to a problem, your brain may have drawn your attention to clues from your surroundings without you being aware of it. Experiments with children show that they used the shape of the light bulbs, clouds, even shadows on the ceiling or cracks in the wall to resolve problems they had been discussing before taking a rest break.

You can make use of this capacity of the brain if you:

● spend time elaborating the problem so the brain is absolutely clear what you are looking for. 'Day-dreaming' alone is not enough;
● give the brain some space to work on the problem;

● enter a relaxed state of mind for a while;
● return to the problem after a break.

You can send the brain on errands

As the brain will work on a problem when you are not consciously thinking about it, you can give it directions about what you want it to do. You need to be precise about what you want, and be prepared to wait. For example, if you know where the Buddha was born but can't remember and want to know, the brain will often deliver the answer a few minutes or hours later. Sometimes, it sends the message in code: you may find yourself thinking about an Indian film or Indian music or food, even though the only link with the Buddha is India. Be aware of this so you are ready to spot the clues.

Sleep on it

Work on a problem before you sleep. Identify the core questions as far as you can. List the things that are puzzling you. Write these as questions. Focus on one or two questions that are really key.

Whilst you sleep, your brain may continue to work on the problem. It may not. However, you increase the chances of your relaxed, unconscious mind working on the problem whilst you sleep. Keep paper and a pen by the bed as you may wake up with lots of ideas.

The brain likes to be fed and watered

Greenfield (2001) describes the brain as the greediest organ in the body. Although it is less than 2.5 per cent of our body weight, when the body is at rest the brain uses up 20 per cent of the body's fuel input. It consumes oxygen from the air we breathe and glucose from the carbohydrates we eat, burning these off at ten times the rate of any other body tissue. A good diet assists the brain. Over time, starving the body of carbohydrates will reduce the fuel that the brain needs in order to function.

Our bodies are mostly water. Water conducts electricity – and the messages our brain sends and co-ordinates are ultimately electrical impulses. These are affected by dehydration. When we are dehydrated, we reduce the efficiency of our brain as well as the general functioning of the body. Drinking water increases brain efficiency; other drinks do not have the same effect. We need about eight glasses of clear water a day, taken in gradually over the day.

The brain uses energy to process food and drink. After a large meal, you can become drowsy as the brain diverts its resources to deal with digestion. A big meal or drink is best avoided just before an exam or interview.

'The brain is fundamentally a chemical system' (Greenfield, 2001). The chemicals ultimately come from what we feed the body. Nicotine, for example, puts the body into survival mode, raising heart rate and blood pressure, whereas creative thinking is associated with more relaxed states. Various oils have also been associated with the way the brain functions (Stordy, 2000).

For most people, a varied diet provides the small amounts of a very wide range of chemicals that the body needs.

📖 Reflection   Nourishing your brain

- How well do you feed and water your brain?
- How much water do you drink each day?
- Does your diet help or hinder your brain? If you are unsure, speak to somebody at your student health centre.

You can take your brain for a walk – physical exercise

Our brains first developed to manage movement and to respond to the environment whilst moving. The brain is stimulated by movement. It has been shown that mice learn better after a period of brisk exercise, as the supply of endorphins and other chemicals to the brain is increased.

In humans, a very large part of the motor cortex in the brain is devoted to the fine motor movements of the fingers and mouth (for using tools, writing, playing an instrument, speaking). If you want to stimulate your thinking, take a walk, play an instrument, draw, *do* something.

Activity: Exercising the problem

When working on a problem, take a brisk walk for about 20 minutes before returning to study. What is the effect? Do you come up with any ideas about your study whilst walking?

If you are required to sit and listen, find ways of increasing your personal engagement. For example, in long presentations or lectures, it is natural for the mind to wander after a few minutes. You can manage this process by:

- deliberately diverting yourself from listening for a few seconds at regular intervals. You can time this to coincide with when the speaker pauses or changes a slide. Otherwise, the brain will automatically 'switch off' but at less well timed occasions, and without you noticing;

- Listening actively, in a questioning way, jotting down your questions and opinions;
- Making notes: this can be an act of 'translation' of ideas from someone else's speech into your own words and ideas. Your listening is more active if you are choosing what to note, considering how to summarise, turning the talk into a diagram, and looking at how different aspects link up.

The brain won't work well when it is upset

When we are anxious, our body releases chemicals, such as adrenalin, which put us on the alert for danger. It is a very ancient bodily response, to help us survive. Our eyes look for movement at the periphery of our vision, so that we can detect danger and we become more alert to noise, ready to react. We are easily distracted by our environment. Resources are diverted to large muscles in the arms and legs so that we can fight or run.

If we are anxious about an essay or exam, we can have the same adrenalin and survival response. As the body is then ready for large movements, we confuse it if we simply sit still. When we read or write or use the computer, we focus our attention on a small central space

whilst our eyes want to look around for danger. We give mixed messages to the brain.

When we are stressed, the brain is not interested in 'thinking' tasks: it wants us to move, to escape, to survive. The more distressed we become at not understanding something, the more the brain diverts energy away from the thinking brain to the survival brain. Some strenuous activity, such as exercise, a brisk walk, housework – anything which uses the arms and legs – uses up the excess adrenalin, leaving us more relaxed and able to concentrate.

Strategies for managing stress and thinking positively can 'trick' the survival brain into believing that everything is OK, even if we do not fully feel or believe that at first. This allows us to use the parts of the brain needed to work out a complex solution. If we get too stressed, it becomes necessary to get help from somebody who isn't – and who can think more clearly.

The brain works well when it is excited and engaged

The brain likes to be stimulated and engaged. When tasks are not challenging enough, the brain finds it hard to stay focused. If tasks are too difficult for its current level of experience, the brain may become stressed. To work well, the brain needs to find a task that is stimulating but not a threat its current level of competence.

If you look for the interest in a task, you are more likely to find it manageable than if you dismiss the task as too difficult. When we are excited or frightened, similar sets of chemicals are released in the body. We can direct the brain on how to interpret those chemicals. If we approach complex thinking problems as 'difficult', we may feel ourselves 'freeze up'. On the other hand, if we choose to look for the interest and excitement in them, we are less likely to 'go blank' and more likely to use the expertise we already have.

The brain likes to be refreshed

Although the brain enjoys being stimulated, the mind can become too busy. It becomes cluttered with thought and benefits from being 'stilled'

Read through the whole activity first. After that, all you have to do is be in the present moment whilst watching your breath.

- Sit so you are upright but comfortable. You may find the activity easier if you close your eyes.
- Watch the way that your breath enters and leaves your body. Notice whether it is cool or warm. Notice whether your breaths are long or short, easy or laboured. Avoid changing the way you are breathing – just notice the detail. The exception is if your breathing is noisy: breathe as quietly as possible.
- Your mind will wander. This is natural. Avoid forcing it. Just notice when it wanders and gently return your attention to your breath.
- As ideas enter your head, tell yourself to 'let go' of them. If you notice that you are getting uncomfortable, shift very slightly and slowly, and then focus on your breath again.
- You may find that really interesting ideas and thoughts enter your head, or that you have become lost in a dialogue about an event that happened that day, or that you remember how angry you are with someone. The brain finds it difficult to let you remain quiet with just yourself in the present moment. Don't explore interesting ideas or try to remember them just now. Let them vaporise or fly away.
- You may think that your brain is too smart, clever, fast-moving, idea-filled, and imaginative for you to benefit from this exercise. The exact opposite is true.
- This task is almost impossible for most people. However, noting which justifications you find for not doing it tells you a great deal about yourself, if you can work it out. Simply acknowledge the frustration or other emotions, and again, just let go of them.
- Smiling relaxes the face muscles, making this activity easier. If you feel agitated, remind yourself that you have created the luxury of doing nothing but breathing and being with your own mind in the present moment.
- Each time you 'let go', you clear and energise your mind. You give it a break. You allow it to stop worrying and give it an opportunity to relax and do nothing.

At first you may not notice any difference. However, doing this for 20 minutes several times a week develops better mental and emotional awareness. Sometimes, the activity will leave you feeling clear-headed, relaxed and calm.

occasionally. This is one of the most difficult things to achieve. One way of practising this is outlined above.

Creativity

Most people equate creativity with a particular kind of person. You may have associated creativity with being an artist, designer, performer or inventor.

Most of us underestimate our capacity for creativity. We may compare ourselves to great artists, for example, ignoring all the occasions when we have used our minds and resources creatively to deal with the situation we are in. We all have our own spheres where our natural creativity shines. This might be, for example:

- knowing the right things to say;
- seeing the funny side when things go wrong;

- finding ways of avoiding work and inventing unusual but convincing excuses;
- co-ordinating the activities of several children so that they are all entertained, occupied and safe;
- making patients feel at ease before an operation;
- cooking a special meal on a budget;
- soothing the waters when people are arguing;
- finding the perfect present for other people.

📖 *Reflection*   Personal creativity

- If you think of creativity in the ways suggested in the list above, what kinds of creativity do you show in your life? For example, what things do you do that seem easier for you than for some other people that you know? Do you have your 'own ways of doing things' for certain tasks?
- In which areas of your life would you like to be more creative?
- Do you feel comfortable with the idea of yourself as a potentially creative person?

Creative problem-solving

Previous chapters looked at problem-solving when managing tasks, yourself and other people. The magic element in all these situations is coming up with something new when it is needed – the 'creative spark'. This is often the hardest part of problem-solving. It is easy to sit waiting for inspiration, expecting an answer to fall from the sky. This chapter looks at strategies you can employ to oil the brain and assist it in generating ideas when needed.

The 'many quickly' approach

If you have one solution, look for five, ten, twenty more

Those who feel they know the answer to a question rarely look for a better one. Also, looking for one solution can take longer than ten possible solutions. We can be so concerned about finding the one 'right' answer that we block our thinking. If we look for ten solutions,

our thinking can be more relaxed: we will not use nine of the ideas so it is safer to have some bad ones. Even if we then only find six ideas, we still have lots to work from. The chances of finding the best idea first time round are quite remote. The more alternatives we consider, the more likelihood of finding the best solution.

Phrase brain-stimulating questions

In the first activity, you were asked to consider the use of a shoebox. This usually prompts one response, as the wording of the question suggests there is only one use. However, if asked, 'How many uses can you think of?' people usually generate many more responses. The way we phrase the question influences the way we approach a problem.

📖 *Reflection*   Multiple solutions

Jot down your responses to the following:

- How many uses for a shoebox can you think of in three minutes?
- For one problem that faces you on a regular basis, how many possible approaches to solving this can you generate in five minutes?

You probably found many more uses for a shoebox this time round. Answers people give include: carrying shoes; storage; for making a doll's house or garage; a door stop; carrying things; hiding things; a sandwich box; stepping on when the floor is wet; cardboard; rattling things as a musical instrument; protection from the rain; holding CDs; a small bench or seat; for babies to tear up; holding pencils; a treasure box for children; to decorate as a gift box; sending something in the post; papier mâché; food for goats, etc.

📖 *Reflection*   Multiple solutions

- How typical is it for you to push yourself to keep looking for more answers?
- For which activities would it be most useful for you to adopt this kind of approach?

Just a minute

It may seem paradoxical, but it is often more productive to give yourself a short time limit to generate ideas. The brain can leap into action better if it knows it has a time limit. This does not usually work well if you leave things to the last minute, as you need to be relaxed. Approach the task in a 'playful' way.

Try it. Give yourself just *one* minute to jot down everything you can think of to solve a problem you are working on. If you do not generate any useful ideas in that time, you have lost only a minute.

Play with time

If an activity is likely to take three hours, leave at least four hours to complete it, but aim to complete it in two. If you plan to allow more time than you need, you reduce the need to 'get it right' first time. Less stress can mean more creative thinking. You will also have more time to fine-tune your answer and deal with emergencies. The time challenge creates just enough excitement to generate adrenalin to help with the task and reduce 'sluggishness'. If you have too much time, it is easy to start too slowly or work at a slower pace. Set off at a good pace, aiming to finish at an earlier target time rather than your absolute deadline.

'What if' questions . . .

'What if . . .' or 'Supposing . . .' questions stimulate the imagination. The wording suggests an imaginary state that is safe to explore (it isn't real so it can't do any damage) but which might provide real answers. If you reach a point where your ideas feel stuck, use 'what if . . .' questions. For example:

- 'What if . . . we designed a model that worked on its side/upside down/in reverse . . .'?
- 'What if . . . we asked the people who are going to use the building what they will use it for?'

- 'Supposing . . . we ate ten small meals a day rather than any big ones?'
- 'Supposing . . . we drew our reasoning rather than using words and numbers?'
- 'What if . . . witnesses were never visible to the accused?'

'What if' questions open up an area for exploration.

> ### Activity: What if . . .
>
> Take one problem or issue that you are working on at present.
>
> - How many 'what if...' questions can you generate in three minutes?
> - Select three of these.
> - How many responses can you brainstorm for each question in three minutes (each)?
> - Jot down any leads that arise from this activity. If there were none, take a walk or a break and then repeat the activity.

Generative thinking

There are many techniques that can be used to generate ideas and they are not difficult. An attitude of mind is the most important factor. Many people censor ideas at a very early stage if the ideas do not immediately seem sensible or useful.

Suspend judgement

Negative attitudes strangle creativity. We often dismiss the embryo of a good idea because we will not risk appearing foolish. Creativity, however, involves risks, mistakes, and 'bad' ideas as well as good. Only one in ten or twenty ideas will lead anywhere. To be creative requires the capacity to suggest ideas without immediately worrying about whether they are 'right' or what other people will say.

Nolan (2000) cites research which shows that when people's ideas are judged or dismissed, the number of ideas that are put forward drops dramatically. We tend to become more cautious and anxious if our suggestions are not welcomed, adopting a 'survival' response to avoid being discounted again.

Suspending judgement means:

- encouraging others to suggest ideas;
- avoiding negative self-judgements such as 'I am not a creative person';
- giving all ideas a chance to flow;
- being willing to express 'bad' or 'silly' ideas;
- noting all ideas in the early stages, without immediately evaluating them;
- being willing to look at all ideas for hidden potential;
- not assuming that a good idea holds all the answers;
- avoiding self-criticism if good ideas do not emerge quickly.

Creative thinking requires a light touch

Reflection   Self-censoring

- How far do you censor your ideas to avoid appearing foolish?
- What allows you to let your imagination work more freely?

Right- and left-brain thinking

Usually, when we work on problems, we use logical, sequential, ordered thinking. Sometimes this is referred to as 'left brain' thinking, although thinking is not strictly compartmentalised in that way. Logical thinking is a necessary part of arriving at a solution to most tasks. However, such thinking tends to run along tramlines, following predictable routes. If you do not already know the answer, the tramlines may not lead anywhere.

The kind of thinking associated with the 'right brain' requires a lighter touch. It does not respond well to being forced. It works well with direction and a clear goal, but not if the mind is too rigidly focused on a particular outcome. It works when you 'hover' over an idea, or play with it, teasing out possibilities. Right-brain thinking is rather like holding a small bird in the palm of your hand: If you hold the

intention or goal or idea too tightly, you crush or suffocate it.

You can see this when you know the answer to a question but cannot remember it. The harder you try to capture it, the more the answer seems to elude you. Sometimes, playing with the idea or letting it rest works better than forcing it.

Other generative thinking techniques

Chapter 7 describes a range of other generative thinking strategies. These are useful for developing open reflection, but can be used more generally. These include:

- Brainstorming
- Free association
- Day dreaming
- Free writing
- Drawing and doodling.

Synthesis

Synthesis is an important aspect of creativity. At a simple level, combining any two items creates a new entity.

Synthesis as play

The 'Creating from two' activity invites you to play with ideas. Most of the time, ideas do not lead to earth-shattering discoveries. However, even apparently strange and silly ideas can lay

Activity: Creating from two

Imagine . . .

Take any item from the Animal list and any item from the Machine list and imagine them combined into one new object. Choose as much or as little of each item as you like, as long as you 'borrow' at least one item on each side.

Animal	Machine
Giraffe	Car
Penguin	CD player
Dolphin	Radiator
Octopus	Motor bike
Monkey	Book shelves
Snake	Oven
Dragon	Garden hose
Ant-eater	Fridge
Zebra	Speed boat

Experiment
● Do this at least three more times with two different objects each time.

Draw it
● Make a diagram or sketch of one of your creations (even if you 'cannot draw'). What further ideas or details does this generate?

Describe it
● Describe your creation in words. What further ideas or details does this generate?

Apply it
● If you haven't done so already, think of at least three ways your creation could be of use in everyday life (these do not have to be sensible or 'real' applications).

How many ways can you apply this strategy to your academic work or job? Give yourself three minutes to generate a list.

Activity: Synthesis of life experience

Think of two activities where you use very different skills and personal characteristics (such as in seminars, at work, sport, dancing, music, travelling, being with a difficult family member etc.).

Write a list of the skills and qualities for each in the columns below:

	List 1: activity:	List 2: activity:
1.		
2.		
3.		
4.		
5.		
6.		
7.		
8.		
9.		
10.		

● Take any item from list 1 and consider a way that it could be of use in managing your second activity.
● Take any item from list 2 and consider a way that it could be of use in managing your first activity.
● Repeat this at least once more.

📖 In your reflective journal, jot down:

● Which of these are the most practical to put into operation?
● What would be the benefits of transferring these skills and qualities to new situations?

down connections in the brain that one day might help you find the solution to a problem you do not yet know exists.

When you have a problem to solve, you can organise your ideas in lists, chunks or diagrams and then chop these up and rearrange them in new combinations. You can write or draw each on a separate piece of paper and shuffle these about until you come up with the best combination or arrangement.

Play is about:

- having a go;
- finding new things;
- stimulating the mind;
- suspending worry about getting it right;
- allowing the mind to relax;
- experiment;
- 'letting go';
- informality;
- reduced structure (though not necessarily 'no structure').

Play is unpredictable. You may be playing with one idea, looking for a solution, and find that you are suddenly struck by the answer to something completely different that has been puzzling you for a long time.

📖 **Reflection**　On being playful

- How comfortable do you feel about the idea of 'playing' with solutions to academic work?
- Where do you allow yourself to be most playful?

Making connections

Expertise connections

In the synthesis activities above, you were, in effect, looking for and making connections. As you saw in earlier chapters, whenever you are working on a problem, the early stages are best spent in looking for connections and patterns between the current problem and:

- any similar problems or situations you have encountered before;
- other problems you are working on or subjects you are studying;
- the skills needed and those you have already used elsewhere;

- your areas of personal expertise, even if these seem far removed.

Unlikely connections

It is logical to look for expertise connections. However, right-brain thinking can benefit from almost any set of connections. As the brain likes to be entertained, it will pay particular attention to what it finds curious or unfamiliar. It can use any change in your surroundings or experience to find unexpected connections with a problem you have been grappling with.

You can assist the brain by searching out new perspectives in an active and interested way. Be prepared to let what you see, hear or experience change your views or inspire you. Some ways of doing this are:

- walk a different way round the campus or town: you will see different layouts and patterns;
- go into shops that you do not normally visit;
- examine unusual objects;
- browse books that do not normally interest you;
- speak to students from different subjects about themes in their study;
- talk to people about their work and life experience;
- make friends with people from different walks of life;
- find opportunities to talk to or work with people of different ages;
- take a bus journey; visit a new place;
- do something you do not usually do: draw, dance, sing, act, run, yoga, learn a language;
- look at an object from a new perspective: draw it upside down or with both hands at once;
- listen to different music;
- draw or write with the hand you do not usually use;
- use a different medium to describe a problem (paint, model clay, use graphics, sing it, dance it).

Search for 'the missing links'

When breaking your routine with a new activity, act 'as if' the answers or the clues that you are looking for are in that book, object, music, conversation, journey, etc. Search out connections between the problem you are addressing and the new activity. Use language structures such as:

● 'This is similar to my problem because . . .' or
● 'My problem is like this journey/statue/house because they both . . .'

Do this 10 or 20 times. The least likely connection may prompt a useful solution. For example, doing a degree is like going for a walk because:

● you can plan a specific route;
● you can select alternative routes;
● they can both take you to unexpected places;
● the end of both can seem a long way off;
● they both require some effort;
● they both stimulate the mind; etc.

Networks

Networks follow the natural habit of the brain to look for patterns. Making notes in patterns to explore a problem is usually much quicker than writing in full sentences and paragraphs. You can use single words, phrases, images, symbols, or colour to indicate an idea. If you prefer, you can create 'webs' of links using images rather than words. Networks can be very liberating as there are few rules to follow. You can:

● start anywhere on the paper;
● move from that focus point to anywhere else on the paper;
● generate other focus points where one set of ideas meets another set;
● write as much or as little as you like at each point. (A word or short phrase usually works best. However, if your creative flow is stimulated by the process, go with the energy. You can return to the rest of the pattern once you have captured your idea);
● take the ideas anywhere you like, developing new connections: it is not a 'map' of what already exists but a new structure that you are creating;
● let your mind take you for a walk;
● be focused and logical or 'day-dream' and 'play', depending on what suits.

Information contained in networks is easier to remember if you:

● write in 'joined-up writing' (cursive script). It is easier for the brain to recall a continuous movement. Avoid capitals as these are harder for the brain to process;
● write so that you can read the writing without turning the page around;
● avoid using words such as *no, never, isn't, won't*, etc.) as these are harder for the brain to process;
● use colour, symbols and shapes that make sections of the pattern stand out as interesting in their own right;
● take pauses to look for connections you might have missed;
● ask 'what if . . .?' questions about links that initially look unhelpful;

- work on the same problem more than once, designing a different network for each. On the second or third time, you may make very different sets of connections;
- for your last or working model, develop the pattern into an overall image or shape that you find easier to remember, such as a real object. Use a different shape for each topic. You then have only one 'item' for your short-term memory to recall (see the 'expert chess player' section, p. 152).

There is an example of a network on p. 165.

There is an example of a network on p. 165.

Activity: Networks

- Do something relaxing, such as going for a walk.
- Then take a large piece of paper and as many coloured pencils, pens, paints as you like.
- Make a network for a problem or issue that you are working on at present. (See p. 165 for an example.) Hold the idea quite lightly at first and let your pen play with ideas.
- Follow the networks guidelines above.
- When you are finished, look at the overall shape that your map makes. Look for a real object or recognisable shape (flower, house, wheelbarrow, table, castle, etc.) that you haven't used before for this exercise. Draw in a few lines to outline the shape.
- Alternatively, use a distinctive image or style within the network to help you remember it.
- Consider how else you could make this pattern more memorable so that you can recall the different sections easily.

Lateral thinking

Much of the ground-breaking work on 'thinking about thinking' was developed by Dr Edward de Bono, who created the term 'lateral thinking'. Dr de Bono encourages unconventional ways of looking at a problem, playing with the most unlikely solutions and then looking for an aspect that might actually work. Lateral thinking values humour, looking for opportunity in the 'accidental', a willingness to do things in new ways, and exploring all ideas.

For example, a de Bono statement might be that aeroplanes should land upside down, or that a car should have square wheels (de Bono, 1994). By working 'as if . . .' this were a serious proposition, this creates an opportunity for really examining all the taken-for-granted processes such as the tyre pressure, tyre threads, braking devices, puncture problems and so forth. In practice, real-life advances have been made through such forms of thinking.

Activity: Crazy questions

- Generate as many apparently 'crazy' 'what if . . .' questions as you can for a problem or issue you are working with at present.
- Select one of these and work through what would need to be changed in order to make this work. If possible, do this in a group.
- What light were you able to throw upon your problem by looking at it in a different way?

As if . . . it were them

You can also brainstorm solutions to a problem from the perspective of different people. This can generate a different set of responses from those you make 'in your own voice'. Imagine yourself 'in the shoes' of somebody who you think would have sensible things to say about the problem.

Activity: As if . . . they were solving the problem

- Put the 'sensible you' aside for a moment.
- Select at least three people who you think would have an interesting perspective on a problem or issue you are addressing at present. You could include your lecturer or employer or somebody who inspires you or a character from history that you find inspiring, etc.
- Put yourself into their shoes. Imagine their voice talking about the issue. How would they move their hands, head and body? Would they smile or frown? How would they describe the problem?
- What advice would they give you?
- Jot down the ideas that emerge.

Network: creative thinking

Wear different hats

Dr de Bono (1995) devised a system of imaginary hats, each a different colour and representing a different approach to thinking. When you 'wear' each of these hats, you address an issue in a completely different way. In effect, you give your mind permission to let go of one way of thinking for a while, and explore a different approach.

Although de Bono has a specific series of hats, you could devise whatever set of hats works for you: a practical hat, a dreamer's hat, a philosopher's hat, a mechanic's hat, a chef's hat, a poet's hat. Alternatively, you could devise a set of coats or shoes that suggest different ways of working and thinking.

Activity: Design your creative thinking wardrobe

- Imagine at least six hats that represent different types of people, occupation or approaches. If you prefer, use shoes, coats, chairs, etc.
- Describe or draw these if it helps you to imagine them clearly.
- Which kind of hats (or shoes, etc.) do you associate with: reflecting, planning, relating to others, analysing, finding information, writing, evaluating? Try these on when you perform these tasks!

Thinking upside down: sabotage

It is usually easy to think catastrophically. Most of us are quite good at imagining all the things that could go wrong. Use this ability to good effect by playing with the idea of deliberately doing everything wrong. The more the wording is exaggerated, the more inviting this task can be.

For example:

- What 20 things could I do, deliberately, to waste my time at college and have zero to show after three or four years of effort?
- What can I do so I feel more pressurised, irritated, thoroughly miserable, and miss all deadlines?
- What are all the things I could do and say in the seminar group to really inflame the situation and make everything thoroughly explosive?
- How can I really work myself up into a stressful state so that I make the job interview as difficult as possible?

It is usually easy to generate a long list of items to such questions, attesting to our native wit in knowing what we should and should not do in most situations. Once the list is generated, create a second list alongside it, writing the positive solution to each potentially 'catastrophic' action. It can be remarkably easy to generate ground rules or an action plan using this technique.

Activity: Sabotage

- Select one problem that you are working on at present or a forthcoming event that is important to you.
- Brainstorm all the ways you could make this a miserable flop. Pay attention to the details that could ensure it all goes horribly wrong.
- Then go through your list and identify the positive action that you can take to avert each method of sabotage.
- Your second list contains the basic ingredients of a constructive action plan.

Working with raw material

Most of the strategies discussed above are 'early-stage' techniques. They emphasise letting ideas flow. Structure, selection, criticism, censoring, and evaluation are not helpful to the process of generating early ideas.

However, creative thinking does not stop here. The first stage develops a mass of material, which is like undifferentiated dough or clay. The next stage is to shape this into something that works. This means playing and working with your ideas:

- *Analyse*:   What are the interesting aspects of each idea or suggestion?
- *Evaluate*:   What could each suggestion contribute to an understanding of the issue or to finding a solution?
- *Synthesise*:   Which aspects of each idea would work well together?
- *Spot gaps*:   What is missing? For what else do you need to generate ideas and solutions?
- *Elaborate*:   Add details to fill gaps and clarify ideas.
- *Select*:   Which ideas do you want to take forward, and which do you want to leave to one side for now?
- *Organise*:   Structure your ideas into a relevant pattern. This may be a diagram, flow-chart, model or piece of writing.
- *Plan*:   Draw up an action plan to put your ideas into effect.

Develop the narrative

Write down how the whole solution or plan will work from start to finish. If you prefer, talk it through using a Dictaphone or computer. This is the narrative. This can allow a different set of ideas to flow. Focus on the aim (to develop a solution) rather than on the quality of the writing at this stage.

Creating the narrative may be a stop–start process. The halts are also part of the creative process. They usually indicate precisely where you need to dig deeper to ensure something will work well. Geologists, for example, look at the surface of the ground for signs of a break or a change or something that 'doesn't fit' or doesn't match. This 'glitch' or 'bump' is a sign that something is worth investigating below the surface. The same is true for the creative process. It is the bits that seem to be getting in the way of finding a solution, the tricky bits, that lead to creative and sound solutions.

When you hit a 'bump' or the narrative stops, it is important to return to the early-stage techniques again, brainstorming, free-writing, discussing, developing networks of ideas. Focus on the area of difficulty. Then return to the narrative until you hit the next 'bump'.

Creativity and risk taking

Behold the turtle. He makes progress only when he sticks his neck out.

James Bryant Conant

Creative thinking requires risk taking. Most of us have been trained from a very early age to be logical, sensible, not to act the fool. It can be hard to work against that training and to remain confident in what we are doing. It is easy to feel embarrassed or anxious about what others will think.

Creativity and emotional self-management

Nolan (2000) argues that an education aimed at developing innovative, creative thinkers must begin at the emotional level. If we do not have the emotional stamina to deal with other people's opinions, then we divert our creative energies into protecting ourselves from being judged. We won't be able to risk other people's opinions of us.

Creativity carries an element of anxiety and stress. Goleman (1995) has described the physiological reasons for this. It is a natural part of our biology to resist negative feedback. However, we can develop our mental attitudes so that we are less affected by fear of criticism. Goleman's work suggests that the better we are able to manage our anxiety, the more we can think freely and creatively (see Chapter 3).

Calculated risks

The creative risks we take may not pay off. In the early stages of generating ideas, it is a good idea to take risks. At this point, ideas are only on paper.

As you move towards developing an idea, costs come into play. There may be costs in terms of time, money, resources, the environment, or personal prestige. It is then important to limit the risks, without necessarily dismissing the possibility of taking a risk. This means considering such issues as:

- The consequences of a course of action: who will be affected; what are the costs to all parties?
- What are the possible benefits? Who will gain? How significant are the advantages compared to the disadvantages?
- What are the chances of success?
- Can you really afford the solution?
- Is the risk worth it?
- Can you deal with the consequences if it does not work?

Not all risks are worth it. Some will pay off; others will not. You need to be sure that you and all the affected parties can cope emotionally and financially with the consequences if things do not work out as hoped.

Taking responsibility

Because creativity involves risk taking, it also involves taking responsibility for one's own actions. This means:

- thinking through the needs and interests of all parties, including yourself;
- being able to accept the consequences of your own actions;
- planning safety nets where necessary, so that other people do not get hurt;
- being aware of legal and ethical responsibilities.

If you are being creative in the way you approach an essay or experiment, this may simply mean being prepared to accept a low mark if the tutor does not agree that your novel ideas meet the requirements of the assignment. Check what possibilities are open to you, especially if you really need to get a high mark. On the other hand, you may wish to push the boundaries, no matter what the cost. That is your decision.

If, on the other hand, you are designing products for the public or making decisions that affect people's livelihoods, you need to consider a wider range of issues that will become your responsibility, such as:

- health and safety requirements;
- legal requirements;
- financial issues;
- ethical considerations.

Activity B: Memory for patterns (2)

This activity is the second part of the activity on p. 153. Time how long it takes you to memorise the following set of letters, so that you are able to reproduce them without looking.

S h u t   t h e   d o o r   n o w

Compare this result with the time it took you to do the original exercise above. Then return to that page.

Closing comments

This chapter emphasises that creativity is both a state of mind and a way of developing the mind. Creativity is accessible to everybody. Strategies which develop creativity require relaxation, playfulness, a light touch and enjoyment in order to be most effective. Our level of creativity, and hence our ability to be a creative problem-solver, will be affected by our attitudes and beliefs, our sense of humour, our emotional self-management, our health and well-being. Creativity does remind us that mind and body function as an integrated whole.

Creative thinking strategies are unpredictable. They can be time-consuming. It is hard to say how long 'thinking' or creativity will take. When work is left until the day before a deadline, there is not time for the brain to tease out the connections between things, and for you to mull over possibilities. It is also harder to stay relaxed and open to creative possibilities when a deadline is looming.

On the other hand, creative thinking may lead to answers in a small fraction of the time taken by left-brain thinking. Time spent in play, musing, synthesis and making connections can lead to innovatory ways of seeing and thinking.

Further reading

De Bono, E. (1994) *De Bono's Thinking Course*, revised and updated (London: BBC Books).

De Bono, E. (1995) *Teach Yourself to Think* (London: Penguin).

Greenfield, S. (2001) *The Human Brain: A Guided Tour* (London: Phoenix).

McCormick, R. and Paechter, C. (1999) *Learning and Knowledge* (London: The Open University).

Van Oech, R. (1990) *A Whack on the Side of the Head: How to be More Creative* (London: Thorsons).

The art of reflection

There is only one corner of the universe you can be certain of improving, and that's your own self.

Aldous Huxley

Learning outcomes

This chapter offers opportunities to:

- understand what is meant by 'reflection'
- understand the importance of reflection to evaluating and improving personal performance
- identify different kinds of reflection for different purposes
- develop methods for improving your reflective skills
- understand how to communicate the results of your reflection to other people.

Introduction

If you have a fleck of bright green paint between your eyes, or egg on your chin, you cannot see them as they are too close to your eyes to be visible to them. Without a mirror or a comment from other people, you could pretend there was nothing to see. This won't, of course, prevent others from seeing what you cannot.

Similarly, we are usually too close to ourselves to be aware of the things we most need to know. We can easily fail to recognise what may be very evident to other people. Fortunately, we can stand back occasionally and reflect about such things as our aims, responses, feelings and performance. Well-developed skills in reflection can help us to:

- gain a more in-depth and honest picture of ourselves;
- become more aware of our hidden motivations, our thinking styles, and of how we appear to other people;
- develop a better understanding of what affects our own performance and progress;
- develop our insight and judgements;
- gain more control over our own thoughts, emotions, responses and behaviour so that we

are in a better position to achieve what we want to achieve.

Reflection as a challenge

The reflective process is challenging. We do not always like to discover the truth about ourselves: it can be embarrassing to find we have walked around for several hours with a dab of egg yolk on our chin. We would rather believe it wasn't there or that nobody could see it. The same is true of the reflective process. When it works well, we discover things that make us feel uncomfortable. Our natural reaction is to pretend they do not really matter, or to look for an excuse, or to blame someone else. The things we most need to know can be the hardest to hear.

It takes time and practice for people to develop good reflective skills. Don't be discouraged if you think reflection does not come naturally to you. This book structures reflection on a wide range of issues. If you have undertaken some of the reflections and activities, then you will already be developing a sense of what is involved.

Reflection and Personal Development Planning (PDP)

All British universities are required to provide Personal Development Planning (PDP) for students. This is defined as a 'structured process of reflection'. It will be assumed that by the time you leave university, you will know how to undertake structured reflection in order to develop your understanding of:

- yourself, your motivations, choices and behaviours;
- what you want to achieve;
- how to plan, follow through, review and evaluate a course of action;
- how your responses and performance affect other people;
- how to take action to improve your work or learning to the benefit of yourself and/or others.

Why reflection is important to you

As a student, you are expected to take responsibility for your own progress. University students are expected to develop into independent thinkers, capable of evaluating their own performance, drawing conclusions about what they did well, what went wrong, and how to improve. Your success will depend, to a large extent, on yourself.

Develop confidence in your own evaluation and judgement of your work. This will be required of you once you enter the work force. The feedback you receive from tutors and other students gives you a rare opportunity to compare your own evaluations with those of other people.

Bear in mind that even experts can be wrong. Much of university assessment is an approximate art. You need to be clear in your own mind about what is required and see for yourself whether or not you have achieved this, irrespective of what anybody else thinks. Your evaluations should be based upon sound criteria rather than a general feeling that you are right and your lecturers are wrong. Consider the differences between your own evaluations and the feedback you receive from others. Those differences may hold important clues about how

to achieve better grades and to improve your performance generally.

The 'reflective practitioner'

Many areas of work now require a 'reflective practitioner' approach which is built into the work cycle in some way, such as through reviews or appraisal. Typically, this means taking personal responsibility for:

- your continuing professional development (CPD);
- making a fair and reasonable evaluation of your personal experience, strengths, qualities and skills;
- identifying ways of using your strengths well within your professional area;
- identifying personal limitations and areas that could be improved through training, practice or informal learning;
- recognising the effects of your own responses and behaviour and taking responsibility for these;
- making useful contributions to team discussions;
- improving individual and team performance
- identifying your own contribution to the results of a task, project or outcome;
- your own mistakes and your team's mistakes

Your current programme may include reflective activity. If not, the self-evaluation questionnaire on p. 172 can help you to decide where you need to work next.

What is 'reflection?'

Reflection is a type of thinking. It is associated with deep thought aimed at better understanding. It includes a mixture of elements, such as:

1. Making sense of experience
It is important to note the difference between 'experience' and 'learning'. Experience can be the basis for learning and development. However, just because we have been through an experience does not mean we have learnt all there is to learn about it – or even that we have

Self-evaluation on reflective practice

For each of the following statements, rate your responses as outlined below. Note that the rating for 'strongly disagree' carries no score.

Rating: 4 = *strongly agree;*   3 = *agree;*   2 = *sort of agree;*   1 = *disagree;*   0 = *strongly disagree*

'I am very confident that I . . .'	Rating
1. know how to use logs or reflective journals	
2. understand myself very well	
3. challenge my own thinking sufficiently	
4. spend sufficient time looking for relevant links between different things	
5. spend sufficient time 'making sense' of what I learn and experience	
6. spend sufficient time thinking about the significance of what I learn	
7. spend sufficient time thinking about how to improve my academic performance	
8. spend enough time thinking about the effects of my actions and behaviour	
9. make an accurate evaluation of my own strengths	
10. know how to apply my experience and skills to novel situations	
11. am aware of my personal limitations	
12. am aware of my own personal development needs	
13. always consider all options before arriving at a decision	
14. am always aware of all the motivations underlying my behaviour	
15. always take full responsibility for my own part in events	
16. spend enough time thinking about how to improve my skills in dealing with other people	
17. spend enough time thinking about how I could make a better contribution to groups I am in	
18. spend sufficient time thinking about the significance of other people's actions	
19. spend sufficient time thinking about the significance of what other people say	
20. can reflect accurately about my emotional responses to events	
21. could draw upon my reflections well for assessment purposes.	
22. spend sufficient time thinking about how to use the feedback I receive from others	
23. know how to use reflection effectively when applying for jobs	
22. am clear about the different kinds of reflection that are open to me	
21. do not need to develop my skills of reflection any further.	
Add up your score	**Total**

Interpreting your score

You have a score out of 100. This is a rough guide to your strengths as a 'reflective practitioner'. If the score is less than 100, then there is more work that you could do to develop your reflective skills.

● What are your priorities for improving reflection?
● Which *one* thing could you do this week in order to develop your reflective abilities?

learnt anything at all. Reflection is an important part of the learning experience. It is where we analyse experience, actively attempting to 'make sense' or find the meaning in it.

2. 'Standing back'
By 'standing back', we gain a better view or perspective of an experience, issue or action. It is not always easy to reflect when caught up in the midst of activity.

3. Repetition
Reflection involves 'going over' something, perhaps even several times, in order to look at it from several points of view or to check nothing has been missed.

4. Deeper honesty
Reflection is associated with a striving after the truth. It is through reflection that we can come to acknowledge things we find difficult to admit in the normal course of events.

5. 'Weighing up'
Reflection involves a sense of even-handed judgement or evaluation – it usually involves 'weighing things in the balance', taking all things into account rather than just the most obvious.

6. Clarity
Reflection can bring greater clarity, as though seeing things reflected back in a mirror. This can be useful at any stage in the process of devising, carrying out or reviewing activities.

7. Understanding
Reflection is associated with opening up to learning and understanding at a deeper level, including gaining insight into concepts that are difficult to access by other means.

8. Making judgements
Reflection involves an element of making judgements and drawing conclusions.

📖 **Reflection**   First thoughts

Before looking at the definitions below, jot down a few thoughts on the following:

- What do you think 'reflection' is?
- Is all reflection the same?
- What uses do you make of reflection?
- Do you value reflection as a process?

Reflection in everyday life

Reflection is a natural activity. To a greater or lesser extent, we all spend time going back over what we have said or done, or what we wish we had said and done. Often, reflection accompanies hindsight: we realise long after an event how things might have been different, or how some small event was more significant than we realised. This is reflected in everyday expressions:

- 'If only I had known then what I know now . . .'
- 'With hindsight, I realise . . .'
- 'I could never have imagined that doing X would result in Y . . .'
- 'Now I realise where this leads, I wouldn't do it again . . .'
- 'If I had the chance, I would do it all over again.'
- 'It was worth it/it wasn't worth it/it was worth the risk.'

In other words, we review what was said or done, weighing up the consequences and considering what the alternatives might have been. We evaluate whether we would do things differently if given the chance again or whether we were right first time.

Basic steps for reflection

If you are new to reflection, the following steps outline some basic features of reflection to help you get started.

- *Small regular bites*   Keep a regular journal or log. Write something in this at regular intervals. Little and often is better at first, so that you develop the habit of reflection. Seven minutes every weekday evening is all that is needed. Alternatively, you may prefer to take half an hour once or twice a week.
- *Be specific*   Choose one small aspect to focus on for each entry. This will develop your critical thinking better than writing on a superficial basis about your whole day.
- *Aim at improvement*   Choose something that was difficult or 'sticky' during your day. Think through what gave rise to the problem. Consider how you might achieve a better outcome next time.

Brief critical entry aimed at improving performance

How good were my people skills today?

Today was useful as I realised I am still interrupting people when they are talking. I cut right across Mary today during the seminar break. I realise this was not very skilful or considerate. Mary looked annoyed. I just ignored this at the time because I was embarrassed. It would have been better to have apologised as soon as I realised. I will next session. I have to take more care not burst in when other people are talking. Maybe I could ask Joe and Ali to point it out to me for a while so I notice it more.

Descriptive entry

The following is an example of poor reflection. It simply describes what happens and focuses on other people. The writer doesn't take personal responsibility for actions nor plan to improve performance. It doesn't take the writer forward.

In the seminar break today, Mary was talking and I wanted to say something. She had been talking for a few minutes already and I hadn't said anything. I was interested in what she was saying but then just interrupted. It was a simple mistake. I didn't mean to upset her. Mary carried on talking for a moment and then decided to stop. She looked angry. Everybody just looked at me as if I was in the wrong. I didn't even talk for very long. Peter said I had an interesting point. Then we went back in the seminar and Mary avoided looking at me all the way through.

- *Focus on yourself* Avoid using reflection as a way of blaming and taking out anger on others, even if you feel they deserve it. Focus on your own role, and how you can make a similar situation more manageable next time. This takes you forward.
- *Use prompts* Select an activity from the book and use this to structure your reflection.
- *Critical rather than descriptive writing* Reflection involves critical, analytical thinking. Weigh up the strengths and weaknesses, costs and benefits, decisions and outcomes. These are thinking skills required for most academic work. Avoid descriptive writing that simply recites what happened, or who said what.
- *Have a purpose* Reflection should be directed to a purpose. It is better to write a short entry that is meaningful than a long one which is simply pages of description. Find a topic that is useful to you. What do you most need to improve? What do you need to think through?
- *Find the right questions* Consider the right questions for structuring your reflection. It is easier, when you start out, to answer questions that give shape to your thinking. See p. 175.

- *Review* After a few weeks, read back over your entries. Look for the main themes in what you have written. Consider what action to take next.

Types of structured reflection

There are many models for reflection. You are unlikely to need them all. Browse through the chapter and see which activities most appeal or are most useful to you at present. The types of reflection introduced below are:

- question-based reflection
- open reflection
- synthetic reflection
- developmental reflection
- evaluative reflection

As you will see, there are overlaps and connections between these different types of reflection. Each type may be useful for a different task or for different stages of a task. As you develop your reflective ability, you will find that you begin to move quite easily between these different methods to suit the task in hand. Your tutors may also be able to guide you about the types of reflective activity that are most suitable for your subject.

Question-based reflection

Question-based reflection is a highly structured form of reflection; it is used extensively throughout this book. The method is relatively simple. Generally, a series of questions is given under a set of headings. Question-based reflection has a number of advantages:

- it prompts and guides you through the reflective process;
- it helps ensure you don't miss out any essential elements;
- it can give shape and direction to the subject of reflection, reducing vague discussion and 'waffle';
- it enables everyone in a group to reflect on the same set of issues in a particular way in order to make direct comparisons on specific issues;
- questions increase motivation to produce a response and can sharpen thinking.

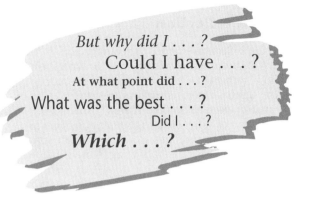

But why did I . . . ?
Could I have . . . ?
At what point did . . . ?
What was the best . . . ?
Did I . . . ?
Which . . . ?

Who does it suit?

Question-based reflection is associated with analytical, serial, left-brain thinking. It tends to suit people who like to work in a logical, ordered or controlled way, and who appreciate some external direction.

Activity: Setting questions

Select an activity that you engage in regularly or you wish to improve.

- In your reflective journal, jot down a list of at least ten questions to structure your reflection about your performance.
- Answer your questions.
- What did you find out about your performance by questioning it in this way?

Example

Question-based reflection

Question
How did I make use of feedback for my course-work?
Response
I read through it, I accepted most of it, I identified themes that need to be addressed.

Question
Did I make the best use of the feedback I received on my report?
Response
At the time I thought I had made good use of the feedback. I did read it and I set myself priorities for action. However, looking back, I don't think I took it seriously enough. I wondered if the tutor had been too harsh on me, so when I did my essay for the next tutor, I didn't really follow through on the advice I had been given. I then got some of the same feedback again. I realise I ignored my own priorities.

Question
How can I make more effective use of feedback?
Response
I need to set myself a realistic target. I tried to take on too many changes at once last time and then got discouraged. I need to speak to my tutor to work out one or two changes that would make the most impact. Basically, I need to be more focused and accept that I cannot change everything at once.

Open reflection

Open reflection methods encourage you to 'let go' of some concentration, and 'go with the flow' rather than trying to control the process too tightly. Open reflection can seem 'unstructured'. However, there is usually a structure of some kind to the method, such as working from prompts, working through several stages in a process or following semi-formal rules.

The benefits of open reflection are:

● it makes it easier to get started on a task as it helps you to generate thoughts and ideas;
● it allows the imagination free rein so that a relatively uncensored set of associations can be formed;
● unexpected ideas may emerge, which can be energising and exciting;
● it can be more personally relevant than working through questions set by somebody else.

Open reflection is good for generating ideas, but not always for structuring and making sense of them. It can help to combine open reflection with other methods to structure your thoughts effectively and make meaning from experience.

This method of reflection suits people who like to work in organic ways, and who appreciate things evolving in new or original ways. Open reflection can be conducted in an orchestrated way (a tutor guides the process) or can be personally controlled.

The various methods of open reflection are discussed below.

Brainstorming

Brainstorming is a very simple and quick technique. Take a large piece of paper and a pen. Write the problem or question down somewhere on the paper – the centre is often a useful place but you can choose wherever suits you. Write down every idea or solution that comes into your head. At this stage, do not evaluate or judge what emerges – just let the ideas flow.

Brainstorming is one of the most widely used techniques for generating ideas quickly. You can use it to start the process of reflection, as well as for writing essays or other assignments.

Activity: Brainstorming

● Select a topic that you need to think about this week – or brainstorm ideas about an ideal birthday gift for someone you know.
● Write the topic somewhere on the paper.
● Give yourself five minutes to write down everything you can think of about the subject.
● Avoid judging your ideas as you go along; just write down whatever comes into your mind.

● Once you have finished the brainstorm, consider each suggestion in turn. Cross out the least useful. If other ideas emerge as you do this, jot them down for consideration too.

Discussion

Discussion can be a very valuable form of reflection. It has the advantage of offering multiple perspectives. Paired or group discussions may raise challenging questions that you, as an individual, may wish to avoid. Such questions are often the ones we need most to address – so discussion-based reflection can keep you on your toes.

Discussion, unless strongly chaired, can tend to drift in many directions. It is more creative if only a limited number of prompt questions or statements are used. This allows the discussion to wander broadly over the topic. For a more controlled discussion, set more questions and time limits for responses. If the discussion veers away from the agenda, don't dismiss the tangents straight away. The tangents may be giving you important clues about the target subject, or about how well the group is working together, or how you might approach a particular problem.

Day-dreaming

Without forcing the issue, let your mind drift over the target subject. Day-dreaming about the target subject is more likely to occur if we give the subject serious and detailed consideration, and then do something very different for a while. Day-dreaming is not something that can be forced, but it can be encouraged and nurtured. Keep pen and paper, a tape recorder or a lap-top computer nearby to capture ideas as they occur. Reflections that arise in this way are easy to forget. Sometimes, there is a natural movement from this more relaxed reflection towards more analytical questioning, as you become aware of what you are discovering.

Networks

These are useful for letting your mind develop an idea in a visual way that follows the way the brain works. See p. 163 for details.

Free writing

Writing as a reflective tool is different from writing intended for an audience or tutors. Its aim is to stimulate thinking, not to communicate a message to others. This means that the writing may look, sound and flow differently from other writing that you do. Your method will be quite different from any other person's. You may just pick up the pen and write; you may write words and phrases rather than sentences; you may scribble and draw as you write; you may write in verse. In other words, you assess the value of this writing for yourself, in terms of whether it helps you to reflect and achieve your own aims.

Reflective freewriting, like other free writing, will probably take more than one draft:

- a draft that generates ideas;
- a draft that explores some issues in more detail, going off at tangents and with more details;

- later drafts with more structure, as you begin to draw conclusions from your reflection and write them for others to read.

Example

Reflective free writing

A good day. Enjoyed the session. Made contributions. Really liked it when we saw video and discussed the video. I got very involved in the debate, which surprised me. I hadn't thought I felt so strongly. Not sure why I do. Why do I? I don't like the design of the bridge. Ugly. Not that though. More . . . Reminds me of history lessons more than engineering. Hated history at school. Maybe not a good reason for me to respond to a design now. Or maybe it is. Maybe other people will feel the same way. What else influences my responses apart from history lessons? I like sculptured surfaces . . .

The above example may not make much sense to you, but it did to the person who wrote it. He knew the issue he was trying to explore and this was just his first step.

Activity: Free writing

Choose a subject that you want to think about this week. This may be the same as one you considered for a previous activity.

- Give yourself ten minutes to write down, as fast as you can, any thoughts that come into your mind on this subject.
- Unlike brainstorms, where you just jot down any phrase, for free writing aim to link the thoughts to some extent. Consider how one idea connects to others. Monitor, lightly, where your thoughts are going. As in the example above, this does not have to be a very developed process.
- When you have finished, read through what you have written. Look for *one* key theme or idea. Highlight or underline this.
- Give yourself a few minutes to free-write on only that *one* theme.
- Then highlight a *second* theme and free-write on that.
- You will find that your ideas on the subject are starting to develop.

Drawing and doodling

Drawing and doodling can be used to distract you from controlling your thought processes too closely, allowing your mind to take you where it wishes. You may find that the drawing and the reflection have little in common. On the other hand, you may wish to analyse your drawings for clues about how your mind is working. You could need to check whether your interpretation made sense when weighed against other evidence.

Caricatures, cartoons, paintings or other graphic means may be your preferred methods for reflection, for exploring past actions or events and for getting a feel for their meaning.

Activity: Doodle

- Select a new topic for reflection.
- Take a piece of paper and scribble in the middle.
- Either doodle as you think about the subject or draw a picture or diagram of it. The image does not have to be of good quality: it is simply a tool to distract you from concentrating too hard on the topic.
- If ideas emerge that you want to jot down or develop, then let yourself do so.
- After you have finished, consider how far you find this method suits your learning style.

Generative thinking

The strategies suggested above are associated with generative thinking styles. The strategies and approaches developed in Chapter 6, 'Thinking outside the box', can support the development of this way of working.

Synthetic reflection

Synthetic Reflection involves a 'bringing together' or a 'synthesising' of different aspects and perspectives. It is useful for giving shape to a series of reflections or making sense of earlier stages of reflection. It helps you find the meaning behind your reflections, thoughts and actions. It also stimulates creative thinking.

Advantages of synthetic reflection

Synthetic reflection is useful for:

- seeing links and connections;
- gaining a sense of the 'bigger picture';
- gaining a concrete overview from where to begin more detailed analysis;
- giving shape or structure to the reflective process;
- drawing reflections together into a coherent whole.

Synthetic reflection is associated with gestalt, holistic, or right-brain thinking. It suits people who like to spot clues, solve puzzles or put things together into new forms. Artistic endeavour and synthetic processes are closely associated. Linking can be made in logical or creative ways, so synthetic reflection can suit those who like order and those who like to work organically. The importance of developing these modes of thinking is highlighted in Chapter 6, 'Thinking outside the box'.

As synthetic reflection helps to draw things together, it can be used to follow up reflection based on free writing or discussion.

Look for links and themes

Synthetic reflection is an active type of reflection. You are looking for links, connections and leads in material you have already produced. Use it to search out hidden themes that are there on the page but which you may not yet have noticed. Going over the material, rewriting it, colouring it, highlighting it, illustrating it, will help you to focus on each theme.

Developmental reflection

Whilst any method of reflection can assist the process of personal development, the following methods focus specifically on understanding and improving your performance and achievement.

Monitoring performance

You may be asked to keep a log or journal as part of your course. Even if this is not a requirement, it is a useful practice. Many employers require logs to be kept of actions taken, along with the rationale and outcomes. These may be used in team meetings or in reviews in order to assess the effectiveness of project decisions.

Example

Monitoring performance

Project Group: reflection

20th February
I chaired the project group meeting again today. This went better than last time. I was able to keep the group to the agenda. Unlike last time, this time I did not let people just bring up new topics as they felt like it. I was quite tough, for me. I summarised points well and the feedback on this was good.

Unfortunately, the meeting still ran over time. I did find it difficult to break in to interrupt the flow when Carla and Ian started arguing. I am not sure whether I should speak to them before the meeting, or whether I should just cut across them, which might seem rude. I am worried because they speak loudly and it would look bad if nobody could hear me when I try to interrupt. Because I didn't keep these two in check, we ran over time. Time-keeping looks like my big challenge, but really the issue is about knowing how to interrupt people. This is my next priority. I have arranged to speak about this to my tutor.

Transferring skills

Chapter 2 demonstrated that expertise can be used in diverse contexts. However, skills do not transfer automatically. Skills are likely to be 'transferable' only if we:

- identify the sub-skills implicated in an activity. It is easy to overlook the wide range of sub-skills that are integrated into a rich experience;
- make specific attempts to draw parallels between one activity and another, searching out the comparisons;
- are able to see how one situation is similar to the other. If we cannot see those parallels, then we may believe ourselves incapable of

dealing with situations that are well within our actual competence.   (Butterworth, 1992)

It is worth giving time and thought to what we have achieved in any one situation and considering its applicability to other situations. The self-knowledge gained may help us later in new situations.

Example

Transferring skills

I have been working with children in a local school, helping them with their mathematics. The main developmental points for me were in taking responsibility for others and in using 'plain English'. However, I am also much better now at organising information so other people can use it.

The teacher pointed out that when I first started at the school, I launched straight in and tried to finish as much of the worksheet as I could. Now, I structure the work much better, so the children know what they are learning. This is partly good communication. However, I am also developing skills in structuring information. I look much more closely at how to break down instructions into small chunks that the children can take in at once. They don't like it if I have to repeat instructions.

I have found that this is useful when talking to adults too. In my part time job, I now do this when giving guidance on technical problems. I find I don't have to go over information so many times. This way of thinking seems to be helping me to plan and structure my written assignments. My tutor says I write more clearly.

📖 *Reflection*   Spotting your skills

In your reflective journal, write for a few minutes about any one *new* activity that you have undertaken recently. Consider things such as:

- What skills you already had that you used for the new activity?
- Were there any ways you adapted your usual ways of thinking or doing to help you with the new task?
- Did you discover anything about yourself by doing something new?

Example

Transferring skills

I was very anxious about writing an essay as I hadn't written one before. My programme mainly uses report writing. Reports are very structured whereas I couldn't see how essays fitted together.

I spoke to a third-year student who talked me through the process. He pointed out that the discussion part of my reports is quite like an essay. If I take out the different sections of the report, such as the method and results sections, and remove all headings and tables, I have the core of an essay already.

I find it easier to write the main part of an essay as if I was writing a report. I use headings and write a paragraph under each of these. This helps me see the structure of my writing. I have noticed I need to check my paragraphs are linked because sections of essays flow into each other more than sections of reports. I then remove the headings when I am ready to hand in the essay.

Reflecting on your academic development

Take time to stand back and look at the big picture regarding your academic development. Consider:

- Are you sufficiently motivated to achieve well academically? How could you increase your motivation?
- How coherent are the choices you are making for options or electives? How will these choices help you achieve your longer-term ambitions?
- Are your choices giving you a strong enough specialist base?
- Will your choices make you stand out as distinctive with interests and capabilities beyond your subject specialism?
- What are the most stimulating aspects of your current learning?
- What is blocking your progress in any area? Are your study strategies still relevant or do they need to be revised?

Academic choices

I wanted to study nothing but chemistry as that interested me most but I am concerned that this will look boring when I go for jobs. I am also interested in travelling abroad. I couldn't see how the two could fit together as I imagined myself in a large British factory near where I grew up.

The Careers Service showed me some case studies of career paths that people from my programme had taken, and I was struck by the opportunities that are available through some big companies for working in international branches. I am not sure yet whether to take a language, which I could start from scratch. This would make it easier to get picked for a placement abroad in the future. However, a specialist IT option might be more useful.

I also need to look at the opportunities open to me if I take a subsidiary in a subject such as health science or nutrition. I have put some time aside next Thursday to look through materials in the Careers Service library.

You could reflect on differences in your performance from one topic or option to another. For example, you may experience a sudden drop or increase in your marks, or find you are more successful in some areas than others. You can begin to investigate this by techniques such as:

- listing how you approach each subject differently;
- free writing about your attitudes or approaches to each subject;
- brainstorming differences between the topics and how you will manage these.

Reflection on assignments

I spent a long time on my last assignment and was disappointed with the marks. This time I spent less time and yet my mark was better. It seems to me the main difference is that I really thought a lot about what the question meant this time. All of my work was very focused on addressing the title. It felt like I really knew what I was doing – so it took less time. I spent more time, though, just working out my initial plans. I think I have made a breakthrough in the way I go about my assignments.

What I need now is to know how to work out what is needed for my land-surveying option. I can't really see how to work out the problems in the same way. I suppose I haven't actually tried applying my 'breakthrough' method to surveying yet, so I don't know if it will work or not.

Reflecting on your professional development

Take time occasionally to consider your short- and long-term professional development. For example:

- What skills are you developing? Are there obvious gaps in your profile of skills and experience? Will these matter when you apply for jobs?
- Are your programme choices the right ones for the type of career you have in mind?
- Are you focusing too much on study at the expense of other experience which would help your career?
- Are you making the best use of all that university has to offer to develop your skills, experience and CV?
- Is there some kind of work experience you could undertake to develop your people skills in the workplace?
- Are you making good (and early) use of the Careers Service and its resources?
- Would it be useful to have a mentor from the area you are considering for a career?

Reflecting on your personal development

Reflection isn't useful only for academic or work-related contexts. You can use it to look hard at any area of your personal development. For example:

- Are your life ambitions changing in any way?
- Are your values and beliefs undergoing any changes? What is influencing such change?

Example

Professional development

I have noticed that many job adverts require good team-building skills. There is not much opportunity on this programme to work in teams. I am worried that this will be a weak point when I come to apply for jobs. I have heard that there are volunteer activities being co-ordinated on campus and I will follow this up this week. Some of that might involve team work.

Another alternative might be to study an elective that includes team work in its skills profile. Unfortunately, I haven't found one that interests me. I might have to choose one that is not especially interesting. I would rather work in a team that was involved in real-life activities rather than study, as I think employers would prefer that . . .

- Are you giving sufficient time to friends and family?
- How are you taking care of your health?
- What are you doing to manage stress?
- What are you doing to ensure a good 'work/life balance'. Do you get time to enjoy yourself without undermining your work and study?

Example

Personal development

I have been working very long hours at college and at work recently. I added this up to 65 hours last week. I was supposed to go to my brother's birthday party but in the end had to work an extra shift as it was double pay. This was good from the money angle, but my family was really disappointed. I am not getting the right balance.

I need clear breaks with no work or study. I have to start planning out my time so I get time to rest and enjoy myself occasionally. Just stop. I have noticed that I am not sleeping well. It would be better for me to start earlier and then finish off earlier in the evening. Studying late just keeps me awake at night, rattling it all round in my head.

I am also neglecting my interest in music. I would really like to spend more time listening to recent releases. I could do this by . . .

Evaluative reflection

Questionnaires and checklists

Self-evaluation questionnaires are useful starting points for self-evaluation:

- the questions help to define the field, indicating the areas that are important to consider further;
- the questionnaire can be used in a 'before' and 'after' way, enabling more precise comparisons between answers given at different times;
- it is often difficult to answer a questionnaire with a straight 'yes' or 'no'. Those questions that resist easy answers prompt longer answers, indicating what the real issues might be for you;
- questionnaires are usually good starting points. They are not particularly useful if used in isolation from other reflective methods.

Critical event

One good way of finding out more about yourself is through an in-depth analysis of a single event. To begin with, select an occasion that was of some importance to you such as:

- the first time you . . . ;
- the last time you . . . ;
- a very difficult occasion;
- a test of your values;
- a test of your abilities;
- a test of your will-power;
- a test of character;
- a turning point in your life;
- a time you realised something unexpected about yourself or other people.

If you undertake this exercise several times you have valuable materials for reflecting on your performance. Consider:

- What themes emerge?
- What noticeable areas of improvement are there in your performance over time?
- What areas did you highlight for further action that you did not then attend to? What do you think is preventing you from doing so?

Example

Critical event

I undertook a student project for MMM Manufacturers, spending one afternoon a week working with their development team. I was responsible for designing paper-based materials that made their new software easy to use for short-contract workers. I worked alongside the IT-development team in Human Resources, and one of these acted as a 'line manager' . I piloted my materials with ten part-time workers, and used their feedback to make some major changes.

The paper-based materials I produced were used by the company. That was a success, but the work experience was an important event to me for very different reasons. First of all, I had no confidence that I could work in that kind of environment or work to deadlines. I proved to myself that I could be relied on to carry out a job well.

I had been very anxious about piloting the materials. I imagined that people would be very critical and that I would get upset if I was criticised. During the pilot, I was determined to listen to what the part-timers had to say, as I wanted my materials to work. They said some very positive things but they also pointed out a lot of aspects that needed to be changed. I surprised myself. I stayed very calm and encouraged them to say what they really felt. What they said was actually very sensible – I could see how most of it would improve the materials.

I learnt the value of feedback as I was able to put it to good use. I also learned how important it is to allow people to be critical. My main achievement, from my perspective, was in 'taking it on the chin'. I accepted what was said without being devastated that everything wasn't perfect in the first place. This is something I have not been able to do in the past so I feel this has been an important turning point.

This experience will help me in my seminar group. For example, I used to see all feedback as a kind of attack on me . . .

📖 *Reflection* Critical event

Select one event that is of key importance to you. Consider:

● What happened generally – the context?

● What did you do – your own role?

● What were the outcomes or consequences of your actions?

● What alternative actions could you have taken?

● How might you prepare differently for a similar occasion

● How did your performance or action differ from your performance on other occasions? What were the reasons for this?

● How did you use or how could you use feedback from other people?

● What is the one main area where you need to focus to improve your performance? What do you need to do in order to take this forward?

● What did you gain and learn from the experience?

Write down your answers to each of the above questions so that you have a record to which you can refer on future occasions.

See Chapter 9, p. 236.

Using feedback

As a student, you will receive regular feedback on your work in ways you may never experience again. Such feedback, provided by experts who want you to succeed, is an extremely valuable resource. You can use it as the basis of reflection on your development by:

● Reading it! – and reading it again a few days later, as you probably will not be objective the first time you see it;

● considering whether the comments are unexpected;

● considering whether you agree with the comments. If not, what are the grounds for your disagreement?

● deciding if you want to see similar comments on future work. If not, what steps can you take to change or improve that area of your performance?

● considering sources of support available to you (books, web pages, tutors, support services) to address areas for improvement.

Latifa could always find constructive use for her tutor's feedback.

Put time aside at least two or three times a year to read through a set of feedback sheets, pen in hand. Jot down any emergent themes as these may be losing or gaining you marks on a consistent basis.

Recording reflection

Keeping personal records of some kind is integral to personal development work. Your university may require you to keep a log, journal or portfolio and give you very precise directions about what to include and how to present it. Alternatively, you may be asked to devise your own records and presentation. Most of the resources associated with this chapter are reproduced in Chapter 9 for easy use.

Logs and journals

There are different ways of keeping logs and journals. You can:

1. Note down all aspects of a particular experience, such as the fine details of an observation or experiment or how you designed a product. Some subjects require you to note this objectively (without comment);

others require you to reflect upon what you observe.
2. Keep a daily or weekly diary on a particular theme.
3. Keep together all the influences, inspirations, sketches and thought processes that led to a final product or outcome. This is particularly true of art, design and other creative programmes.
4. Record all the information you consider significant about your learning. This could include items such as:

- the general topics covered;
- exhibitions, placements, visits, field trips, etc.;
- your feelings about the programme, teaching methods, students and your responses to these;
- contributions you make in class;
- things you find difficult – and how you address those difficulties;
- thoughts about your learning styles and habits, and the appropriateness of these for you and your learning goals;
- ideas that arise from your study;
- what you find most stimulating in your current study;
- how your studies relate to real life;
- how theory covered in class is relevant to practical or case work you are undertaking;
- what you are learning about yourself through your interactions with others;
- tips and strategies you are gathering;
- what you are learning about how you manage your emotions;
- sources of inspiration.

Maintaining a journal

Keeping a reflective journal can be very challenging, especially staying motivated to make regular entries. It takes determination, good planning and a far-sighted approach. It also means having a strong sense of responsibility for your own development over time. Keeping a journal requires the 'stick-with-it-ness' Edison referred to above (p. 106). The benefits tend to arrive very gently and may not be noticeable for a long time. Even if you cannot detect them easily, the benefits are likely to be there.

Evaluating progress on learning goals

Current learning goals (*see Action Plan*)

Targets and milestones

Action taken to achieve the goal ('What have I done so far?')

Evaluation of performance so far ('How well am I meeting my targets? How sensible were the targets? Do they need to be changed?')

What feedback have I received from others?

How have I made use of this feedback?

Things I have learnt about myself, other people or the task so far.

Strong points about my attitude, approach and performance.

Things I could improve about my attitude, approach and performance.

How I have changed?

Next steps?

Other comments

Signed _____   Date _____

Using your reflective journal

Reflective journals should be easy to use. This means:

- easy to carry around;
- a book you like to open;
- numbered or labelled so you can find previous entries easily and quickly. Use headings and dates for each entry.

A loose-leaf folder has the advantage that you can enter your responses to activities. However, you may prefer to keep a diary or portfolio, as these can serve different purposes.

Format for a journal entry

As well as impromptu entries, such as those listed above, you may find it helpful to work to a format to explore your progress on current goals. One format is given on pp. 185–6. Ideally, this should be used in conjunction with an action plan (see p. 102).

Personal statement

Personal statements are important tools for making real use of ongoing observation, reflection and evaluation. They are characterised by:

- being written in a more formal manner than reflection for personal purposes;
- drawing together learning that has taken place;
- identifying themes (from a portfolio or journal) and summarising these;
- identifying the overall path that developmental work has taken over a period of time;

Example

Personal statement

This semester, I took three modules in Business Studies. These covered project management, business communication and entrepreneurship. I was able to draw out several themes that ran across the three modules.

First of all, the communication skills were important in identifying ways of varying a message so that it comes across to very different audiences: client groups, bank managers, the buying public, products aimed at different age groups and at people who purchase for those client groups. We also focused on communication within teams.

Communication skills
Communication skills were important to my entrepreneurship project as I was part of a team that took a product (light-weight collapsible bikes) through from idea to design to market. We drew up a business plan that we presented to a funding panel. There was an accountant on the panel who gave us feedback on our presentations. Although our group did not win the funding, we were given valuable advice on what a business plan should look like and how to communicate its strengths when asking for funding.

The entrepreneurship students were not all from a business background: some were from product design, fine art, engineering, marketing and multi-media. One important lesson was in discovering that students from each discipline use very different ways of describing their work process and the product than we expect from a business perspective. Although we learnt that we have to find a common vocabulary, a shared way of communicating, we could have approached this is in a more organised way and avoided some misunderstandings. Communication for team-work across disciplines is an area that I would like to investigate further.

Team work
The product designers and engineers, in particular, approached their work in ways that the business students found challenging. This meant that we had to establish ground-rules for working together as a team. This took several attempts because our starting points were so different. We had not anticipated this and did not realise at first that this was the case. In the beginning, each of us was unwilling to compromise on methods we had been trained in.

However, as the deadlines drew closer, we made a choice to develop a hybrid way of working that met the needs of the project rather than what we thought we should do as 'business students' or 'design students'. This felt like a risky strategy but we were encouraged by our tutors, who gave us some useful tips on how to negotiate a strategy…

- identifying the lessons that have been learnt;
- evaluating current performance;
- making recommendations for future improvement;
- identifying action that needs to be taken.

The emphasis of a personal statement may differ depending on whether it is written:

- at the beginning of a programme;
- as developmental work within a programme;
- for assessment or submission at the end of a programme;
- for a specific purpose such as a job application.

Position papers

A position paper is a 'snapshot' of where you are now, which draws together reflections on your personal development. Typically, its format follows a time-line from past to future. You are usually asked to:

- look back over past experience and identify what you have learned from your experience;
- evaluate your current position;
- project forward to where you wish to be;
- decide a plan of action that takes you from where you are now to where you wish to be in the future, using your past experience;
- identify how you will be able to recognise when you have achieved your goals.

To write a position paper, you can draw upon entries from your reflective journal, responses to activities in this book, self-evaluations and action plans. A possible structure is suggested below, organised through a series of questions. You can use these to guide you, selecting relevant questions. Where possible, include references to texts you have read in order to support your reasoning.

Orientation

Aspirations and motivation: where am I going?
- What are your aims for your future? Where would you like to see yourself in five or ten years' time? (Be imaginative and bold.)
- In what ways do you think your programme will help you to achieve those aims?

- What skills and attributes do you want to develop whilst at university?

Review

What do I bring from my past?
- What has led you to the present stage in your study or career?
- What has inspired you? (Give references where possible.)
- How has your past learning and life experience equipped you for this course and for being a student now? Evaluate the knowledge, qualifications, skills, attitudes and experiences that you bring with you and which are relevant to your study and goals.

Appraisal

Where am I now?
- What skills and abilities will be required of you as a student on this course?
- What are your main strengths and weaknesses as a student on this course?
- What will you need to improve in order to do well?

Planning

How will I achieve my aims?
- How do you plan to achieve your ambitions and study aims? What are you going to do, when and how?
- What targets have you set as milestones (to what time-scales)?
- What difficulties might you encounter?
- In what ways might you sabotage your own success? What steps will you take to prevent yourself or others from sabotaging your success?
- How will you keep yourself motivated?
- What other preparation and planning do you need to undertake?

Evaluating progress

What have I achieved?
- How will you be able to recognise that you have achieved your aims?
- What changes do you expect to see in yourself, your work, and in the attitudes of others when you have achieved your aims?

- How will you be able to demonstrate to others what you have achieved?

Extrapolation

What have I learned?
- What have you learned about yourself or your learning that was unexpected in some way?
- How might this learning help you more generally with your studies, life and work?

References

Include references to books, films, music or other sources that have inspired you on your journey to where you are today. Include references to all materials you have used in writing the position paper.

Example

Sample introduction

In this position paper, I demonstrate how my past experiences and future objectives are influencing my current study on a degree in media technology. The paper is based on an in-depth consideration of my previous life and learning experiences, and shows the ways in which prior learning has provided me with skills, knowledge and personal qualities that are relevant to my present studies. In particular, I draw attention to the range of skills and insights I acquired through working as a volunteer last summer and how these, unexpectedly, have provided me with starting points for design work on the degree.

My main aim is to use this qualification to advance my professional career. This position paper outlines both the areas I need to investigate in order to improve my career prospects and my reasons for the module choices I have made for next year. It also looks at skills I need to improve next year to improve my course marks. In addition, I demonstrate how the programme I am on and the decisions I am making will help me to achieve my goals.

A reflective essay

Purpose

Some programmes set reflective essays as marked assignments. The contents of the essay will vary depending on the focus of the programme and the purpose of the essay. For example, some programmes ask for a reflective piece of writing at the beginning of programmes in order to encourage students to focus on their goals and learning needs. Other programmes set an essay at the end of a module to draw together their learning and identify their next steps. Usually, you will be given specific guidance on what is required for the essay.

Structure

Reflective essays differ from position papers and personal statements in that they follow an essay format. Like any other essay, a reflective essay will have:

- a specific title: you must structure your essay to respond to the question contained within the title;
- an introduction that identifies your overall position and prepares the reader for what to expect from the essay;
- a main body divided into paragraphs: this does not usually contain any headings or bullet points;
- a conclusion that sums up the main points: this does not introduce any new material;
- references to source materials within the text;
- a list of all references at the end of the text.

Contents of a reflective essay

Typically, a reflective essay will contain a selection of the following elements.

Personal aims and goals
- Why did you choose your programme: what were your aims and objectives?
- Have these changed since starting the programme? In what ways and for what reasons?

Expectations
- What were you expecting from the programme?
- What did you expect from yourself?
- What led you to form these expectations?

Programme learning outcomes
- What are the learning outcomes for modules you have taken so far?

- What skills development is linked to the modules you have taken?
- How do these outcomes and skills correspond to your own aims and goals?

Other activity
- What else do you do outside of your programme in order to achieve your personal goals or to supplement your learning for the programme?

Learning goals and targets
- What are your current areas of strength in relation to your programme, career or life ambitions?
- Which areas do you need to improve?
- What are the priority areas for improvement as 'learning goals'?
- What are your targets, milestones and time-scales for meeting these learning goals?

Personal reflection
- What methods have you used for reflection?
- How do you use reflection?
- A detailed example of how you developed and evaluated your performance in one area.

Use of feedback
- What kinds of feedback have you received from tutors, students, employers or other people?
- How do you feel about this feedback?
- How have you made use of this feedback?

Evaluation of personal choices
- In practice, how far does the programme meet personal goals and interests?
- Would any other programme or set of modules be more suitable for you?
- What other subject choices, additional modules or supplementary programmes would help you to meet your personal goals?

Evaluation of learning
- How well are you achieving the learning outcomes of your programme?
- What else have you learnt through the programme?
- What are you gaining, additionally, from your programme or from university that was not part of your original goals?

Evaluation of the programme
- How does each module or aspect of your programme contribute to your professional and personal development?

Evaluation of personal performance
- How well are you achieving your personal goals?
- How well have you engaged with your programme (Attendance? Punctuality? Level of interest? Contributions made in class? Efforts to make personal meaning of the course material? Additional reading or work undertaken?)
- How far do you consider you have taken responsibility for improving your own learning?

Personal development
- How have your opinions, attitudes, beliefs or values changed since starting at university?
- In what ways have you changed as a person since starting at university?

Critical incident
- Identify an incident that illustrates your approach to your learning.
- What does this incident demonstrate about you?
- How does this incident relate to any theories of learning you have covered on your programme?
- What did you learn from this incident?
- See the reflection on p. 183 above and the Critical Incident Sheet in Chapter 9, p. 236.

Progress files and portfolios

What is a progress file or portfolio?

Progress files were described in the Introduction (pp. 1–13). A progress file or portfolio of personal records is simply a file where you keep together relevant information about yourself. These assist the process of reflection. It is useful to keep and update a portfolio of information that you can call upon to:

- go over your reflections;
- monitor your progress;
- keep important documentation together;
- keep feedback in one place;

- use for sessions with tutors, careers advisers and support staff;
- help staff write your references;
- write your CV and job applications.

Contents of a portfolio

You may find it useful to include some or all of the following in your full portfolio.

A contents page

Divide the material in your portfolio into sections. Number and label these so that you can find material and update it easily: see p. 226. Use a detailed contents page to direct you to materials.

Summary

Include a personal statement or position paper. Aim to be selective and specific, identifying key themes and bringing out what you have learnt. The position paper should refer precisely but very briefly to evidence contained within the portfolio.

Formal documents

- Certificates of any qualifications;
- your academic transcript;
- references and testimonials you have received;
- an example of a recent piece of marked work is also useful when seeing support tutors.

Developmental documents

- Completed, dated, self-evaluation questionnaires;
- responses to any activities in this book or similar activities;
- feedback from tutors and peers for past assignments and your commentary on these.

Planning documents

- Documents you completed about your current goals and aspirations, such as what you want to achieve from the course, where you see yourself in five to ten years' time, who or what inspires you, what motivates you, and what you need to do to achieve your goals;

- your updated action plan to achieve academic or other goals;
- details of priorities you have set, including milestones, targets and deadlines, and how far you kept to these.

Documents relevant to future job applications

- A profile of vocational, technical, academic and other skills you have developed;
- an updated summary of your education and training, including school, college, training courses and relevant short courses;
- an updated list of all work experience, with the dates, addresses of employers, a brief job description, main responsibilities, skills or qualities demonstrated, and what you learned from doing that work which is of value to your current aspirations;
- a curriculum vitae (CV) – a Careers Adviser can help with this;
- examples of experience that demonstrate typical job competences.

Personal papers

You may like to include personal material that you think relevant to your personal development, such as photographs, letters, school reports, poems, quotations, job descriptions or articles. These may relate to:

- sources of inspiration;
- things that motivate you;
- charts of your progress to date;
- things that remind you of what you wish to achieve;
- things that you find reassuring when stressed.

Presenting your reflection to others

First-stage reflection

Most of us engage quite naturally in very deep reflection when we do it in our own time and way. It is important to capture such reflections in a way that suits our personal styles. However, such 'first stage' reflections are in raw form. They are not usually accessible to other people and are not necessarily in a form that is useful to you.

Second-stage reflection

Second-stage reflection is characterised by:

Time   Leaving time between the initial reflection and the current stage of reflection.

Summary   Second-stage reflection seeks out and summarises key themes and salient points, noting down where more detailed evidence can be found in the portfolio.

Insight   Identifying what has been learnt – especially the less obvious learning. This will refer to broad themes rather than specific subject knowledge. It will bring out issues of relevance and significance rather than focus on data. During second-stage reflection you come to appreciate the deeper and subtler aspects of your learning.

Communication   It is at this point that you are ready to consider presenting the results of your reflection to others. The context will determine what it is appropriate to show to others. For most purposes, you will need to remove:

- material about your personal life you wish to keep private;
- personal details about other people;
- repetitive or irrelevant material;
- unnecessary examples;
- materials produced by other people, such as guideline materials, tutor notes, copies of background reading, lecture notes, etc.

Submitting selective portfolios

If your tutors are going to mark your portfolio, they will look for:

- *how well you summarise your insights into your learning* (or the subject of the portfolio). Most marks are likely to be given for the reflective essay, position paper or similar document, which draws together the main points;

- *how well you select and edit relevant information for inclusion in the portfolio.* Large, unedited portfolios that contain all the information you could possibly gather on a subject are unlikely to impress. Bulk does not usually gain marks. The tutor is likely to give marks specifically for skills in selecting, editing and cross-referencing;

- *how well the evidence and examples you refer to in the portfolio really do support the point you are making.* If you say the evidence demonstrates a particular skill or insight, it must be a very clear example;

- *how well the portfolio is constructed:* clear contents; all documents labelled; the summary writing makes exact cross-references to the page where the evidence can be found. Use a highlighter pen or number the lines to indicate exactly where the tutor should look to find the evidence. If you make vague references to long documents, the tutor will probably not accept the reference;

- *how well you select one or two good pieces of evidence for each main point you make.* More than one piece of evidence is usually not needed or wanted.

In other words, good guidance for portfolios is:

- include a contents page and a strong summary document (e.g. position paper or essay);
- label and signpost clearly;
- back up your main points with good evidence;
- cross-reference your argument clearly to evidence in the portfolio;
- include only essential evidence;
- keep it light (your tutor may have to carry it home!).

Reflection is not something that comes easily to everyone. However, there are many different strategies that can be used to develop the process. Reflective abilities develop over time and with practice.

● Put time aside on a regular basis to reflect upon your performance.
● Use a structured approach. Make use of activities in the book if you are not sure where to begin.
● Read back over your reflections on a regular basis. Look for themes.
● Consider regularly how far you have achieved personal goals.
● Find approaches that suit you and your programme.
● Look for changes in yourself, your actions, goals or values.
● Notice and celebrate your achievements.
● Be positive about the process: over time, you will see the benefits.

Further reading

Boud, D., Keogh, R., and Walker, D (1985) *Reflection: Turning Experience into Learning* (London: Kogan Page).

Buzan, T. (1993) *The Mind Map Book* (London: BBC Books).

Cottrell, Stella (2003) *The Study Skills Handbook*, 2nd edn (Basingstoke: Palgrave Macmillan).

Mezirow, J. (ed.) (1990) *Fostering Critical Reflection in Adulthood: A Guide to Transformative and Emancipatory Learning* (San Francisco: Jossey-Bass).

Schon, D. A. (1989) *The Reflective Practitioner: How Professionals Think in Action* (London: Temple Smith).

Chapter 8

Successful job applications

The more I want to get something done, the less I call it work.

Richard Bach

Work and play are words used to describe the same thing under different conditions.

Mark Twain

Learning outcomes

This chapter offers you opportunities to:

- develop an awareness of what employers are looking for
- consider what you want from an employer and your first job as a graduate
- plan ahead towards the jobs you want
- make use of progress files, personal records and personal statements
- make a strong job application
- write covering letters, CVs and competence statements when applying for jobs
- develop effective interview skills
- use the application process to improve your performance.

Introduction

Applying for a job you want usually means developing the skills and qualities that go with that job. Such skills and qualities are not developed overnight, so the earlier you start the process of thinking and planning towards a job, the more successful you are likely to be.

This chapter guides you through the processes and considerations of applying for your first job as a graduate. It enables you to think and plan ahead towards careers and jobs that interest you. It leads you through the basic processes so that you have undertaken the appropriate reflection and action to improve your job applications. It also offers specific guidance on preparing for the interview so that it is a more predictable, manageable and successful event.

In this chapter, you will gain an introduction to the general state of the employment market, and the kinds of skills employers want. It is worth remembering that almost half the jobs available to graduates are open to students of any discipline. Your career may lie in an area that has very little relation to the subject you have been studying. This means that the opportunities open to you are very wide indeed.

It also means that employers may have much more interest in everything you have learnt outside your subject discipline. This can be quite a difficult fact to acknowledge when the subject has been the focus of your attention for several years. If you do nothing but study in that time, you may find it more difficult to compete for jobs against students who have planned ahead towards a career whilst studying.

You will be a stronger candidate for a job if you can talk about how the job meets personal aims (see Chapter 1). It is important that you appear knowledgeable about the skills and qualities required for jobs that interest you. Many employers will be interested in hearing about the steps you have taken so far to develop such skills, either through your studies or outside of the curriculum.

Smart students plan ahead, seizing the opportunities and creating opportunities for themselves. For example, almost all jobs now require a broad range of people skills, task-management skills and personal qualities as well as subject knowledge. Most employers value candidates who can show they have experience of working well with other people and managing new tasks either in a team or by leading a team. If opportunities for developing these skills and qualities are not available through the curriculum, good forward thinking includes planning how to acquire these skills outside of the curriculum. Earlier chapters in this book will also help in developing those skills.

What do employers want?

Minimum effort, minimum cost

Employers usually want an easy life when it comes to employees. They want to get the job done with minimum cost to themselves. This means they want people who are skilled, confident, able to get on with a job with minimum direction, and who are not likely to create difficulties for the company. This formula will translate differently from one company to another. For some, it means they will only recruit people who are already trained and skilled. For others, it may mean that new recruits are expected to read work situations well, learning quickly on the job, with minimum disruption to colleagues and supervisors.

Soft skills

Apart from specialist skills and knowledge, employers consistently argue that they want graduates to have better 'soft skills'. Soft skills

are those skills which are often hard to measure but which oil the wheels of any work situation. The top ten, according to research by TMP Worldwide Research (1998), are:

1. oral communication;
2. team-working;
3. listening;
4. written communication;
5. problem-solving;
6. relationship development;
7. adapting communication style;
8. time management;
9. sharing knowledge;
10. influencing others.

It is noticeable that most of these involve 'people' skills. Some companies refer specifically to 'problem-solving within teams'. Most work involves dealing with other people, either as colleague, client or the public. Most work involves working through solutions to new situations and problems as they arise, usually on an informal basis working closely with colleagues. Many work contexts are complex, requiring an understanding of how each person's contribution assists or hinders others further along in the process. This is very different from the way most school and university study is organised, which is normally on a very individual basis.

Skills in context

When employers refer to communication skills, time management or problem-solving, therefore, they are usually referring to a team or company context, not to an individual effort. Words such as 'written communication' mean different things to those in an academic context. For example, whilst it is true that university does develop writing skills, employers usually want particular kinds of accuracy, speed, clarity, precision, style, layout and sensitivity to different audiences.

Employers do value the skills developed by a university education, but are frustrated when academic contexts are given as the only examples of skills. They prefer to see examples of using those skills in real-life contexts.

For example, 'presenting a seminar' is often given as an example of oral communication.

Delivering a speech develops courage, as well as speaking skills. However, most jobs require formal presentations only on very rare occasions. Taking and managing questions at the end of your presentation, or contributing to seminar discussions, are likely to develop more relevant skills than delivering the paper.

Moreover, the bulk of oral communication used in most jobs is two-way communication, usually with colleagues, the public or clients. The associated skills are those of establishing rapport with others, conveying information exactly, expressing yourself clearly and accurately, listening, summarising what others say, dealing with difficult people, negotiating your position, offering criticism, taking criticism and adapting your communication style to suit varied circumstances.

It is useful to build a 'rounded portfolio', developing skills in work or community contexts. This can be developed through a wide variety of work-related learning opportunities,

I have made this letter longer only because I have not had time to make it shorter.

Blaise Pascale (1655)

such as sandwich programmes, part-time work, projects for employers, voluntary work, helping in local schools or youth groups, running student groups, or helping with the Student Union. The Careers Service and Student Union can give advice about a wide range of local opportunities.

Activity: Skills in context

Take at least seven different pieces of literature written for the public. Include two different types of newspaper, some leaflets on public information, advertisements, trade magazines, bank or building society information, or shopping information. Browse through these, comparing the writing style with that used in higher education. What are the characteristics of such writing? What writing and thinking skills would it take to produce them?

Collect literature from the areas of work that interest you. Browse through these, comparing the writing style with that used in higher education. Consider, again, what are the characteristics of such writing? How do they differ from what is expected for academic writing?

- Where else do you develop your written communication skills outside of academic contexts?
- How could you develop skills in writing for a non-academic audience?
- What skills have you gained from your academic writing that will be useful to any context?
- Complete the written communication competence sheet on p. 286.

Reflection — Oral communication skills

- What could you do (or have you done) to develop oral communication skills suitable to work contexts?
- What skills have you gained from academic tasks involving oral communication that will be useful to a work context?
- Complete the oral communication competence sheet on p. 288.

Employability skills

In 1998, the Committee of University Vice-Chancellors (the CVCP) commissioned research by Coopers and Lybrand to identify 'employability skills' for graduates. They produced the following list (CVCP, 1998):

1. Traditional intellectual skills
- Critical evaluation of evidence;
- the abilities to argue logically, apply theory to practice;

- to model problems qualitatively and quantitatively;
- to challenge taken-for-granted assumptions.

2. The 'new' core or key skills
- Communication;
- application of number;
- information and communications technology;
- improving one's own performance;
- working with others.

3. Personal attributes
- Self-reliance;
- adaptability;
- flexibility;
- *nous*;
- creativity.

4. Knowledge about how organisations work
The report points out that it is important that employability skills include this fourth area, and 'not just the first three'.

The 'personal attributes' section is worth noting. This refers to 'intra-personal' skills (see Chapter 3) and creativity (see Chapter 6). Intra-personal skills include the ability to manage oneself, one's attitudes and emotions, especially when working with other people. Personal and emotional self-management is expected as an individual responsibility. Employers want people who can use common sense ('nous'), creativity and initiative to resolve issues. As work contexts change very rapidly, employees are required to cope with and manage change. They need to be adaptable to changing circumstances, ready to move where the need is, and develop new skills as required. This is very different from workplaces of the past, where there was more of a 'production line', same-job-for-life mentality.

The DfES Skillsbase website

In June 2000, the Department Education and Skills launched the Skillsbase website. This includes, amongst other things, an analysis of the DfES's *Employer Skills Survey* (based on 27,000 employers) and downloadable reports on skills. This can be found at www.skillsbase.dfes.gov.uk. The Skills Task Force

commissioned by the government found that the key skills of communication, problem-solving and team-working were 'identified as those most demanded by employers and where the gap between supply and demand is most critical'.

The percentage of management, professional and associated professions had risen from 27 per cent of the workforce in 1971 to 37 per cent in 1999, and was expected to rise to 40 per cent by 2010. The Skillsbase found that managerial skills were being expected at lower levels in the work hierarchy. There is a growing demand for the following skills:

- *organisational skills*: knowing how to manage tasks, monitor performance and develop the business;
- *thinking and problem-solving skills*: strategic thinking, conceptual skills, analysing information, solving problems, making decisions;
- *people skills*: managing relationships in the work place.

Skills and earning
The task force found that managerial posts, health and finance professions, and 'generic skills' such as communications skills, problem-solving and team-working, were those most likely to bring higher earnings. The database gives details of relative increases in earnings for different professions. It is a useful site to browse to find out about employer needs across the workforce.

Advertisements

Advertisements for jobs usually list the most important features of the job, including skills that are currently wanted. Browsing through the job advertisements associated with career areas that interest you will help you form a picture of the skills that are most valued by the kinds of employers you wish to work for.

The employer's WIIFT

Bright and Earl (2000) recommend that when applying for jobs, candidates should always keep in mind 'an employer's WIIFT'. WIIFT stands for 'What's in it for Them?' They want to know what you have to offer to the company. If you simply 'sell yourself' you may come across as only interested in you. The more you know about the employer and the work available, the more you can identify how your own skills and experience will bring benefits to that company.

Activity: Job advertisements

● Find at least 20 advertisements for jobs in career areas that interest you. Look at the Careers Service vacancy bulletin and main national newspapers. Alternatively, browse some of the web sites given in the Resources section at the end of the book (p. 294).
● Which skills are referred to the most often (count them)?
● Complete competence sheets (pp. 257–91) for the skills relevant to your career interests and place these in your progress file.
● What opportunities are available to you to develop these skills further?

What do you want from your first graduate job?

In Chapter 1, you considered what your vision and values were for the next ten years. You may have changed your mind about these as you worked through the book. Mature students may have a good idea of the job they want when they leave university, but it is not unusual for younger students to have only a vague idea of the kind of work they might enjoy. This is partly because they have not been tested in the workplace and have not had the opportunity to build confidence in many skills such as leadership and team projects.

Your first few jobs as a graduate may be traditional 'graduate' jobs. These are jobs that offer reasonably good salaries, and which set out to recruit new graduates. They tend to be skilled work and recognise the value of a degree. However, many graduates enter jobs that give them general work experience, with the aim of building their skills and personal portfolio. This is especially true of students in creative professions, where it is often expected that graduates will enter at a lower rung and plan for the longer term. Work experience is key to many jobs.

Your first step is to think what it is you aim to gain from your first jobs after graduating. You may want time to work on personal projects, such as travel or developing your artwork, taking a break from work. You may prefer to work part-time on more than one job, or to spend time on agency work whilst you build additional skills. Do you intend to walk straight into a particular job? If this does not happen, what other jobs could carry your career or life plans forward?

Whatever job you choose, it is unlikely to be for life. Consider what there is to be gained from the opportunities available rather than panicking that the perfect career opening does not seem to be available to you straight away.

Choosing a job

Know what is right for you

The Careers Service will have a wide range of paper and electronic resources, including psychometric tests, which will enable you to pinpoint the kinds of work that suit you. If you completed the activities in Chapters 1 and 2, you should have a good idea already of the general direction that you want to take in life. When applying for jobs, consider how far each job advances, in the short or long term, your life vision. Consider how far it is in line with your values and beliefs: it will be hard to come across well in interview if the job contravenes basic beliefs and values.

Consider the best route

Some jobs receive thousands of applications – they are very popular and the reality is that almost every applicant will be disappointed. That does not mean that it is impossible for you to be in a job that suits you.

Know all your options

Too many graduates select the most obvious jobs. Talk to the Careers Service so that you have an idea of the range of jobs open to you. More than two out of every five jobs are open to

Activity: What do I want to gain from my next job?

- On the table below, indicate with a tick if the item is something that you would like to gain or develop in the next (or first) job that you take. Put more than one tick if you feel this is very important.
- Then go through the items you have ticked and rate them in order of importance (1 for the most important, 2 for the next in importance, and so on).

From my next job, I want to . . .	Important to me?	Order of importance
1. gain work experience in a new field		
2. enhance career opportunities		
3. earn more money		
4. increase my job satisfaction		
5. work in accordance with my values and ethics		
6. work better hours		
7. work in better surroundings		
8. work near home		
9. work with people more like myself		
10. take on more responsibility		
11. broaden my mind		
12. give myself more challenge		
13. know myself better		
14. develop technical skills		
15. develop a wider range of skills		
16. work with a wider range of people		
17. develop problem-solving skills		
18. develop inter-personal skills		
19. develop a broader set of interests		
20. make friends		
Other things:		
1.		
2.		
3.		

📖 **Reflect**

In your reflective journal, consider:

- What do I really want from my next job?
- What would most persuade me to apply for a particular job?

any graduate. Identify which jobs have fewer applicants and whether any of these would suit you. They may provide easier entrance routes to the job you prefer over the longer term.

Plan long term

Consider unusual routes to your desired destination. Work experience, travel or gaining skills that are short in demand but relevant may all provide unexpected routes.

Starter posts

Companies tend to be loyal to their own personnel. It is worth thinking about entering at the bottom or in a less competitive post, and aim to work towards the job you want from inside the company. Consider interim jobs that you could fill for a few years that would provide a sideways route into the job you want.

Choose jobs you can do

Every employer receives a large number of applications from people who have not read the information about the job correctly. If you have very few of the qualifications, skills and experience required, you will not be short-listed. You could have spent your time making a stronger application for a job that is within your competence.

Consider smaller companies

Many students want to work for large companies and these are often the ones invited to careers fairs at universities. However, many small and medium-sized companies also recruit graduates. These can provide very good opportunities to develop experience.

Reflection   Routes into work

In your reflective journal, consider:

● What kinds of jobs are you most interested in?
● What are the statistical chances of you gaining that job as a first job? Your Careers Service will give you details of what to expect.
● Brainstorm alternative routes into that job. Which of these would you consider? Which are you most likely to succeed in?

What do you want from an employer?

For your first job as a graduate you may want to look for specific characteristics in an employer – or you may just want to get a foot on the employment ladder. Local and personal circumstances will affect what kind of choice is available to you. However, the following points are worth considering.

Investors in People

A number of companies have gained Investors in People (IiP) status. This means that the company has demonstrated a commitment to the training and development of its employees. If an employer has IiP status, they are more likely to welcome questions at interview about how they develop their staff. They are very likely to ask candidates about what steps they take to ensure their own professional development.

Equal opportunities

Legislation on race, sex and disability is aimed at protecting against unfair practices and discrimination. Many employers will make a reference to being an 'equal opportunity employer'. This means, usually, that they are keen to be seen making efforts in equal opportunities. It does not necessarily mean that all aspects of work at the company will affect all workers equally, nor that discriminatory practices do not take place. However, if equal opportunities matter to you, you may feel more comfortable at a company that has an equal opportunities policy that extends beyond the basic legal requirements. For more information, see www.cre.gov.uk (Commission for Race Equality), www.equalops.co.uk (equal opportunities), or www.ability.org/emp.html (disability).

Career opportunities

Some companies expect their graduate employees to move very quickly from one post to another. This may mean travel, very varied work, and opportunities to gain experience in a number of areas. Some provide opportunities to work or travel overseas. Larger companies will usually detail such opportunities in their graduate literature. It is reasonable to ask questions about this at interview. Smaller companies are not usually able to create such opportunities so this may affect the type of company that would suit you. However, a small company may be growing quickly and would offer a different kind of opportunity to employees who were with them from the beginning. For information about different kinds of companies, see

- www.bloomberg.com (international and entrepreneur site);
- www.companieshouse.gov.uk (lists all UK public companies);
- www.vault.com (lists what it is like to work for named companies).

Graduate apprenticeships and company schemes

Some companies offer programmes to bridge the time between university and work. Sometimes this is of an apprenticeship nature, offering training for a reasonable but relatively low salary (or no salary). These are useful for gaining experience of a new work context. Other companies offer outstanding opportunities to work on a particular project in a workplace but under supervision from the university. Your university Careers Service or Work-Based Learning Unit would have details of such programmes.

Your 'bottom line'

A first job can offer experience and training that will be of use in future applications. You are well advised to accept less than the ideal employment in order to gain that first step. However, you should be clear in your own mind about what is and what is not acceptable to you. This may relate to the level of pay, working hours, location, behaviours, being the only person of your sex or colour, lack of reliable transport, or something personal to you. You should be clear where you will not compromise on issues such as:

- personal safety;
- health and safety;
- disability access;
- unfairness, bullying or discriminatory behaviour;
- working hours you consider to be unreasonable.

Plan ahead

Make opportunities

You will see from the section below that career planning does not start with applying for jobs in the third year at university. Employers will be looking to see whether you know how to make use of the opportunities that surround you, whether you have planned ahead and have thought through what they, as employers, want. They will want employees who know how to spot and use opportunities, think on a broad front, and can plan ahead for the good of the company.

They will look to see how you spotted, created and used opportunities on your own behalf, in the first instance. If you did not do this for yourself, they will be less convinced that you could do this on behalf of their company. Ideally, your planning should start in your first year, so that you are in a strong position by the time you apply for jobs as a graduate.

Develop a rounded portfolio

When you apply for a job, the subjects and extracurricular activity you have been engaged in will count. When you apply for jobs you will be considering:

- 'How have I used my time?'
- 'What have I done that makes my application stand out?'
- 'What will make this company consider me rather than somebody else?'
- 'What evidence have I got that I can deliver the skills they are asking for?'
- 'What experience can I offer?'

The subject and grade of degree are relevant, but are only a small part of the story for most jobs. You will not get a job simply because you have a 'first class' or '2.1' degree. That may be one of ten things the employer will consider, if at all, and is possibly the least important on their list.

When people invest in stocks and shares, they are advised not to put all their money into one investment, but to develop a rounded portfolio that includes different kinds of investment. If one company fails, the others may still earn money for them. Your time at university is a similar kind of investment. Your time and your energy can be invested entirely in study, or they can be spread out over a wider portfolio. Your degree is obviously your largest and most important investment at present, but it does not have to be your sole investment. In addition, there are also 'smart' ways of putting a degree together, so that it counts for more in some circumstances.

A rounded student portfolio will contain 'investment' in at least three of the following:

- the degree subject;
- complementary subjects;
- a broad set of skills that could be transferred to the workplace;
- unusual technical expertise;
- work experience;
- volunteer activity;
- contributing to the community;
- a position of responsibility;
- general career awareness;
- awareness of the professional field or the companies where you want a job;
- evidence of taking responsibility for personal development needs or training.

When to use the Careers Service

The Careers Service can give you excellent advice from your first year at university, so that you can plan the best possible route towards the jobs that will interest you later.

The Careers Service should be able to guide you to put together a rounded portfolio. They can advise you on how to spend your time as a student so that you:

- choose an interesting but relevant selection of subjects;
- understand which skills are relevant to the field of work that interests you;
- know how to make the best use of work experience;
- plan and prepare well in advance for the areas that interest you;
- are aware of the range of opportunities available to you through the university, locally and further afield.

Many also have 'job shops' or similar, to help you gain student jobs whilst studying. You may find it helpful to browse websites that give career guidance for graduates. For example, see:

- www.prospects.ac.uk
- www.gradunet.co.uk (advice and jobs for graduates);
- www.hobsons.com (guidance and jobs for school leavers, young people and graduates);
- www.insidecareers.co.uk (guidance and jobs for graduates).

📖 *Reflection*   Developing your personal portfolio

In your reflective journal, consider:

- How are you currently planning ahead so that you have a better chance of gaining the job you want after you complete your degree?
- In your case, what else are employers likely to be looking for apart from your degree?
- Which aspects of the 'rounded portfolio' are you already working on?
- Which aspect will you work on next? How will you go about this? Who will you speak to first about this?

Activity: The Careers Service

- Visit the university Careers Service in person or electronically within the next three weeks.
- Find out what services are available. Is there a website?
- Find out how you can make best use of the service.

Plan to stand out

Employers see hundreds of similar people, all wanting the same job for similar reasons, and all holding similar certificates and qualifications. This is one reason why Careers Services ask to see undergraduates early, so that they can give advice about planning forward towards the job-application stage. You can prepare to 'stand out' from other applicants by various means:

- *Choose unusual subject options as electives or subsidiary subjects.*
  Employers are likely to be interested in why you chose unusual options. They may appreciate that you have a broader outlook, or they may be able to use the subsidiary subject in some way. You should plan to choose companies that are likely to appreciate the subjects you selected. For example, you may choose to take a language as an option and look for companies that deal with overseas clients or have overseas branches. Be prepared to answer questions about what it was that interested you about the options you selected, and the links you can make between this, your subject and your career plans.

- *Choose smart combinations*
  Consider combining different subjects. For example, lawyers, accountants or designers work for all kinds of businesses. A law student who has studied two modules of sports science will look more appealing to the sports industry. Similarly, the media industries or an architectural firm might be more interested in a business graduate or accountant who had undertaken some study in their own areas and knew the field and terms of reference.

- *Do something different*
  An unusual interest, study abroad, travel, a curious combination of languages, success in a competition, holding an exhibition of your work, voluntary work and similar activities can provide a spark of interest in employers. They are likely to ask you questions about these if they interview you.

Making use of progress files and personal records

Chapter 9, 'Recording Achievement', offers a range of resources to assist you in charting information that you will need to call upon for applications and interviews. When you complete the information there, you will have most, if not all, of the material you need about yourself to apply for almost any job. It is particularly important to focus on the section on personal competences and the competence sheets (see pp. 257–91).

> **📖 Reflection**   Stand out from the crowd
>
> In your reflective journal, consider:
>
> - What is it about you that would make you stand out on an application form so that you increase your chances of receiving an interview?
> - What is it about you that would make you stand out on in an interview so you will be remembered out of a large number of interviewees?
> - What can you do now or during the year to develop your profile in this respect?

All of the chapters in this book have been designed to assist you to plan towards your future, develop personal insights, devise strategies for improving personal performance, and understand the skills that are required in many occupations. If you have worked through the activities in this and earlier chapters, you will have developed a good picture of yourself, and the kind of career that might interest you.

When completing your application or preparing for an interview, you will find your 'personal statement' (Chapter 7, pp. 187–8) is of particular value. A good Personal Statement will summarise your goals, your achievements, how you went about improving your personal performance and how you have learnt from your experiences.

> **Activity: Update personal records**
>
> - Put time aside to update your progress file this week.
> - Which aspects of your progress file need updating?
> - Which three of the competence sheets on pp. 257–91 would you find most useful for the jobs that interest you? Your answers to competence questions need to be very brief and very specific.

Browse your personal records or progress file to prepare for the application process. These will remind you of what counts in your life, what you aim to achieve, what you have achieved and what you have to offer in a job.

Making the application

Read the documentation

First read the documentation you are sent. You will usually receive one or more of the following items.

General information

This will tell you more about the company, work conditions, and sometimes includes information about matters such as pensions, holidays, bonuses, and so forth. If it does not, you may wish to ring the personnel department at the company to find out more about these and to ensure that you are happy with the conditions on offer. Read carefully about the company, and follow this up on the Internet, or through the Careers Service if it is a large company. Make sure you are happy with the record and ethics of the company. Large companies expect you to know something about them. All employers expect you to know something about the general area of work, whether from experience, from having talked to others or from some basic research.

A job specification

This will outline the responsibilities of the post and what the post-holder is expected to do, building on information that was contained in the advertisement. Check that this does match what was said in the advertisement and that you are still interested. Tick off all the responsibilities that you can manage successfully. It is unlikely that any candidates will be outstanding in all the areas that the employer requires, so do not be put off if there are one or two areas where you consider yourself to be weak. Consider what the essentials are and whether you could cope with these.

A person specification

The person specification will list the qualifications, experiences, skills and qualities that the employer is looking for. Sometimes these are divided into 'essential' and 'desirable'.

It is unlikely that many candidates will meet all the essential requirements. You will need to make a judgement about your suitability for the job if you do not meet some of the essential requirements. For example, some qualifications are very specific, such as for a qualified engineer, or an educational psychologist to administer tests closed to the public. If you lack those qualifications, it is not usually worth applying. However, sometimes relevant experience and skills can be considered as alternatives.

Ensure that your overall application refers to all of the items on the person specification. Typically, an employer will tick off each specification that has been addressed successfully, and then add up the 'ticks'. If you merge two or three characteristics into a single paragraph or example of experience, the employer might not spot this, which may cost you the interview.

Person specifications usually include:

- a *requirement for qualifications*: 'educated to degree level', 'preferably a degree in a business subject', 'a degree in a care subject', 'preferably with a higher degree (MA)';
- *skills specific to the job*: 'experience and ability in managing a team', 'experience of working with the public', 'at least two years' experience of working in X';
- *general skills*: it is common for employers to ask for 'ability to work as an effective member of a team', 'excellent communication skills', 'ability to work independently', 'a good self-starter';
- *willingness to accept particular work conditions*: 'ability to work flexible hours', 'willingness to work across several sites', 'must be willing to travel'.

Information about how to apply

Read carefully to see whether the employer asks for a CV or other information to be sent in, and whether specific directions are given about completing the application form. Do exactly what is asked because if there are thousands of applicants, the employer may choose to read only those applications that are completed correctly. If they ask for a CV, send one (see below). Some specify that you should *not* send a CV – they will throw it away unread. Some specify that they wish you to complete the form in a particular colour ink, as they need to scan the form into the computer.

Equal opportunities form

This form is usually for the personnel department of a large company and should not be available to the selection team. Large companies need to monitor that they are following equal opportunities policies, and to monitor for potential bias. If the form is not completed, it may make the company appear to be more successful at equal opportunities than they are, as the percentage of people they appoint from under-represented groups may appear to be a high percentage of those who actually apply.

An application form

Not all employers use these. If they do, you must complete it. If it has space for a long personal statement, you can usually word-process this on a separate sheet, writing 'see attached' on the form. People with disabilities who cannot complete a form by hand should be able to request electronic or other means of applying.

Complete the form

Complete the form, following the directions closely:

- ensure the form is completed neatly. Good impressions do count. If you are likely to make mistakes, complete it in a light pencil first;
- use a good pen: avoid blotchy biros, pencils, pens that make your writing look spidery and messy;
- write neatly; do not write in capital letters;
- be honest and accurate: the company is likely to check on information you give them, either immediately or at a later date;
- be complete: do not leave gaps in work or recent educational histories. Include all relevant training. Complete all requests for information;
- refer clearly to all skills, qualities, qualifications and experience.

Qualifications

Ensure that you write all the names of qualifications in full, either in the space provided or in your CV or covering letter. The employer may not know what is meant by abbreviations. This is especially important if you are applying for a post in a country different from the one where the qualification was gained. Find out what is the local equivalent of your qualification, and indicate this in the covering letter, so that the employer takes it into account.

If you have your degree results, you do not need to go into details about school history unless you are asked for this, or unless a particular school qualification is relevant to the job. However, if you have good A-level grades or equivalents, it is worth mentioning these.

Write the personal statement

This is an important part of the application process and requires time and thoughtful consideration. Lay it out neatly and clearly so the main points can be found easily. Attach a word-processed personal statement to your application form. If you were asked to send only a CV or letter of application rather than an application form, it is a good idea to include a personal statement to accompany these.

Use your personal records

This is the time when you will make most use of your personal records of achievement such as progress files. If you maintain good records and competence sheets, such as those recommended in the next chapter, it will be easier to select appropriate information to complete your personal statement. Read through your records to remind yourself of your strongest competences and the best examples of your experience.

Employers will want to know that you are capable of achievement, so it is important to identify which of your experiences and responsibilities can be described as achievements and successes. If you have only held one or two positions of responsibility outside of the home, ensure that it is clear what your role was. If you held a post on a student society or have held down a job, consider what your achievements were during that time. For example, turn a sentence such as:

As Social Secretary, I was responsible for organising social activities for the student body.

into a more detailed statement such as:

As Social Secretary (2001–2), I was responsible for organising activities for a student body of 14,000 people. I successfully ran over 30 events, involving 5000 people. Satisfaction surveys were conducted and these received excellent feedback. I also increased the budget by 10 per cent over the year.

Write to the person specification

Go through the person specification and job specification in detail. It is a good idea to copy all the person specifications onto a wordprocessor, and make each into a separate heading. Write a paragraph to address each specification, giving at least one good (but brief) example of where you use the skill or attribute at present. For example:

Example

Specification: 'ability to work as an effective member of a team'

As part of my current part-time job, I am a member of a team of ten people. This requires me to work towards common goals to strict deadlines. The employer has provided two training days in team-work skills. I have been asked to stand in as deputy team leader on several occasions, which attests to my team-management skills. I feel I am a good team member as I am ready to listen and act upon other people's ideas and am confident in making my own suggestions. I also have extensive experience of problem-solving in small groups as part of my degree. I completed a successful group project, which received good feedback from tutors. My main roles in that group were as meeting co-ordinator and data researcher.

Refer to the job

In the statement, include a few sentences in which you clarify why you are interested in the job and what you have to offer to the employer. Select three or four skills or qualities that you think are particularly relevant and list these as benefits that you can offer to the company. This will indicate to the employer that you are serious about this particular job. It will suggest you have thought about its needs and have selected it on the basis of your own suitability.

Writing a covering letter

If you have included a personal statement, your covering letter can be brief (as shown in the example on p. 207). If not, your letter should cover many of the points raised in the personal statement section above. Your covering letter should:

- be clear, to the point and businesslike – avoid waffle and anecdote;
- refer clearly to the job for which you are applying, including any reference number that was given;
- state where you saw the job advertised;
- be proofread: it is evidence of your ability to give 'attention to detail' and of your communication skills;
- refer to your confidence that you can meet the requirements of the job, and that this is outlined in your personal statement.

If the employer's form offers very little space for details about your employment history, use the covering letter to bring out your responsibilities for key posts and the skills and training acquired. State these briefly. Select only those aspects that are relevant to the post for which you are applying.

Use the letter to bring out any other qualities, skills and experience that you have which would be relevant to the post.

Competence-based applications

A number of employers are starting to use competence-based applications. These are looking to see which candidates can demonstrate the best examples of the skills, qualities and experience needed for the job. Usually, such jobs are open to a very wide range of people. The employer is likely to take account of 'transferable' skills acquired in very different situations from the job under consideration. This can be an advantage if you have developed

Your name	Amit Evans
Your full address	1111 Apple Avenue Summertown, London
Your postcode	BB1 11B
Your contact details	Tel: 11111 0303030; Mobile phone: 22222 0303030 Email: agevans@freemail.happy
Date	31 August 2003
Employer contact name **Employer address**	Ms Samantha Browne Alpha Conferences 222–228 Olive Grove Berryfield BB1 XXX

Dear Ms Browne

State the name of the post, its reference, and where and when you saw it advertised

I am very interested in the post of Assistant Conference Manager (ref. AAP/223/01) advertised in the *Guardian* on 27/8/2003.

Give brief details of your experience and suitability. Refer to your competence sheets

I have recently completed a degree in Business and Economics. As part of my degree, I undertook a project for an events company that mounted conferences for employers locally and nationally. As well as providing me with experience of event planning, I thoroughly enjoyed the atmosphere and the opportunity to meet a wide range of people.

I have worked in sales and with the public for many years. I hope my ability to speak and write several languages will be of additional benefit in the conference world.

Indicate that you know something about the company and why you feel it is the right appointment for you

I am particularly interested in working in a new and growing organisation such as Alpha Conferences with an international dimension. I would like to feel I had contributed to the development of a new company in its early stages. Your commitment to employee training is impressive and I would be keen to further my own professional development.

Indicate when you would be available for work

I live locally and would be ready to start work at short notice. I enclose my CV, as requested, and would appreciate the opportunity of an interview to discuss the post further. I look forward to hearing from you.

Use 'sincerely' when you address a named person

Yours sincerely

Sign the letter

[signature]

Type your name beneath

Amit Evans

skills but wish to change your field of work. However, such jobs also tend to attract a very wide range of applicants, so care needs to be taken to select the best examples of your experience for each competence.

Typically, competence-based applications use an application form and allow very small, specific amounts of space for you to complete details about each competence. You will probably be told not to send additional sheets or a CV. This means that you must be very precise and succinct in summarising your competences, in order to include the maximum amount of information about yourself in the space available.

The competence sheets on pp. 257–91 will help you to identify the relevant information and to develop skills in writing brief summaries of key information. Competence-based applications are time-consuming, so it is useful to keep good and updated personal records so that you can identify information quickly.

Curriculum vitae (CV)

This used to be the most common form of document required by employers, However, it is less in demand than it used to be. Agencies often request CVs, and some employers respond to CVs even when they do not have a job on offer. There is a wide variety of acceptable CV formats. However, as an employer may spend less than a minute reading your CV, whatever format you choose needs to be pleasing to the eye and contain a few key details that will make the selector choose you for interview (see the two examples on pp. 209, 210).

Content

CVs must include:

- full name;
- date of birth;
- home address;
- contact details (phone, email, mobile, fax);
- educational history;
- qualifications;
- employment history;
- interests and other information (relevant

training, languages, certificates, driving licence).

Incorporate, in the relevant sections, a few key details that indicate levels and breadth of responsibility and experience.

Layout and style

Presentation

Presentation is extremely important to CVs. Employers may receive hundreds of CVs, and may conduct the first selection on the basis of presentation skills. If so, they are more likely to eliminate CVs that are too long, which clearly omit essential sections, or which are handwritten or badly typed. Your CV should be:

- divided into clear sections with headings;
- laid out in legible lists or tables for sections on educational history and employment;
- easy to read;
- brief and concise;
- relevant to the job.

The whole document should be in the same font. Use larger fonts and bold or underlining or italics for headings. Each main section should have the same level of heading (the same font size, style and format). Avoid colour, images, unusual or hard-to-read fonts. Avoid 'gimmicks' and special effects.

Language

Use words that emphasise action (verbs). Look for opportunities to include words such as:

> achieved, contributed, co-ordinated, organised, established, demonstrated, accomplished, applied, implemented, initiated, created, set up, developed.

Use words and phrases that demonstrate qualities that employers will value, such as:

> attention to detail, positive outcome, achievement, success, effectively, efficiently, care, creativity, team work, meeting deadlines, co-operation, value for money, time-saving, problem-solving, self-starter, coping strategies, negotiating, networking, flexibility, versatility, creativity, innovation, entrepreneurship, profits, leadership,

Amit Geraint Evans

Personal details

Date of birth: 10/10/1978

Address: 1111 Apple Avenue, Summertown, London

Tel: 11111 0303030; Mobile phone: 22222 0303030

Nationality: British

Postcode: BB1 11B

Email: agevans@freemail.happy

Educational history

1997–2001	University College of England, Broad Street, Berryfield, BB1 22K
1990–1997	Albertina Sisulu School, Juniper Street, Hollyacre, YY1 22Y
1982–1989	Oak Primary School, Blethyn Avenue, Llanpwll, XX1 XX2

Qualifications

2001	BA Hons. Business and Economics	2.1
1997	A-level History	Grade A
1997	A-level Economics	Grade C
1997	A-level Business Studies	Grade D
1995	Seven GCSEs (five A*)	

Employment history

1997–1999	Phantom Books, College Street, Berryfield, BB1 33B	Part-time shop assistant	Two days a week; responsibilities for sales and dealing with the public; 1998 promoted to assistant supervisor.
1990–1996	Juniper Papers, Juniper Street, Hollyacre, YY1 22X	Newspaper round	Maintained the same job for six years.

Positions of responsibility

Dates	Position	Organisation	Achievement
1999–2001	Student mentor	Holly FE	Coached three pupils in maths. All successfully passed their GCSE Maths.
1999–2000	Treasurer	University Rowing Club	Successfully managed accounts and increased profits by 15 per cent.

Skills and competences

As part of my degree, I undertook a team project for a local employer, Berryfield Employer Forum. We successfully set up a new processing system, which we devised to meet the employer specifications. This was adopted by the company. I took a lead in contacting the employers and encouraging them to take part. The project developed my team-building and negotiation skills, as well as familiarising me with events planning. I feel this experience will be of benefit to a post in your conferencing company.

Interests and achievements

I enjoy walking (British Isles; Germany) and rowing. I was a member of the rowing team that won the Community Shield (2001). I enjoyed working on a Mentoring Schools Programme organised by a local FE college, and felt a sense of achievement when pupils' number-skills improved.

Other information

I speak and write, fluently, in Punjabi and Welsh, have GCSE French, and communicate well with a wide range of people. I am used to dealing with the public. I am computer literate and familiar with most business and project software. I am a good self-starter, and enjoy working to tight deadlines. I am keen to develop my expertise in the conference and events business.

Anna Leroy

Personal details

Date of birth: 10/10/1968
Address: 1112 Apple Avenue, Summertown, London
Tel: 11111 0303031; Mobile phone: 22222 0303031

Nationality: British
Postcode: JJ1 11K
Email: aaleroy@freemail.happy

Educational history

1997–2001   University College of England, Broad Street, Berryfield, BB1 22B
1979–1987   Gotama School, Blossom Street, Oakfield, OO1 22Y
1972–1979   St. Ann's RC Primary, Super Road, Ashby, AA1 2AA

Qualifications

2001   BA Hons. Psychology, Grade 2.2
1997   Access to University, Social Science Foundation Course
1996   GCSE English, Grade 2
1994   GCSE Maths, Grade 2
1985   1 GCSE and four CSEs (grade 1)

Employment history

Dates	Employer	Post	Responsibilities
1998–2002	Berry Lawyers, Sharpe Street, Berryfield, BB1 3BB	Part-time legal assistant	Assisting solicitor prepare cases for court; dealing with clients.
1992–1997	Accomb Solicitors, Tailor Road, Oakfield, OO1 22B	Part-time legal assistant	Assisting solicitor prepare cases for court; dealing with clients.
1986–1992	J. J. Field, Solicitors, Tailor Road, Oakfield, OO1 22X	Full-time Administrator/PA	Managing all aspects of a legal office; dealing with the public.
1985–1986	H. Smith Associates, Ash Road, Oakfield, OO1 22P	Administrative assistant	General office duties.

Positions of responsibility

Dates	Position	Organisation	Achievement
2000–2001	Volunteer tutor	University Volunteer Bureau	Tutored a deaf student on a local Access programme. Student has been offered a university place.
1992–1994	Secretary	Oakfield Playgroup, Ash Road, Oakfield.	Established a thriving playgroup involving 40 families; it still exists. Co-organised meetings and events.
1999–2000	Chair	Mature Student Association	Worked with a team to organise 30 meetings and events.
1985–1989	Chair	Oakfield Residents Association, Alder Street, Oakfield OO1 22A	Successful management of an association of 2000 residents; chaired over 50 meetings.

Skills and competences

My work and life history demonstrates that I am a natural organiser. I can see where there are opportunities and will take the lead in creating new groups. I am used to multi-tasking, and have managed to study and maintain family life without taking absences from work. I am very determined and highly motivated. My work in legal companies helped me to develop a wide range of analytical skills and people skills, which I have developed further through my programme and in the organisations that I have helped to run.

Interests and achievements

I enjoy playing an active part in community events and am generally good with people. I am keen to work in a profession related to the caring professions, where I can make use of the knowledge and skills gained through my Psychology degree.

Other information

I have a full driving licence and the European Computer Driving Licence. I am ready to start work at short notice. I am currently taking a course in basic counselling skills.

decision making, priority setting, competitiveness.

Product

The completed CV should be:

● word-processed;
● printed on A4 paper;
● unfolded and sent in an A4 envelope;
● on good-quality paper;
● of 'top copy' quality.

CVs for different purposes

You may need more than one CV. The basic CV should be brief, fit on one side and contain standard information. Academic CVs tend to be longer. If you are looking for an academic job, then include conferences and seminars to which you contributed a paper or workshop, all research projects with details of who funded these, and details of all publications. When applying for a job, adapt your basic CV to fit what you know about the company and the requirements of the person specification.

Competence statements in CVs

Traditionally, the rule for a CV is that it fits on a single page. If you have a large number of qualifications or jobs, the information may need to fit onto more than one page. In either case, use only a few words to list the responsibilities associated with each item.

Bright and Earl (2000) argue that candidates who include a brief competence statement within a CV have a good chance of being short-listed. They found that there was no particular place on the CV where it was better to position the competence statement. When you have elaborated your competences (see Chapter 9), you may wish to use short competence statements in your CV.

Sending uninvited CVs

Some employers do file and use CVs sent to them when they have not advertised for a post. Many will not, as those using equal opportunities practices usually will advertise all posts. If you have rare and marketable specialist skills, such as high-level IT skills, then the opportunistic CV can be particularly useful.

If you do send CVs on an opportunistic basis, you will need to include additional information. The employer will need to know, for example:

● the kinds of job that interest you – using job titles if possible;
● whether you wish to work full- or part-time;
● the salary range that you will accept or a figure that indicates the salary level you expect;
● which parts of the country you are willing to work in;
● the size and kind of company you are interested in working for;
● what your ideal job would be.

These CVs may be slightly longer – but do aim to stay under two pages. Include more details about your skills, experience and what you can offer. Your enthusiasm and interest should radiate from the CV in order for it to be considered.

Using the Internet

'Ultimately, I think the internet will become the primary means of advertising and looking for work. The enormous size of the audience and specificity of positions that it offers makes the traditional media forms (e.g. newspapers) seem obsolete and vastly over-priced'.

Tom Campbell, futurologist, *New Media Knowledge*, in Chapman (2001)

A source of jobs and advice

In 2000, two-thirds of graduate recruiters were recruiting through the Internet, and nine out of ten students were using the net for career purposes (Association of Graduate Recruiters). There are several hundred job sites on the web, such as www.monster.co.uk and www.gradunet.co.uk. In addition, there are career advice resources on the net, some aimed at students. Some employers will send job details and accept applications and CVs by email. A list of such resources is given in the 'Resources' section at the end of this book.

Put your CV on-line

Large recruiters may provide their own facilities for you to create a CV using a 'wizard'. This is not simply a question of putting up the CV as you have already typed it. If you do this, you will probably lose most of the presentational features such as font style and layout: it may look fine on your screen but look messy or bizarre when viewed on the employer's screen. You will usually need to write in your details for each site. This takes time so it is worth researching the best recruitment sites for the jobs that interest you. Use a plain-text version to 'cut and paste', using the same font throughout and without using tables or formatting. This will save you time. Leave at least half an hour to do this for each site.

Some employers may simply ask you to send a CV as an attachment. If so, use a rich-text format so that you increase the chance of it printing with the desired layout and presentational features on the employer's printer.

E-mail cover letters

If you send an application by email, include a covering letter. This should follow the same general principles as any other cover letter. In other words, it should be brief, relevant, to the point, summarising your interest and what you have to offer to the company. Email responses can be signed off as 'Best wishes' rather than 'yours faithfully'.

Referring to disabilities

Many students with disabilities are unsure whether they should mention a disability at interview or not. Legislation introduced in 1995 should protect your rights if you have a disability, but employers are still not always aware of what to do when faced with a candidate with a disability.

Should I tell the employer?

There is no easy answer to this. If you need particular help for the application process, the interview or the job, then you will need to disclose the disability. If you do not, then it may not be relevant and it would be an individual decision whether you say anything. You must ensure that you would not leave employers in a position where they could not meet their health and safety responsibilities to you or the public if you do not disclose.

How should I bring up the subject in interview?

If you have not needed to change the interview in any way because of the disability, then the employer may not be aware of the disability. Personnel usually keep this information confidential. It is probably best to assume that the employer knows little about what the disability means and may have very confused or exaggerated ideas about what different disabilities are.

Choose a positive way of introducing the disability. For example, identify the additional skills and qualities you have acquired because of the disability. It is likely that you will have developed additional skills and personal qualities to manage the disability alongside study, work and other people's attitudes. This may have become such a way of life that you underestimate how many skills you have developed in this respect. For example you may have:

● IT skills (awareness of different ways of making electronic material accessible, which the company might need in order to meet disability legislation);
● people skills (familiarity in dealing with other people's discomfort, embarrassment or rudeness; familiarity with a wider range of people; awareness of how people respond to 'outsiders'; greater ease in dealing with people with disabilities, who form a large minority of the population);

- creativity and problem-solving skills (you will probably have had to find new ways of performing a range of tasks, some of which called for ingenuity);
- self-management skills (disabilities usually call for greater application, determination, self-motivation and endurance).

No two people are alike

Your disability and your strategies for dealing with it, as well as your individual characteristics, will mean that you are different from any other person with a disability that the employer has met. However, the employer may have had a bad experience employing a person with a similar disability. Even though it should be obvious, it is worth mentioning that no two people with the disability respond in the same way, so that the employer starts with a cleaner slate in considering your application.

Be clear about your abilities

The employer may have very mistaken ideas about what a person with your disability can do. They may underestimate your capabilities. Outline, briefly, your achievements. For example:

> I gained excellent feedback from my work placement, where I helped to design a new door operation system. I was able to call upon the design and IT skills that I had developed through my degree, and feel these would be very useful for this job too.

> I worked as volunteer technician for three years for a local theatre group. This brought me into contact with a wide range of people. Many community groups used the theatre. I feel this experience has developed my expertise in finding technical solutions at very short notice and on a tight budget. It also showed me that I enjoy working with older people. These skills and qualities should stand me in good stead for this post.

Outline briefly how the disability does affect you

If possible, present this in the context of what you can do, or the strategies you have developed in order to achieve a result. For example:

> My writing skills are good when I use speech-to-text software. I am very familiar with X software. I work quickly and I have a clear writing style. I can proof-read but it is useful if someone else checks the final version.

> I organise my time so that I change between tasks every few minutes if I can, so that I keep changing which group of my muscles I am using. I tend to keep two or three different tasks on the go at any one time. This is usually very efficient, because I do not get bored, and it fills in the natural pauses that occur when you wait for responses from clients.

Mention ways that the disability will affect you at work and what your needs will be.

- 'I need to jot down verbal instructions and then I can work through them.'
- 'The wheel chair requires a width of X cm.'
- 'I am sensitive to light and will need to work in dimmed light or wear glasses with tinted lenses, which I will provide.'

Preparing for the interview

Mental preparation

If you have made a sensible job choice, were able to meet the 'person specifications' and have thought through answers to likely questions, you should feel confident that you have a reasonable chance of being considered for the job. The majority of applicants do not receive an interview, so if you have been offered one, this is already a success. Focus on being calm and on the questions you can answer. Remind yourself of your interest in the job and of what you have to offer the employer. Make sure you sound convincing to yourself. It is natural to feel anxious, but avoid feeding your anxiety by negative thinking.

Prepare for likely questions

Preparing for the more obvious questions will help you to feel confident about answering at least some questions well. This gives you more room for error on other questions. The section below gives an indication of the kinds of questions that you can expect.

Two-minute answers

When preparing your answers, aim to complete any answer in one to two minutes. The interviewer may wish to ask between six and ten questions, as well as using time to ask the question and make comments of their own. It is unlikely the employer will wish the question stage to last more than 20–30 minutes. If your answers are long, they may not be able to ask all their questions, which means you will be disadvantaged if they award points for each answer.

Identify your strong points for each question

Before the interview, identify what are the strongest points you can make for each likely question. A strong answer will refer to experience, achievement and success. It will also be specific: give at least one example, with reference to the scale or importance of the achievement, including one or two key pieces of data if relevant.

Prepare points to include in the interview

Use the interview to bring out your strongest points. Be very clear what these are in advance so that you bring them in when an opportunity arises. Before the interview:

● List your strongest five achievements, qualities or attributes;
● sum these up in less than 20 words;
● think of which questions you may be asked where you can bring in these five points;
● be ready to bring them in elsewhere if they do not arise naturally.

Sense of time

Practise speaking aloud and timing yourself so that you develop a sense of what two to three minutes feels like. You should build up a sense of how much you can say within that time, without sounding rushed. You can cover a number of relevant details in two minutes if you are precise and to the point.

Presentation

Employers expect candidates to be smartly dressed and presentable: you may need to act as

> ### Activity: *Speaking time*
>
> Look at the example below. How long do you think it would take to deliver? Read it aloud at a reasonable speed, with expression, and time yourself.
>
> Q: 'Have you worked in a caring post before?' (The candidate has not done so.)
>
> A: 'My most relevant work experience has been in acting as a student tutor to three young children in a local school. Those children were very vulnerable, and I had to develop skills which are typical of those needed in care posts. For example, I focused on building a rapport with the children, watching for non-verbal cues, and being sensitive to their feelings. I had to be prepared to wait and work at their speed. I also had to consider the wishes of the teacher and other parties. I feel I achieved a good relationship with the children and their teachers. I negotiated work schemes with the teacher and each child. The teacher said that they all made an improvement and I received very good feedback, so it seems to have worked well. I think that gives me a good foundation for this post, and I particularly look forward to working with children and parents.'
>
> ● What do you think are the strong points about this answer?

the public face of their company at some stage. Pay attention to details such as clean hands and fingernails, polished shoes, and a smart bag. This is true even if you will not be expected to dress smartly in the job.

In the interview

First impressions

Although the whole interview is important, you can make the interview run more smoothly if the first minute is well managed. This requires only a few simple actions.

● Look clean and smart.
● Be on time.
● Ensure your right hand is free in order to shake hands.

- No matter how you feel, smile and appear relaxed.
- Look pleased to meet the interviewers. Shake hands firmly, look them in the eye, and listen when they say their names.
- Move calmly so that you do not crash into furniture.
- Sit upright, alert and interested for the interview.

During the interview, avoid apologies and regrets. Work with the situation as it is, not with what might have gone better. Tell yourself that the interviewers' questions are interesting and manageable – keep considering what it is they are looking for in an employee and what examples you can give them to reassure them that you can meet their needs.

You do not need to be magical, a super-brains, or word-perfect. Everybody stumbles on some words and questions. Avoid gimmicks, 'hard sell' and theatrics. Be natural. If possible, imagine you are being interviewed by an interested relation of one of your friends or colleagues. Although this seems obvious, many candidates do not come across as genuinely interested in the job, easy to get on with, honest or natural.

Keep it simple

It is not unusual to ruin a potentially good interview by trying too hard to impress. If you demonstrate a reasonable degree of calm, interest and enthusiasm, you will already be well placed.

Employers may take a number of approaches to selecting a candidate. They will usually look for a 'good fit' between what they want and what the candidates can offer. This is partly a question of skills and experience. However, the majority of candidates short-listed for interview will probably be well matched for skills and experience. Possibly, none may meet all the requirements. All will meet about 75–95 per cent, with different kinds of strengths. If the employer needs very specific skills which are in short supply, the person with the best skills will get the job.

However, the probability is that the choice will come down to inter-personal skills and behaviour demonstrated in the interview. The interview is about meeting you and seeing what you are like: the employer already has information about your skills and experience. The employer or interview panel will want to choose someone who:

- can do the job with minimum training and supervision;
- seems like a reasonable, sensible person, with common sense, whom colleagues could work with;
- answers their questions, rather than delivers a sales pitch;
- will 'fit' the post; who seems to suit the work temperamentally;
- looks as though they will 'fit in' generally.

Team work and supportive working climates are important so it is understandable that interview panels will favour people who seem to have the right characteristics to suit their work environment. This is usually a question of apparent personality. Under equal opportunities legislation, interviews should not discriminate on the grounds of sex, race or disability. However, personality and other characteristics can become confused in people's minds. If you suspect discrimination, you have legal rights.

It is important to project yourself as mature, reasonable and friendly. It may help to focus on this rather than struggling to make 'perfect answers'. Many people come across as very stilted, and even bizarre, in interview because they are nervous. Focus on the needs of the panel – what they are looking for – rather than on 'selling' yourself.

During the interview

Put yourself in the employers' position. They are likely to interview at least four people during a period of two to three hours. They may be interviewing dozens of people over several weeks. Even four interviews in a row can be tiring. It will be appreciated if you:

- provide brief answers which are to the point;
- provide clear examples;
- provide exactly the information you are asked for;
- are ready for predictable questions so that you can answer promptly.

Avoid

- long, winding answers that go off the point;
- 'interesting anecdotes';
- giving several examples if you are asked only for one;
- giving a long background to your answers.

Opening questions

Employers tend to start interviews with one or two questions to settle the interviewee. Here are some typical questions.

'Have you had a good journey?'

This is politeness. Answer very briefly.

'Tell me a little about your programme'

Two or three sentences will suffice. Draw out unusual features as these may reflect well upon you.

'Why do you want this job now?'

Be as specific as you can. Include reference to something about the company that appeals to you. The employer wants to know why you want to work at this company, and that you have done some homework about the company, not that you are desperate for a job. Indicate what you think you can offer to the company.

'Where do you see yourself in 3/5/20 years' time?'

The employer is looking to see whether you are realistic and whether you are a good match for the job. They may be checking to see whether you are likely to leave within a few months or weeks of appointment. You may not know your plans five years into the future but give a strong answer that indicates you have an idea of what you want to achieve. Refer to the kind of experience you hope to achieve from this job that will further your own aims in a few years' time. Your answer should suggest there is benefit to yourself as well as the employer in you being offered this post.

'What do you find interesting about . . . advertising/engineering/nursing, etc?'

The employer may interview many graduates who appear to know nothing about the company or its work. Such candidates are unlikely to be appointed unless they possess very highly valued skills in short supply. Find out about the industry and the company – at least enough to hold a conversation for a few minutes.

'Tell us about yourself'

This can be the most difficult question as there is so much to choose from. It is, therefore, a question for which you should prepare. Play safe by referring to your career ambitions and why you think these suit your personal characteristics and experience. Keep it very brief. The employer may be looking to see how aware of your audience and how concise you are, rather than being interested in your life.

Person specification and competency questions

You can expect to receive several questions that relate to the person specification. Although you will have given this information already when you applied, employers may ask similar questions to ones you believe you have answered. This may be for several reasons:

- The panel may not have been involved in the short-listing process and may have received your details at the last moment.
- The panel is seeing many people. They are likely to remember what they hear rather than what you have written.

- Do not assume that just because you have given the answer in the paperwork, the panel will have read it. Give a full answer in case they have not.
- The panel is looking at your people skills. They know you know the answers to most questions, but want to see how well you communicate information to other people.
- They are 'double-checking' to compare your verbal answers with those on paper.

Competence questions

For competence-based applications, most questions usually relate to the competences in the person specification. This means you can prepare for these with reasonable confidence. Think of unusual angles for the question. A competence question may be phrased in very different ways. For example, a question on dealing with difficult people might be phrased as:

- 'From your life and work so far, give the best example of a time when you had to deal with a difficult member of the public.'
- 'Can you give us two or three examples of a time when you . . .'
- 'Think of an example when you dealt badly with a member of the public. What did you learn from that occasion and how has this affected the way you would approach a similar situation now?'
- 'What kind of advice would you give a new member of staff who had not dealt with the public before?'
- 'What professional development have you undertaken in recent years to improve your capability in dealing with members of the public?'
- 'What is the worst example of you dealing with a member of the public? What did this teach you?'

Catch-all questions

A number of questions tend to appear in many job descriptions, and mean different things depending on the type of job.

'Team work' may be used to mean:

- good at people skills;
- easy to get on with;
- a nice person;
- has specific skills in negotiating with others;

- has experience of working in project teams.

'Leadership' could be used to refer to:

- willingness to speak on behalf of the group;
- a strong vision that carries other people – such as directing plays or setting up student groups;
- a tendency to be the person chosen to act as group chair;
- experience of running a project;
- experience of running a major project.

'Good self-starter' may mean:

- enjoys working on their own;
- will accept a job that offers little support;
- works well independently;
- can start a new job without supervision;
- has good problem-solving skills;
- can take on major projects in almost any area;
- is a responsible worker.

'Flexibility' may mean willingness to:

- fit in;
- work with a wide range of people;
- work unusual or long hours;
- change schedule at short notice;
- respond quickly to crises;
- work at different locations;
- travel;
- help out different departments in emergencies;
- change departments;
- find solutions to a wide variety of problems.

It is important to work out, from the level and nature of the job, what kind of interpretation to use. It is also important to gain a balance, so that you can show that you are able to work with and listen to others, but are also able to work alone, take responsibility, and give direction to your own and others' work.

Anticipating questions

For each element of the person specification, consider how you would respond to the following questions:

- Your best example. What is good about it? What worked well? What was your own contribution?

- Two or three brief examples. What do these suggest about the range and breadth of your experience?
- An example from which you learnt something that improved your current performance. If you are asked for your 'worst experience', this may be a useful example as you can emphasise what you learnt that benefits your current performance.
- How you would advise somebody else to perform this competence?
- What professional development have you undertaken in relation to this competence?
- What skills and personal qualities were involved in an example of this competence?
- How regularly do you demonstrate this competence? (This is to check whether your example is a 'one off' or represents your everyday experience.)
- At what level of responsibility do you demonstrate this competence? (This is to check your ability to take responsibility for tasks that involve this competence.)

Other typical questions

Other favourite questions are variations on the following themes.

An example of a highlight from your life or career so far

Be prepared to describe briefly what happened and why you consider this to be a highlight. For example, it may have developed particular skills that would be useful to the company. It may have been an occasion where you took on a challenge or worked at a higher level of responsibility than previously and proved your capability.

An example of your worst mistake

Use this as an opportunity to show how you are willing to learn from mistakes and to put that learning to good use. Avoid using an example that would make the employer worry about employing you. Select the kind of mistake that anybody could make. The employer will also want to see that you are willing to take responsibility for your own actions, rather than trying to lay the blame on others (even if it was

someone else's fault, in your opinion). See the Competence Sheet on p. 284.

Examples of your commitment to personal development

You can expect this kind of question from employers who have 'Investors in People' status, professional organisations and posts related to public office.

What contribution do you think you can make? What have you got to offer?

Refer to specific experience and skills that you have gained and which are likely to be of benefit to the company. Relate your contribution to what has been described in the job specification and to what you have found out about the company. Include personal qualities. If possible, refer to feedback that you have received from employers or from colleagues or team members.

What personal qualities do you possess that would be of benefit in this work?

Select two or three qualities upon which you can focus. Give one or two sentences to sum up where you demonstrated this quality and why you consider it relevant to the current post. List briefly three to five other qualities that you also possess. Leave it to the interviewer to ask you more details about these. Be prepared to give examples if questioned further. See pp. 234 and 241.

A critical event in your life or work that you have coped with

This may be another way of asking about 'worst mistakes' or 'highlights', depending on how it is phrased. You are unlikely to receive all three questions, so you should be able to use the same material to prepare for at least two of these questions. This question is looking for such features as evidence of levels of responsibility you have held, the extent of your coping strategies, your ability to reflect upon and learn from experience, your ability to apply your learning. For some professions, especially caring professions, the critical event question may be used to explore your ability to describe and work with emotions and feelings. In creative fields, this question may be used to see how well you use experience as inspiration for your artwork.

What you learned from . . .
You may be asked why you chose a particular study option or job, and what you learned from these. Focus on what is of use to the employer from the experience. For example, you may have learnt to be flexible, to work with difficult people, to maintain high levels of concentration when working with numbers, to think analytically, to be a stronger person emotionally, to deal with the unexpected. You may like to show how the subject or experience drew out your natural strengths and abilities.

Closing questions

General interest questions
Sometimes employers ask about your general interests at the end of an interview. These usually seem to be easier, and so candidates may relax and let down their guard, revealing a different side to themselves. For example, the employer may ask:

Q: 'I see you are keen on Mexico. What is the interest there?'

It is important to remember that you are still being interviewed. The employer is still looking to see what it is you have to offer the company. Your answer should reflect this. Keep your reply brief: this is not an opportunity to tell the employer all about your pet interests. Your answer might bring out personal qualities or an ability that is useful to the company. For example (depending on the circumstances):

A: 'I am keen to develop my Spanish.' (*Useful if the company has Spanish-speaking offices or customers.*)

A: I wanted to find out about a different culture and have always been interested in Mexican art. (This suggests you have breadth of interests and the confidence to go and find things out for yourself.)

Do you have any questions you would like to ask us?
You do not have to have a question, especially if the information is available in the literature that was sent to you, or is available from Personnel or on the Internet. Avoid unnecessary questions: they may suggest you have not done your homework. The employer will not want the interview to go on too long, so keep to one or two essential questions. Reasonable questions to ask are, for example:

- related to something that was reported recently in the trade papers about the company, especially if it allows them to make a positive response;
- genuine questions that determine whether you want the job. Now is the time to ask these;
- questions about training and professional development;
- whether there is a mentoring scheme for new employees;
- what would the employer consider to be a sign of your success after two years with the company? What are their expectations of you as a new employee?
- who you will be reporting to;
- opportunities for travel, or for secondment;
- what the next step will be? When are you likely to hear the outcome of the interview?

Activity: Sabotage the interview

1. List all the things you can think of to really mess up an interview so that the employer is convinced you are unprepared and unsuitable. You may include comments related to:
   - your clothing;
   - your punctuality;
   - not knowing anything about the company;
   - asking silly questions when given the opportunity.

2. Give yourself advice!
   What advice would you give to somebody else who said they sabotaged interviews in this way? The advice may seem obvious to you – but many people forget the basics. If you are uncertain about how to prevent the sabotage you suggest, speak to a careers adviser at the university.

3. Write a preparation list for yourself in order to ensure you are ready for your interview.

Is there anything you feel we should know that you have not yet had a chance to tell us?

- Some employers are aware that candidates are anxious and may not have given their best answers. If you really feel that you have let yourself down on an answer, this is an opportunity to return to it, if you feel you can now give a better response.
- Before the interview, you may have rehearsed skills and qualities that you feel are important to this kind of job or company. If these have not been referred to in the interview, raise these now.

If we offered you the job, when would you be able to start?

Ensure you are clear about your personal arrangements so that you are in a position to answer this.

Activity: Practise the interview

- Find one or preferably two other people with whom to practise your interview techniques. This may be embarrassing, but it is better to get feedback before the interview rather than after.
- Give details of the kind of job for which you are applying. The other person(s) can use and adapt the questions in this chapter to conduct an interview for your job.
- Give at least 15 minutes for each person's interview.
- Ask for (or give) feedback that is constructive. The feedback should give clear guidance on what is good about your interview performance already, as well as what could be even better.
- Note down the feedback you receive and decide what you will do to improve your performance.

After the interview

After the interview, you will probably remember all the things you wish you had said. It is not always easy to tell whether you were successful. Use the experience to learn more about your performance so that it was not a waste of time, no matter what the outcome is.

Analyse the questions

Jot down all the questions you were asked.

- Which ones were unexpected? Were any of these similar to questions that you had prepared, without you realising? Note the different ways that employers can word questions aiming at similar information.
- Note how many questions you were asked. How long was your interview supposed to last? Take ten minutes off that time and divide the remaining time by the number of questions. How long did the employer expect each answer to be?
- Were your answers too long? If so, practise punchier responses for the next interview.
- Were your answers too brief? If so, think of a good example of your experience that you could use to develop that answer more fully.

Analyse your performance

- Which examples did you use? Were these your best? Remind yourself of your best example so that this stays in your mind next time.
- Did you include all of your best points?
- What went well about the interview? Jot this down and read it before the next interview.
- What could have been better? How would you deal with this next time? Write this down and read it before the next interview.

📖 ***Reflection***   Learn from the job application

- Select one job application that you attended, whether successful or not. If you have not applied for a job interview, now is a good time to practise with a friend.
- In your reflective journal, go through the 'After the interview section' above. Jot down ten things you did well.
- Jot down the three things which are most important to improving your performance at job interviews.

Ask for feedback

Some companies will give brief feedback to unsuccessful candidates. It is worth asking for this. However, be prepared for very general comments such as 'the candidate we selected was the most successful in meeting the criteria'. Some companies refuse to give any feedback, in order to avoid legal repercussions.

Closing comments

This chapter has covered the basics of applying for work as a graduate student. There is a very wide range of materials available to help with specific aspects of the process. If you are very anxious about certain aspects, such as answering interview questions, or writing CVs for the Internet, then there are books to help with every detail.

However, in most cases, the basics are enough. If the employer wants someone with more experience or particular skills, they will employ on that basis, no matter how good your application. The important basic rules are:

- Apply a problem-solving strategy to finding a job. Good preparation is similar to the 'problem elaboration' referred to in Chapter 4.
- Research your options, and look for opportunities that carry you towards your long-term goals.
- Choose well. Unrealistic and unsuitable applications may be a waste of your time.
- Rather than sending out hundreds of applications, select a few applications, research the companies and fine-tune the personal statement or competences so that they are precise, informative, clear and relevant to the job.
- Ensure you keep your personal records or progress file up to date so that you can make a good application at short notice.
- Prepare for the interview. Use the competence sheets in your progress file.

Finally, aim to learn from the experience. You may pass the majority of courses or exams that you take in your life, but it is unlikely that you will be successful in gaining a job for each application. You will gain enormously if you view each application and interview as a chance to gain experience, develop application skills, and learn something about employers or yourself. Reflect on the experiences and keep records so that you can benefit in the future.

Further reading

Bright, J. and Earl, J. (2000) *Brilliant CV: What Employers Want to See and How to Say It* (London: Prentice Hall). (Useful if the jobs you apply for are mostly CV-based rather than form-based.)

Chapman, A. (2001) *The Monster Guide to Jobhunting: Get the Perfect Job, Double Click* (London and Edinburgh: Pearson Education). (Detailed guidance on using the Internet. Useful if you are not already comfortable using the Internet.)

Jackson, T. and Jackson, E. (1991, 1997) *The Perfect CV: How to Get the Job You Really Want*, revised and updated edition (London: Piaktus).

Hodgson, S. (2002) *Brilliant Answers to Tough Interview Questions* (London: Prentice Hall). (One of a number of books that are useful to focus the mind when preparing for an interview.)

Popovich, I. (2000) *Winning at Job Interviews* (London: Hodder and Stoughton). (Traditional but sensible advice on job interviews.)

Chapter 9

Recording achievement

The reward of a thing well done is to have done it.

Ralph Waldo Emerson

Learning outcomes

This chapter offers opportunities to:

- create and build your personal records or progress file
- undertake a profile of current skills and qualities
- map your personal competencies in relation to the 'person specifications' frequently required for jobs, and to questions typically asked at job interviews
- record your education, training and other examples of professional development
- provide personal resources that you can draw upon to write a CV and personal statement when applying for work.

Introduction

Chapter 8 emphasised the importance of advance planning and personal development as part of the process of applying for a job. Chapters 1 and 2 focused on an analysis of yourself, and the vision and goals that should be informing and inspiring such advance planning, in order to assist your career development.

When you apply for a job or attend an interview, you will be required to identify, at speed, the best examples for a wide range of questions. Most of us have the information we need to make good responses – but accessing it at speed is not always easy.

This chapter provides resources for collating information about your experience, and reflecting upon that experience so that you can identify your achievements easily.

It is important to bear in mind that employers will be looking to see not only what experience you have but also what you made of the opportunity: your successes, what you learned from the experience, its significance in your life,

and how you can use the experience to benefit their company. They will want to see how you make use of experience and opportunity generally – so that they feel comfortable that you will make good use of opportunities on their behalf as well as your own. They will use the information you give them to form judgements about your coping strategies, your work ethic, your attitude to work and life, your character, and even the way you relate to others.

Paper or electronic personal records?

You are likely to need both paper-based and electronic personal records. Many certificates, licences and similar records will be provided to you in paper format. It is useful to develop a system of records that holds these together. Moreover, you will be asked to send photocopies or faxes of these to employers, so keeping these together with your personal records will save you time. In addition, you may wish to include reflective notes, examples of your work, photographs, images, and hand-drawn records for your own personal use. These will usually be best in paper form.

On the other hand, some records (such as your CV, education and training history, personal statement, and competence sheets) will need to be updated regularly. This is accomplished most easily if you keep electronic copies. Make paper versions so that you can see them easily when browsing through your records.

Developing your personal records

The Introduction to this book referred to the progress file initiative required of all universities. Progress files should contain records for personal development and career planning, and records that you can call upon to make strong job applications.

Organising your personal records

The contents of your personal records will be particular to you. Whatever you include, it is useful to:

● include a contents page so that you can find records and evidence easily;
● make electronic copies of forms that need to be updated, such as records of your employment history, skills and competences;
● number the items in each section rather than from the front of the file. This will enable you to update sections with minimum effort;
● for paper folders, invest in a large folder (as your records will grow as your work history develops) and section dividers.

An example of a Contents sheet is offered below (p. 226), as a guide to what you could include in your progress file or portfolio.

Records for personal planning

The nature of these records will vary depending on the requirements of your programme. They will also vary according to the importance you place upon your own personal development and the role of reflection in your life.

The various chapters of this book have structured reflection along thematic lines and through a variety of activities and questionnaires. If you completed any of those activities, you will already have compiled a record of yourself, your thinking, your attitudes and your goals. You may find it useful to draw together some of those resources. In particular, you may wish to make a photocopy of your completed responses to some of the following activities. Include copies of the blank pro formas so that you can update your responses.

Include your responses to any activities you choose: it is what is important to you that really counts.

Introduction
● Do I need personal development?
● What are my PDP priorities?

Chapter 1: The vision: what is success?
● Spectrums of success – or knowing what you want
● A personal definition of success
● Personal values
● The long-term vision
● What do I want to gain from my time at university?
● Short-term goals
● Sources of motivation
● Self-evaluation of personal qualities associated with success
● Extending experience

Chapter 2: Start with yourself
● Top forty strong points
● Seven areas for improvement
● Identifying personal expertise
● The best failure
● Make setbacks work for you
● Performance styles, habits and preferences series of activities
● Visual, auditory and kinaesthetic learning styles

Chapter 3: Successful self-management
● SWOT analysis
● Sources of support
● Evaluating your emotional intelligence
● Is there a right answer?
● Primary level for improvement

Chapter 4: Successful problem-solving and task management
- Self-evaluation: problem-solving and task management
- Priority sheet
- Action plan
- Use performance indicators
- Competitiveness audit

Chapter 5: People skills
- Self-evaluation: how good are your people skills?
- People skills needs
- The balloon game
- Contributing to a team
- Identify your team personality
- Evaluating personal assertiveness
- Dealing with a difficult person
- Changing a recurring situation
- Monitoring effectiveness
- Reflections on leadership

Chapter 6: Thinking outside the box
- Self-evaluation of creative thinking skills

Chapter 7: The art of reflection
- Self-evaluation on reflective practice
- Developmental reflection
- Critical event
- Evaluating progress on learning goals
- Log or journal
- Personal statement or position paper

Chapter 8: Successful job applications
- What do I want to gain from my next job?
- Routes into work
- Sabotage the interview

Chapter 10: Drawing it together
- Recognising personal changes
- Developing skills in reflective practice
- Building from strengths
- Transferring skills
- Working at the edge
- Areas for improvement
- Next steps

Records for job applications

Chapter 8 looks at the process of applying for a job, and making best use of information about yourself. A good application will be tailored to the particular job and person specification, which takes time. Good interview answers may require you to reflect upon your experience from quite different angles.

It is extremely common for people to emerge from an interview saying. 'Why didn't I say that?' 'Why didn't I use this example rather than that?' Similarly, it is easy, once the envelope is in the post, to remember information that could have been included to strengthen the application.

The answer is usually in the preparation. Good preparation means that you have much more control over your answers, whether at the application or interview stage. Your memory is primed to call upon the examples you really want to use. Moreover, knowing that you are well prepared will increase your overall confidence, so that you come across as a much stronger candidate.

Basic information

Almost every job application will call for very basic information:

- education and training history;
- employment history.

Although this should be a straightforward matter, information is usually scattered over many different pieces of paper from employers or across several CVs, depending on the nature of the job. It is useful to draw all of that information together in one place, so that you can access it at a moment's notice if the right job appears. Use one file or box to keep all such materials together. Keep a disk of electronic records with your paper records.

Education and training history

At some point you could be asked for all or any of the following:

- Schools you attended (usually the schools where you took qualifications after the age of 15 will be all that is required). You will need the name and address of the school, the date you started and the date you left.

- Qualifications you took, the date, and the result. If you are asked for the awarding authority, that is usually printed on the certificate. If you are offered the job, you will be asked to bring in the original certificates, so it is important to be accurate when you give these details.
- If you took your qualifications in a different country from the one where you are now studying or where you intend to work, ensure that you gather details of the local equivalent for all your qualifications.
- Training you undertook as part of a job. Give brief details of short courses and the dates of these.
- Much learning is informal – a colleague may have shown you how to use a piece of software, for example, or you may have trained yourself in using a piece of equipment. Include brief details of the outcomes of such informal learning (what you can actually do as a result).

You will find it useful to draw all your certificates together into one section of your progress file.

Employment history

Employers will look at your employment history to see:

- whether your work history suggests you have the type and level of experience necessary for the job they are advertising. It is important to check that you use similar wording to that in the job description. Slight differences in the wording of a job title may mean that your experience or response is not relevant;
- if there are any gaps in your employment record. Employers are likely to ask you about any periods of a year or more where no work or education is indicated;
- what your job history says about how often you change job, how likely you are to stay with the company, the kinds of work you have accepted in the past, and your career path. If there are unusual jumps from one job to another, employers may ask you the reasons for this at interview. For mature students, the employer will probably want to see a period of continuity within the work history (at least two years). It is expected that younger applicants may have a number of short-contract jobs. This is also true for certain types of work that are organised in short contracts.

You will be required to give information such as:

- employer names
- employer addresses
- contact details for the employer (telephone, fax, email)
- dates you began and finished work for each employer
- your job title
- your chief responsibilities
- previous employers who can act as referees

Contents of personal records file

Educational history
1. Record of education and training
2. Certificates for all qualifications
3. Degree transcript
4. Evidence of learning

Employment history
1. Record of employment history
2. Contract for current employment
3. Names, addresses, job titles and other contact details for at least three referees
4. References and testimonials (if any)
5. Your National Insurance number
6. P45 or P60
7. Pay slips
8. Pension details for all jobs
9. Analysis of learning through work

Other experience
1. Positions of responsibility in clubs, societies or organisations
2. Achievements (from sports, leisure, social life, etc.)
3. Travel
4. Languages
5. Voluntary and community work
6. Mentoring experience
7. Life experience that developed skills or personal qualities
8. Health and safety
9. Equal opportunities.

Skills, competences and personal qualities
1. Personal profile (skills, experience, personal qualities)
2. Evidence of skills and personal qualities
3. Critical incident sheet
4. Competence sheets for specific skills
5. Analysis of personal qualities

Personal development
1. Self-evaluation questionnaires
2. Reflective documents and activities
3. Extracts from reflective journal
4. Quotations that motivate or inspire
5. Drawings, photographs and personally relevant documents

Overview documents
1. Position statement
2. Personal action plan
3. Curriculum vitae (CV)
4. Analysis of knowledge and experience

Other materials

Record of education and training

Education

On the chart below, record details of your educational history, excluding short courses.

Secondary school (ages 11–16; focus on qualifications after age 14)

Dates (from . . . to . . .)	Name and address of institution or provider	Subjects studied	Qualification achieved (and grade where relevant)	Year of the qualification	Topics covered and skills acquired

Post-16 education (before degree level)

Dates (from . . . to . . .)	Name and address of institution or provider	Subjects studied	Qualification achieved (and grade where relevant)	Year of the qualification	Topics covered and skills acquired

Copy to complete for additional qualifications

University education

Dates (from . . . to . . .)	Name and address of institution or provider	Name of course or programme	Qualification achieved (and grade where relevant)	Year qualification was awarded	Topics covered and skills acquired

Short courses, programmes and training

On the chart below, record details of other training you have undertaken at college, through work, or through private agencies.

Dates (from . . . to . . .)	Institution or provider	Name of course or programme	Qualification achieved, if relevant, and year	Topics covered	Skills acquired

Copy and complete for additional training and qualifications

Informal learning

Other learning developed through work experience, informal training by peers and 'away-days', etc.

Year	Where learning took place	Other people involved	Reason for undertaking the learning	What was learnt? Topics covered and skills acquired

Other qualifications, experience and assets

Driving licence, additional languages, familiarity with other countries or cultures.

1.

2.

3.

4.

5.

Copy and complete for additional information

Evidence of learning

Qualifications are one way of providing evidence of learning. However, employers are often interested in seeing what you have valued about your learning, or hearing what you think you have learnt, in order to see how you demonstrate your skills and intelligence. It is useful to be prepared for such questions.

What has interested you most about your programme?

What do you feel has been the most important thing you have learnt from your programme?

What do you think you have learnt on your programme that could benefit you in the world of work?

In what way is your subject relevant to the world outside of university?

What advice would you give to other students embarking upon your programme?

Record of work history

Starting with your earliest work experience after the age of 16, give details of all work that you have undertaken. You will then have a complete record of the essential information most commonly required when completing application forms.

Dates (from . . . to . . .)	Employer and employer address	Job title	Responsibilities	Experience acquired	Reason for leaving

The most important things I have learnt through my work history that are of benefit to me in other jobs (or in life more generally) are:

1.

2.

3.

4.

5.

Copy and update

Learning through work

Place and date Incident (basic details)	
What I did	
Responsibility involved	
What others did	
What I learned	
Skills I acquired	
Feedback from employer	
Feedback from clients	
Feedback from others	
How I made use of feedback	

Profile of current skills, abilities and personal qualities

The competence sheets below (on pp. 239–40) and in the Appendix cover the most commonly asked themes that you are likely to face in applications and job interviews. However, there are a myriad of other skills and qualities that you may be asked to demonstrate during the application process. For the following activity, you will be asked to look at your wider skill profile, identifying the range of skills and qualities that you possess. The aim of this exercise is to give you a sense of the breadth of your skills and personal attributes. When you have completed the personal profile on p. 234, select *one* skill or quality that is relevant to the types of job you are most likely to apply for. Use the resource sheet on p. 235 to elaborate your evidence of that skill or quality in more detail, as in the example below. Repeat this activity for at least two other skills.

Example

Skill, quality or attribute		Negotiating skills
1.	How and when I developed this skill or quality	I have good negotiating skills. At school: school debating team. Runners-up in 1997 East Region Debating Championship. The modules in year 2 have developed people skills that also assist with negotiating.
2.	Examples of occasions when I demonstrate this skill	**At university** Group project work in year 2: negotiated the work schedules. Good at working out compromises. Part of Student Union team that negotiates student mentor placements. **At work** Negotiate sales. Although junior, I lead on some sales during weekends. **In life** I have small children, so have to negotiate child-care rotas; persuade and encourage others to assist in emergencies.
3.	Evidence that I possess this quality or skill (e.g. reliable feedback from others; qualifications, testimonials, etc.)	**At university** College mentor scheme. Part of team that placed all students who wanted to be mentors. I was an active member of that team and successfully negotiated placements. Good feedback from others. Letter from Student Union. **At work** Reference refers to good people skills. **In life** Haven't missed any work or lectures this year, as successfully negotiated cover when needed.

Personal profile

People

- [ ] Ability to get on with people from different backgrounds
- [ ] Ability to see and understand other people's points of view
- [ ] Dealing with the general public
- [ ] Teamwork
- [ ] Managing other people
- [ ] Teaching or training others
- [ ] Listening skills
- [ ] Communicating clearly
- [ ] Negotiating
- [ ] Helping others to arrive at decisions
- [ ] Being sensitive to others' feelings
- [ ] Caring for others
- [ ] Being able to read other people's body language
- [ ] Dealing with others by phone
- [ ] Being able to cope with 'difficult' people
- [ ] Speaking clearly and to the point
- [ ] Being able to take direction from others
- [ ] Having courage to speak out against injustice
- [ ] Others:

Activities

- [ ] Creativity, design and layout
- [ ] Being able to see the 'whole picture'
- [ ] Researching information
- [ ] Classifying and organising information, e.g. filing
- [ ] Applying theory to practice
- [ ] Being good at argument and debate
- [ ] Making decisions
- [ ] Managing change and transition
- [ ] Setting priorities
- [ ] Working out agendas
- [ ] Organising work to meet deadlines
- [ ] Facilitating meetings
- [ ] Reading complicated texts
- [ ] Word-processing
- [ ] Computer literacy
- [ ] Using the Internet
- [ ] Technical skills
- [ ] Number work
- [ ] Selling
- [ ] Problem solving
- [ ] Getting things done
- [ ] Fund-raising
- [ ] Practical things
- [ ] Seeing how things work
- [ ] Writing reports or official letters
- [ ] Others:

Personal qualities

- [ ] Recognising my own needs and asking for help
- [ ] Being able to learn from my mistakes
- [ ] Staying calm in a crisis
- [ ] Managing stress
- [ ] Being willing to take risks and experiment
- [ ] Demonstrating assertiveness
- [ ] Showing determination and perseverance
- [ ] Setting my own goals
- [ ] Maintaining a high level of motivation
- [ ] Taking responsibility for my own actions
- [ ] Trusting in my own abilities
- [ ] Honesty
- [ ] Commitment to values or ethics
- [ ] Showing attention to detail
- [ ] Others:

Evidence of skills and personal qualities

Skill, quality or attribute		
1.	How and when I developed this skill or quality	
2.	Examples of occasions when I demonstrate this skill	At university At work In life
3.	Evidence that I possess this quality or skill (e.g. reliable feedback from others; qualifications, testimonials, etc.)	At university At work In life

Copy and complete for other skills and personal qualities

Critical incident sheet

1.	Context: brief details of the critical incident. What happened, where, and when?	
2.	My role in the incident. What I did.	
3.	My immediate response to the incident. How I coped.	
4.	How I made use of advice and feedback from other people.	
5.	The longer-term impact of the incident upon my life or work. How important this incident was in the grand scheme of my life. What changed?	
6.	Positive outcomes for me or for other people.	
7.	What lessons I learned from this occasion.	
8.	How I applied what I learned to new situations.	
9.	The impact of the incident upon my values, beliefs, attitudes and motivation.	
10.	Personal considerations and comments.	

Critical incident

During job applications, employers often ask if you can give details of an important event or experience that had a major impact upon your life or work. This is sometimes referred to as a 'critical incident'. In particular, they are looking to see what kinds of things you regard as important (your values), how you managed transition and change, or how well you learn from experience.

It is useful to be prepared for this question, and the 'Critical Incident Sheet' on p. 236 outlines some of the main themes that are worth considering. Even if you are not applying for work, this is a useful exercise to work through from time to time, using either the same incident, or comparing your responses to different incidents.

Responding to competence-based questions

In Chapter 1, you undertook profiles of your skills and qualities in relation to successful executives and to a personal goal. This chapter gives you the opportunity to analyse your personal competences in some depth. The competences selected for analysis are those frequently asked of graduates when they apply for jobs. When you apply for a graduate job, you will receive a 'person specification' that outlines the qualities required for the post. These are prompts to you to outline some details of your ability to meet the job requirements. Increasingly, employers are introducing competence-based applications. These usually ask you to give specific evidence of your competence under a number of headings that they give you.

Whether or not you are asked details about competences at the application stage, it is typical for some or all of a job interview to be competence-based. Having a set of well-recorded competences can significantly boost your confidence in your performance during the application process. If you store these records electronically, you will find that you can save yourself a great deal of time in making each application.

What is a 'competence'?

To be competent means to be able to perform an activity reasonably well and on more than one occasion. To consider yourself competent at a task, you are likely to be able to do what is necessary to achieve a successful outcome without having to check continually what needs to be done, and without supervision. Competence is associated with the notion of repeated performance; simply doing something once is not usually a sign of competence. Competence is often associated with well-placed confidence. It requires proficiency in a set of relevant skills. If you can train or advise others in the area, this is usually a sign of competence.

Describing your competence

In interview, you may be asked to give evidence of your competence from one of a range of different perspectives (see Chapter 8). This can often catch people unawares so that they feel they have not done themselves justice. Similarly, when writing competence-based applications, it is easy to omit details for which the selection panel will be looking. This can make the difference between being selected or not. The resource sheets provided below and on pp. 257–91 will guide your consideration of your competences so that you are better prepared for managing competence-based questions.

Selecting examples

For written applications, you are likely to be given a restricted word limit for listing skills or giving details of one example. In interviews, you may be given time only to describe one example in detail. It is not untypical to hear people say after an interview that the wrong example came to mind. For instance, they may have prepared to answer a question giving a 'recent example' and be asked for the 'best example in relation to the current job' – or vice versa. It is useful to update your records so that you are clear about:

● which is your *one* best example of the competence from your experience. Usually this will be a recent example but sometimes a significant event or achievement may not be recent;
● details of all aspects of that best example;

- two other good examples, in brief;
- what is the most relevant example for the job;
- what is a recent example.

Building your competence

If you find that you are not able to give good examples of competence in any area, you will need to decide:

- Is this a competence that is likely to be required for the kinds of jobs that interest you?
- What opportunities are open to you to develop that competence?

Most employers want to see that you have experience. It is a frequent complaint that people cannot gain experience because they cannot get a job, and they cannot get a job they want because they cannot gain the experience. Students have many opportunities to develop experiences that are less easy to come by once student life is over. Again, this is often not appreciated until the chance has passed. Seize the opportunity whilst you are still a student – and ensure you have a good portfolio of skills and experience by the time you leave.

Completing the 'evidence of competence' sheets

Below are a number of resource sheets to assist you in elaborating your personal competences. On the left are prompts to help you explore the situation fully. You can make your responses in the boxes on the right. You may consider that very little space is provided for each answer. However, it is unlikely that you will ever have as much time or space as is provided here. You will be required to give very brief responses to each question, so your thinking must be clear, precise and succinct.

Employers are looking at your own personal involvement and the responsibility you take for your own actions. Anything which comes across as an excuse or appears to be blaming others for a poor outcome will sound unconvincing. Speak about your own role and take responsibility for what did not work. Identify what you have learnt about how you would do things differently in the future.

They will also be interested in knowing the level of operation: how high-profile was the work, how central were you to events, where did you stand in the hierarchy of people involved? Being able to contribute to projects led by others may be as important as being the leader, as both team work and leadership are prized qualities.

You may find it useful to copy the blank sheets before completing them, so that you can use them again in the future. You may wish to copy the outlines into your electronic records, so that you can update them easily.

In completing the records, it is worth taking time to jot down all the occasions you can think of when you exemplified the competence in action. This will give you a full list from which to select your best examples. Make use of the responses you have made to activities in chapters earlier in this book or on your programme. It can help to have a friend or relation to prompt you if you struggle to find examples. You can call upon the same experience for more than one competence, but it is useful to refer to at least three separate experiences or examples overall.

List of competence sheets provided

One competence sheet is provided here on pp. 239–40. A list of resource sheets for recording other competences can be found on p. 257.

(1) Evidence of competence in team work

1.	The best example.	
2.	The purpose of the team, the nature of the team activities and membership.	
3.	Context: brief details of the circumstances, event or activity when I showed good team skills.	
4.	Level of responsibility in this team. The scale and scope of the work or event	
5.	Personal contribution: what I did; the role(s) I played in the team.	
6.	Example of leadership: (e.g. planning, negotiating, persuading).	
7.	Example of ability to work with others (e.g. accepting others' views, following directions, working out a compromise, etc.).	
8.	What worked well on this occasion?	

9.	The lessons I learned from this occasion.	
10.	What would I do differently on another occasion?	
11.	How typical this example is for me (a daily occurrence/weekly/ occasionally/rarely)	
12.	Brief details of a recent (or second) example.	
13.	Brief details of a third, preferably contrasting, example.	
14.	How do I measure my success for this competence?	
15.	How could this competence be applied to other situations?	

See pp. 257–91 for further resource sheets for recording competences.

Personal qualities

Quality	Where developed	Example of where you demonstrate this quality	How this benefits you in your approach to your life and career	How this quality would be of benefit to an employer or in the workplace

Health and safety

Date:

My general understanding of health and safety issues and legislation

Examples of specific health and safety issues that I needed to be aware of in one place I have worked or studied

Health and safety training I have received

An incident that demonstrates my management of health and safety issues

Copy and update

Equal opportunities

Date:

My general understanding of equal opportunities issues and legislation

Examples of specific equal opportunities issues that I needed to be aware of in one place I have worked or studied

Equal opportunities training I have received

An incident which demonstrates my management of equal opportunities issues

Copy and update

Improving personal performance: evaluation sheet

Date:
Example of where I took action to improve my performance
What needed to be done?
What were the issues?
What made this a priority or a good area to address?
The preparation and planning I undertook
My strategy (plan) for improving my performance

What I did. Any changes or adaptations that I made to the strategy

What worked?

What else could I have done or could I try on a future occasion?

What changed?

What did I learn about my own performance through this experience?

The ways this knowledge is more generally applicable to my study, work or life.

Breadth of knowledge and experience

The ways that my interests and life experiences are of benefit to me at work, college (or in life more generally) are:

This chapter provides resources that can assist in structuring your reflection about your experience. Experiences are more valuable when we are aware of their significance to our lives. They are our richest resource for learning, and yet we often resist slowing down sufficiently to examine what we have gained. It is much easier to move onto the next task – and even to repeat similar mistakes.

The main focus of this chapter has been reflecting on experience in order to be in a better position to move towards career goals. That is because the main aim of most graduates is to gain a job. However, the deepest learning is likely to come from our reflection about our broader life experiences – our vision, values and beliefs, the way we respond to other people, and how comfortably we live with ourselves. There is nothing to prevent you from using these resources to examine more personal questions, as and when you are ready.

These resources are not for use on a single occasion. As you move through your programme and as you gain wider experiences through life and work, you will find better examples to record. At the time, these experiences will appear very vivid in your mind but you will begin to lose the details over time. Write these down whilst they are still fresh. Reflect back upon those same events in a year's time. Often, you will find that you see much more significance in the same events after time has elapsed.

Chapter 10

Drawing it together

Even if you're on the right track, you'll get run over if you just sit there.

Will Rogers

Learning outcomes

This chapter offers opportunities to:

- recognise personal changes and achievements
- review your reflections on personal planning
- update your profile of skills and qualities
- identify your 'learning edge'
- identify emerging personal responsibilities
- plan your next steps.

Introduction

Personal planning is not simply about making a 'plan' and following it. It is a developmental process that each individual moulds to suit their own needs and interests over time. It is about getting to grips with issues such as:

- who you are and the kind of person you want to be;
- the life you want to lead and what you want from life;
- what matters to you and what you want to achieve;
- the steps you will take to achieve your goals;
- recognising changes in your interests and charting out a new plan in line with those changes.

Good planning involves taking steps to ensure you have the information you need at your fingertips when you need it. It involves thinking about possibilities, some of which may seem far-fetched, and starting to put the support and skills in place now that might be useful later.

This chapter offers structured opportunities to review your current position, referring back to activities undertaken in previous chapters, and looking forward to your next step. It looks at the process of managing personal development planning once you are already embarked on the journey of self-discovery and life planning.

Recognising personal changes

Goal inertia

Chapter 1 encouraged you to form a strong vision of what you wanted to be or to achieve. However, your views may already have changed. Each day, our experiences shape us anew. Over time, our aims and goals may become out of touch with who we have become: this is 'goal inertia'.

The 'newer you' is inspired by fresh ideas, moulded by experiences, changed by the knowledge you are acquiring, living in an environment that also changes each day. Is this 'newer you' still inspired by plans made one, three or five years ago?

Activity: Recognising personal changes

Take ten minutes to brainstorm all the differences you can detect between yourself now and yourself three years ago.

	Me three years ago	Me now
Appearance		
Clothes		
Friends		
Interests		
Tastes in music		
Life aims or vision		
Attitudes		

	Me three years ago	Me now
Inspiration		
Personal qualities I want to develop		
People I admire		
People who support me		
Job taken		
Career interests		
Other significant changes		

Review your goals

You may be inspired by the same vision or aims all of your life. However, if you feel that your goals are not inspiring you anymore, you have probably outgrown them. It is worth reviewing your goals from time to time. For example:

- Do the 'Dream' or 'Long-term vision' activities again (pp. 22–4). Compare your current and previous responses.
- Talk to someone about your goals. Ask them to press you into really exploring what you want.
- Take a journey to somewhere you have never visited before. The change of scene can generate new ideas about what you really want.
- Speak to other people about their goals and interests. Broaden your perspective on the options open to you.

Success is a very personal thing. For you, success may mean reaching the stars or it may mean a particular source of happiness that other people would not appreciate.

Success is associated with happiness. Does your vision of your life leave you with a feeling of relative happiness? If the goals you set for yourself are unappealing, or make you feel that you are making more hurdles for yourself in life, or seem to be setting you off on paths towards places that you no longer find attractive, it is probably time for a rethink.

Review your values

Your vision will be strongly influenced by your values – either in what you view as successful, or the behaviours and lifestyle you find acceptable and desirable.

Using the reflective process

Monitoring personal progress

Progress can be measured against your personal goals or against objective criteria such as exam marks. In the grand scheme of life, marks given by others count for much less than:

- the depth of your personal awareness;
- your ability to monitor your own progress;
- and your ability to take action to improve performance without being told to do so.

In order to monitor performance and personal change, you need records. A reflective journal, maintained for your own purposes, is a key tool for monitoring change. If you haven't read through your reflective journal for a while, now is a good time to do so.

Read through ten pages of your reflective journal, preferably from at least six months ago.

- What do you notice about your state of mind at the time? How does it differ from now?
- What things had you forgotten were in the journal that you are pleased to find?
- What things did you mean to do but have not yet got round to doing?
- What else strikes you as interesting from your journal?

Identifying change

Keeping a reflective journal provides material to help you monitor changes in yourself over time. The following activity invites you to look back over your reflection and identify themes and changes in your responses.

Activity: Has your thinking changed?

- Select any three activities from anywhere in the book. Include one you enjoyed and one that you found difficult or resisted.
- Do these again now.
- Compare your responses with those you made previously.
- How do you account for any differences in your responses?

Being a reflective practitioner

Reflective practice is very similar to making New Year resolutions. It is easy to start well, but by mid-year the resolutions are often long forgotten. Similarly, reflection on our goals, performance and personal development may start out well. However, reflection is often an early casualty when there is pressure on our time. You may find that this has been true of you. If so, just take up from wherever you left

off. If you keep doing this, you will find that reflective practice becomes a habit.

📖 **Reflection**   Developing skills in reflective practice

In your reflective journal, jot down your responses to the following.

- What do you feel you have gained from taking a reflective and self-evaluating approach to your academic, personal or professional development?
- How well do you feel you have developed and maintained a reflective approach?
- What steps could you take to improve your reflective practice?

Improving performance

Working with our strengths

One way of improving performance is to identify current strengths and to build upon these. Chapter 2, for example, identified ways of

Activity: Building from personal expertise

In your reflective journal, jot down *one* skill or area of expertise which you feel is your strongest point. This could be a sub-skill such as organising space or drawing up timetables or planning a piece of writing.

- Take two minutes to brainstorm all the ways this skill or area of expertise might be helpful to your future study.
- Take two minutes to brainstorm all the ways this skill or area of expertise might be helpful to work contexts.
- Take two minutes to brainstorm all the ways this skill or area of expertise might be helpful to your life more generally.

Once you have completed this for one skill, go through the same questions with at least two other personal strengths. You may find it useful to update your competence sheets once you have completed this activity.

using expertise in one area to develop understanding in another area. Look back through the competence sheets and other evaluations of your skills and qualities in Chapter 9 to remind yourself of your current strengths. Look back over your learning goals and the areas that you have worked on to improve personal performance. Consider how well you drew on your personal strengths in order to achieve your learning goals.

Identifying 'transferable skills'

To transfer skills from one context to another, it is usually necessary to:

● be aware of the skills (and especially sub-skills) you already use;
● identify which of those skills can be adapted to fit the new context.

The sub-skills are especially important as it is

Activity: Transferring skills

● Select one of your skills or strengths.
● Where did you develop this skill?
● What are the sub-skills and qualities you have developed as part of the overall skill?

Now select one context or situation from the following list. Choose the context with which you are least familiar:

Working with children;
Setting up an arts exhibition;
Designing an office;
Counselling others on a phone line;
Raising money for a charity;
Making a video;
Designing a Web page for a company;
Being the first on the scene of a serious accident;
Organising a conference;
Opening a restaurant.

● Take five minutes to brainstorm all the ways that the sub-skills you identified could be of any use at all in the new context you chose. There will be ways that are not immediately apparent.
● In what ways would you need to adapt those sub-skills so that they fit the new context?

---

usually these that transfer to new contexts. For example, if you are good at working with numbers, the sub-skills might include paying attention to details, sequencing, seeing patterns, logical skills, seeing how numbers relate to words, having the patience to retest all the subsequent stages in a problem in order to identify an error, a good memory for formulas, etc.

If you are good at working with people, the sub-skills and personal qualities involved might include listening skills, coping with other people's anger, seeing things from another person's point of view, being very sensitive to your own feelings and the impact these have on others, taking responsibility for your own mistakes, being able to ask for what you need, etc.

Make the link!

Interconnections between areas of expertise

Very few skills are developed in isolation from others. Our development is usually a complex web of newly developed strengths and relative weaknesses. When we develop one area of expertise, we usually enhance performance in others, even if this is not visible.

For example, people who sing in choirs develop their voices and their musicality. However, they also tend to acquire a good sense of timing in their 'response' to others which can contribute to the development of people skills. A vast array of other skills can be developed from this one activity, such as developing confidence in performing in front of others, team-work, taking direction, following a sequence, attention to detail, sensitivity to mood, etc. The same is true of most other areas of expertise.

The converse is also true. If we are weak in one skill or area of expertise, the ramifications of this will be felt in a wide range of contexts. For example, if we hate sport, this could impact upon our health, our stamina, our opportunities to mix with others, our ability to join in certain conversations, the number of connections we can make with other people, the range of metaphors we have to call upon, our understanding of other people's interest and motivations, etc.

Because of this, the root of difficulties we experience in one area of our lives may lie in a completely different area. For example, poor organisational skills may originate in one of a number of areas, such as poor time-management skills, low motivation, unhelpful attitudes, an inability to say 'No' to too many requests for help, or a lack of responsibility for our own actions. Unless we work on the root cause, the difficulties may not go away.

Raising the game

Recognising your achievements

It may be tempting to feel at times that your personal development could now 'come to an end'. That is usually a good signal for raising your game, setting new challenges, finding a new aspect to stimulate your interest.

One boost to motivation is reviewing your successes. Note what you have achieved so far with your own development and consider the benefits this has brought you.

Activity: Making the connections

Make a list of 3–5 themes that you are working on at the moment. Then identify various sections of the book that can develop relevant skills for improving your performance. For example:

Your goals and how to achieve them: Chapter 1, 'The vision' and Chapter 4, 'Problem solving and task management'.

Managing your responses when working with difficult people: Chapter 3, 'Successful self-management' and Chapter 5, 'People skills'.

Working on problems and looking for creative solutions: Chapter 4, 'Problem solving and task management' and Chapter 6, 'Successful problem solving and task management'.

● Identify the ways that skills developed in one aspect of your life can have an effect upon performance in other areas.

Reflection   Note success

Browse through your reflective journal for the last year – or since your last review. In your journal, note:

● What goals did you work on during that time?
● Which ones have you achieved?
● What are the benefits of having achieved these?

Consider what the effects of these achievements are. These may be changes in your life, successes in your study, the ability to manage a particular situation, or it may be a feeling of accomplishment. Don't be modest. Make sure you include a list of all the sub-skills you developed and your minor achievements as well as the more noticeable ones.

Have you celebrated your achievements? If not: make sure you do!

Reflection   Linking skills and expertise

● What is the area where you have developed most expertise?
● What are the wider range of sub-skills and qualities that have developed as part of that expertise? List at least 20.

● Which one skill, personal quality or area of expertise do you feel you need to improve?
● How would improving this one area also lead to improvements in other skills, qualities, attitudes or areas of expertise?

What do you think is at the root of this area of weakness? What can you do to address this?

Working at your 'edge'

Once you have built your confidence in your own success, you are ready to set yourself greater challenges. This can also mean looking at your approach to challenge itself. Do you welcome challenge? Are you prepared to take on goals that will stretch you?

Indicate how important each of the following is to you achieving well.

(a) I achieve best when I . . .	Very important	Important	Quite important	Not very important	Not at all important
● can see some results quickly	☐	☐	☐	☐	☐
● have feedback from others so I know how well I am doing	☐	☐	☐	☐	☐
● receive guidance or suggestions from other people	☐	☐	☐	☐	☐
● know I am heading in the right direction	☐	☐	☐	☐	☐
● have planned out the whole process in advance	☐	☐	☐	☐	☐
● set short-term targets that I know are achievable	☐	☐	☐	☐	☐
● set goals that I am certain I can achieve	☐	☐	☐	☐	☐
● plan each step closely so as to avoid setbacks	☐	☐	☐	☐	☐
● have a clear vision of where I am going	☐	☐	☐	☐	☐
● have a safety net to fall back on if things do not work out.	☐	☐	☐	☐	☐

Indicate how far each statement below is typical of you.

(b) I am able to motivate myself to work towards a goal even if . . .	Very typical	Typical	Sometimes the case	Not very typical	Not typical at all
● I have to wait a long time to see the results	☐	☐	☐	☐	☐
● It takes years to reach the ultimate goal	☐	☐	☐	☐	☐
● Nobody else is available to tell me what to do	☐	☐	☐	☐	☐
● There is a really difficult challenge	☐	☐	☐	☐	☐
● It is not clear that the outcome will be successful	☐	☐	☐	☐	☐
● The eventual goal is rather vague	☐	☐	☐	☐	☐
● The plan has to evolve slowly over time	☐	☐	☐	☐	☐
● I have to work hard for something that I may not achieve	☐	☐	☐	☐	☐
● There are many setbacks	☐	☐	☐	☐	☐
● Other people think I am aiming too high.	☐	☐	☐	☐	☐

Attitude to challenge

The greatest barriers to success are usually those that derive from our attitudes and fears. The challenge may simply be too great for us at that time. The challenges we set ourselves should be appropriate for our current coping skills, support networks, and emotional well-being. The activity on p. 254 gives an indication of the ways in which you currently cope with challenge.

Using your responses for (a) 📖

- Highlight all the answers to which you responded with a 'Very important' or 'Important'.
- Write these out in your reflective notebook, starting: 'To cope with a new challenge, it is important for me that . . .'.
- As you write, add details or examples from your experience to illustrate how you know this is really true of you

Using your responses for (b) 📖

- Highlight all the answers to which you responded with a 'Not very typical' or 'Not typical at all'.
- Write these out in your reflective notebook, starting: 'I am unlikely to keep going with a new challenge if . . .'.
- As you write, add details or examples from your experience to illustrate how you know this is really true of you.

Interpreting your responses

Your answers to (a) provide you with a summary of the approaches that increase your chances of success with new challenges. For example, you may have indicated that you need support in order to achieve. If this is true of you, you are more likely to be successful if you remain open to guidance from others, plan carefully and set manageable targets. However, see 'The comfort zone' below.

Your answers to (b) provide you with a summary of how highly motivated you are likely to remain even in high-risk contexts. If you indicated many 'Very typical' and 'Typical' replies here, your responses suggest you are likely to respond well to challenge and risk. You appear to be highly motivated and able to manage your own path to success very well. However, see 'The comfort zone' below.

If your responses to (b) were mostly 'Not very typical' or 'Not typical at all', set yourself challenges that avoid most of those circumstances. Your 'edge' is likely to be working on developing your motivation so that you can achieve your goals even when conditions are not ideal.

The comfort zone and 'the working edge'

When we only work to our strengths and preferences, we run the risk of not setting sufficient challenges for ourselves. The 'comfort zone' is where we operate when we are running no risks, setting ourselves no challenges, ensuring we always have a very strong and wide safety net, ensuring we always have more than enough support. A good personal development plan will include areas for improvement that challenge us to work at our 'edge'.

'The edge' is the boundary between the comfort zone and unnecessary or inappropriate risks. It is different for everybody. For one person it might be learning to take advice from others; for another person it may be learning to work more independently of others. For people who avoid risk, the 'edge' might be in learning to set more adventurous challenges. This might entail developing related skills, qualities or attitudes such as managing change, seeing mistakes as opportunities to learn, developing emotional coping strategies, and so forth. For those who take high-risk strategies, the 'edge' might be in developing ways of coping with stress, or developing trust in other people, or in living without high excitement.

📖 **Reflection**   Working at the 'edge'

- What do you feel is the 'edge' you need to work at next?
- What makes you feel that this is your 'edge'? Who could you speak to about this?
- How will you take on this new challenge?
- What support or guidance do you need?

Sometimes it is hard to acknowledge where the edge lies. For example, the kind of advice we dislike the most is often an indicator of where our personal 'edge' lies. We may need guidance on how to work at our edge. As with the 'edge' of a cliff or precipice, we should approach our personal limits with due caution and the right support. It is good to set challenges – but not to go over the edge without a rope.

Final comments

Congratulations on reaching this stage of the book. If you worked through most of the chapters and activities, you will have a very strong sense of yourself, your strengths and what you need to do to achieve your goals.

It is likely that you used the book selectively, picking out activities that seemed most relevant or to which you were directed by your tutors. If there were aspects of this process that you at first resisted, found uncomfortable or absolutely hated but worked through, you have really achieved something. What exactly that 'something' is, is for you to judge.

We are always a 'work in progress':

● There is always more that we can understand about ourselves.
● The range of our knowledge and expertise can always be extended.
● There is always an area of our performance that can be improved.

Our personal development is as dynamic a process as we choose to make it. If we use the reflective approach on a regular basis, we will know ourselves more fully, be more aware of our needs and wants, and more able to achieve what we want to achieve.

> *Seek out that particular mental attitude which makes you feel most deeply and vitally alive, along with which comes the inner voice which says, 'this is the real me', and when you have found that attitude, follow it.*

> William James

Appendix

List of Competence Sheets

(1) Evidence of competence in teamwork – this competence sheet appears in Chapter 9 (see p. 239)

(2) Evidence of competence in working independently

(3) Evidence of competence in exercising responsibility

(4) Evidence of competence in leadership

(5) Evidence of competence in persuading others

(6) Evidence of competence in negotiating a compromise

(7) Evidence of competence in problem-solving

(8) Evidence of competence in project or task management

(9) Evidence of competence in dealing with conflict

(10) Evidence of competence in managing a difficult situation

(11) Evidence of competence in working under pressure or to tight deadlines

(12) Evidence of competence in equal opportunities

(13) Evidence of competence in managing change

(14) Evidence of competence in taking calculated risks

(15) Evidence of competence in learning from my own mistakes

(16) Evidence of competence in written communication skills

(17) Evidence of competence in oral communication skills

(18) Pro forma for mapping other competences

(2) Evidence of competence in working independently

1.	The best example.	
2.	Context: brief details of the work undertaken, for whom and where it was undertaken.	
3.	Level of responsibility for the work in question. The scale and scope of the event.	
4.	Size or scope of the work undertaken.	
5.	Outcomes: what I achieved.	
6.	Contribution of this work to any larger project or team work. How this work linked to the work undertaken by other people.	
7.	How I organised my work in order to motivate myself and meet targets.	

8.	What worked well for this example of independent work?	
9.	What lessons did I learn from this example of independent work?	
10.	How would I manage independent work differently on another occasion?	
11.	How typical this example is for me (a daily occurrence/weekly/ occasionally/rarely).	
12.	Brief details of a recent (or second) example.	
13.	Brief details of a third, preferably contrasting, example.	
14.	How could this competence be applied to other situations?	
15.	How do I measure my success for this competence?	

(3) Evidence of competence in exercising responsibility

1.	The best example.	
2.	Context: brief details of the circumstances, event or activity.	
3.	Level of responsibility on this occasion. The scale and scope of the event.	
4.	Personal contribution: what I did.	
5.	Who else was involved – and what they did.	
6.	Skills I exercised.	
7.	What worked well on this occasion?	

8.	What lessons did I learn from this occasion?	
9.	What would I do differently on another occasion?	
10.	How typical this example is for me (a daily occurrence/ weekly/occasionally/rarely).	
11.	Brief details of a recent (or second) example.	
12.	Brief details of a third, preferably contrasting, example.	
13.	How could this competence be applied to other situations?	
14.	How do I measure my success for this competence?	

(4)   Evidence of competence in leadership

1.	The best example.	
2.	What I believe is meant by 'leadership'.	
3.	Context: brief details of the circumstances, event or activity when I gave leadership to others.	
4.	Level of responsibility on this occasion. The scale and scope of the work or event.	
5.	Personal contribution: what I did.	
6.	Who else was involved – and what they did. How I involved other people, such as delegating authority, or seeking opinions.	
7.	Example of leadership skills I exercised.	
8.	How I took on board the opinions and feelings of other people.	

9.	The outcomes. What happened.	
10.	What worked well on this occasion?	
11.	What lessons did I learn from this occasion?	
12.	What would I do differently on another occasion?	
13.	How typical this example is for me (a daily occurrence/ weekly/occasionally/rarely).	
14.	Brief details of a recent (or second) example.	
15.	Brief details of a third, preferably contrasting, example.	
16.	How could this competence be applied to other situations?	
17.	How do I measure my success for this competence?	

(5)   Evidence of competence in persuading others

1.	The best example.	
2.	Context: brief details of the circumstances, event or activity. Why was it necessary to exercise persuasion?	
3.	Level of responsibility on this occasion. The scale and scope of the work or event.	
4.	Personal contribution: what I did.	
5.	Example of leadership skills involved on this occasion.	
6.	Who else was involved – and what they did. How I involved or worked with others on this occasion.	
7.	Skills I exercised and qualities I demonstrated.	
8.	The outcomes.	

9.	What worked well on this occasion?	
10.	What lessons did I learn from this occasion?	
11.	What would I do differently on another occasion?	
12.	How typical this example is for me (a daily occurrence/ weekly/occasionally/rarely).	
13.	Brief details of a recent (or second) example.	
14.	Brief details of a third, preferably contrasting, example.	
15.	How could this competence be applied to other situations?	
16.	How do I measure my success for this competence?	

(6)   Evidence of competence in negotiating a compromise

1.	The best example.	
2.	Context: brief details of the circumstances, event or activity. Why was it necessary to negotiate a compromise?	
3.	Level of responsibility on this occasion. The scale and scope of the work or event.	
4.	Personal contribution: what I did.	
5.	Example of leadership skills involved on this occasion.	
6.	Who else was involved – and what they did. How I involved or worked with others on this occasion.	
7.	Skills I exercised and qualities I demonstrated.	
8.	The outcomes.	

9.	What worked well on this occasion?	
10.	What lessons did I learn from this occasion?	
11.	What would I do differently on another occasion?	
12.	How typical this example is for me (a daily occurrence/ weekly/occasionally/rarely).	
13.	Brief details of a recent (or second) example.	
14.	Brief details of a third, preferably contrasting, example.	
15.	How could this competence be applied to other situations?	
16.	How do I measure my success for this competence?	

(7)   Evidence of competence in problem-solving

1.	The best example.	
2.	Context: brief details of the circumstances and the problem to be solved.	
3.	Level of responsibility on this occasion. The scale and scope of the work or event.	
4.	Personal contribution: what I did.	
5.	The problem-solving approach I took – my strategy, the alternatives I considered.	
6.	Who else was involved – and what they did. How I involved or worked with others on this occasion.	
7.	The outcomes. What was achieved?	

8.	What worked well on this occasion?	
9.	What lessons did I learn from this occasion?	
10.	What would I do differently on another occasion?	
11.	How typical this example is for me (a daily occurrence/ weekly/occasionally/rarely).	
12.	Brief details of a recent (or second) example.	
13.	Brief details of a third, preferably contrasting, example.	
14.	How could this competence be applied to other situations?	
15.	How do I measure my success for this competence?	

(8) Evidence of competence in project or task management

1.	The best example.	
2.	Context: brief details of the circumstances, project or task selected.	
3.	Level of responsibility on this occasion. The scale and scope of the work or event.	
4.	Personal contribution: what I did.	
5.	The approach I took – my strategy, the alternatives I considered.	
6.	Who else was involved – and what they did. How I involved or worked with others on this occasion.	
7.	The outcomes. What was achieved?	

8.	What worked well on this occasion?	
9.	What lessons did I learn from this occasion?	
10.	What would I do differently on another occasion?	
11.	How typical this example is for me (a daily occurrence/ weekly/occasionally/rarely).	
12.	Brief details of a recent (or second) example.	
13.	Brief details of a third, preferably contrasting, example.	
14.	How could this competence be applied to other situations?	
15.	How do I measure my success for this competence?	

(9)   Evidence of competence in dealing with conflict

1.	The best example.	
2.	Context: brief details of the circumstances or situation.	
3.	Level of responsibility on this occasion. The scale and scope of the work or event.	
4.	Personal contribution: what I did to resolve the conflict.	
5.	The approach I took – why I adopted the techniques or strategy that I did.	
6.	Who else was involved – and what they did. How I involved or worked with others on this occasion.	
7.	The outcomes. How far the conflict was resolved for the short or long term.	

8.	What worked well on this occasion?	
9.	What lessons did I learn from this occasion?	
10.	What would I do differently on another occasion?	
11.	How typical this example is for me (a daily occurrence/ weekly/occasionally/rarely).	
12.	Brief details of a recent (or second) example.	
13.	Brief details of a third, preferably contrasting, example.	
14.	How could this competence be applied to other situations?	
15.	How do I measure my success for this competence?	

(10)   Evidence of competence in managing a difficult situation

1.	The best example.	
2.	Context: brief details of the difficult situation: where it took place, the people involved.	
3.	Level of responsibility on this occasion. The scale and scope of the work or event.	
4.	Personal contribution: what I did to manage the situation and resolve the difficulty.	
5.	The approach I took – why I adopted the techniques or strategy that I did.	
6.	Who else was involved – and what they did. How I involved or worked with others on this occasion.	
7.	The outcomes. How far the conflict was resolved for the short or long term.	

8.	What worked well on this occasion?	
9.	What lessons did I learn from this occasion?	
10.	What would I do differently on another occasion?	
11.	How typical this example is for me (a daily occurrence/ weekly/occasionally/rarely).	
12.	Brief details of a recent (or second) example.	
13.	Brief details of a third, preferably contrasting, example.	
14.	How could this competence be applied to other situations?	
15.	How do I measure my success for this competence?	

(11) Evidence of competence in working under pressure or to tight deadlines

1.	The best example.	
2.	Context: brief details of the circumstances that created the pressure or tight deadlines.	
3.	Level of responsibility on this occasion. The scale and scope of the work or event.	
4.	Personal contribution: what I did.	
5.	What action I took to help me cope with the pressure and stress.	
6.	Who else was involved – and what they did. How I involved or worked with others on this occasion.	
7.	Evidence of ability to work with others under pressure.	
8.	The outcomes. The extent to which deadlines were met or the work completed.	

9.	What worked well on this occasion?	
10.	What lessons did I learn from this occasion?	
11.	What would I do differently on another occasion?	
12.	How typical this example is for me (a daily occurrence/weekly/occasionally/rarely).	
13.	Brief details of a recent (or second) example.	
14.	Brief details of a third, preferably contrasting, example.	
15.	How could this competence be applied to other situations?	
16.	How do I measure my success for this competence?	

(12) Evidence of competence in equal opportunities

1.	The best example.	
2.	What I understand by the term 'equal opportunities'.	
3.	Context: brief details of the circumstances and issues involved.	
4.	Level of responsibility on this occasion. The scale and scope of the issue.	
5.	Personal contribution: what I did.	
6.	Who else was involved on this occasion – and what they did. How I involved or worked with others.	
7.	The outcomes (long term or short term).	
8.	What worked well on this occasion?	

9.	What lessons did I learn from this occasion?	
10.	What would I do differently on another occasion?	
11.	How typical this example is for me (a daily occurrence/ weekly/occasionally/rarely?)	
12.	General awareness of equal opportunities issues and legislation. Experience of working with people from a wide variety of backgrounds.	
13.	Brief details of a recent (or second) example.	
14.	Brief details of a third, preferably contrasting, example.	
15.	How could this competence be applied to other situations?	
16.	How do I measure my success for this competence?	

(13) Evidence of competence in managing change

1.	The best example.	
2.	Context: brief details of the circumstances where change was introduced and why it was needed.	
3.	Level of responsibility on this occasion. The scale and scope of the issue.	
4.	Personal contribution: what I did. How far I initiated the change, or managed my own or others' response to change.	
5.	Who else was involved on this occasion – and what they did. How I involved or worked with others. How I supported others through a time of change.	
6.	The outcomes of my actions or involvement.	
7.	What worked well on this occasion?	

8.	What lessons did I learn from this occasion?	
9.	What would I do differently on another occasion?	
10.	How typical this example is of my life or work experience.	
11.	Brief details of a recent (or second) example.	
12.	Brief details of a third, preferably contrasting, example.	
13.	How could this competence be applied to other situations?	
14.	How do I measure my success for this competence?	

(14) Evidence of competence in taking calculated risks

1.	The best example.	
2.	Context: brief details of the circumstances.	
3.	The nature of the risk involved; the factors that needed to be weighed in the balance.	
4.	Level of responsibility on this occasion. The scale and scope of the issue.	
5.	Personal contribution: what I did.	
6.	Who else was involved on this occasion – and what they did. How I involved or worked with others.	
7.	What I did to manage the pressure and stress for myself and others.	
8.	The outcomes of my actions or involvement.	

9.	What worked well on this occasion?	
10.	What lessons did I learn from this occasion?	
11.	What would I do differently on another occasion?	
12.	How typical this example is of my life or work experience.	
13.	Brief details of a recent (or second) example.	
14.	Brief details of a third, preferably contrasting, example.	
15.	How could this competence be applied to other situations?	
16.	How do I measure my success for this competence?	

(15)   Evidence of competence in learning from my own mistakes

1.	The best example.	
2.	Context: brief details of the circumstances.	
3.	The mistake(s) that I made on this occasion. What circumstances led to the mistake/error of judgement? How I discovered the mistake.	
4.	Level of responsibility on this occasion. The scale and scope of the issue.	
5.	Personal contribution: what I did.	
6.	Who else was involved on this occasion – and what they did. How I involved or worked with others.	
7.	What I did to manage the pressure and stress for myself and others.	
8.	The outcomes of my actions or involvement. How I took responsibility for my own actions.	

9.	What, if anything, was positive about my contribution?	
10.	What lessons did I learn from this occasion?	
11.	What would I do differently on another occasion? How I acted differently on a second occasion.	
12.	How typical is it for me to use a reflective approach to improve my performance?	
13.	Brief details of a recent (or second) example.	
14.	Brief details of a third, preferably contrasting, example.	
15.	How could this competence be applied to other situations?	
16.	How do I measure my success for this competence?	

(16)   Evidence of competence in written communication skills

1.	The best example.	
2.	Context: brief details of the circumstances.	
3.	Level of responsibility on this occasion. The time-scale, word limits and importance of the task.	
4.	The nature of the audience.	
5.	Personal contribution: what I did, including how the writing was suited to the audience.	
6.	Who else was involved on this occasion – and what they did. How I involved or worked with others on this occasion.	
7.	Outcomes. The extent to which deadlines were met or the work completed. What feedback I received.	
8.	What lessons did I learn from this occasion? How I used feedback.	

9.	What would I do differently on another occasion?	
10.	What skills have I acquired through academic writing?	
11.	Awareness of differences between academic writing and that for the career area which interests me.	
12.	How typical this example is for me (a daily occurrence/ weekly/occasionally/rarely).	
13.	Brief details of a recent (or second) example.	
14.	Brief details of a third, preferably contrasting, example.	
15.	How could this competence be applied to other situations?	
16.	How do I measure my success for this competence?	

(17)   Evidence of competence in oral communication skills

1.	The best example.	
2.	Context: brief details of the circumstances.	
3.	Level of responsibility on this occasion. The time limit, scale and scope of the work or event.	
4.	The nature of the audience and how I took this into consideration.	
5.	Personal contribution: what I did.	
6.	Who else was involved on this occasion – and what they did. How I involved or worked with others on this occasion.	
7.	Outcomes. The extent to which deadlines were met or the work completed. Feedback I received.	

8.	What worked well on this occasion?	
9.	What lessons did I learn from this occasion?	
10.	What would I do differently on another occasion?	
11.	How typical this example is for me (a daily occurrence/weekly/occasionally/rarely).	
12.	Brief details of a recent (or second) example.	
13.	Bbrief details of a third, preferably contrasting, example.	
14.	How could this competence be applied to other situations?	
15.	How do I measure my success for this competence?	

(18)   Evidence of competence in _____

1.	The best example.	
2.	Context: brief details of the circumstances.	
3.	Level of responsibility on this occasion. The scale and scope of the issue.	
4.	Personal contribution: what I did.	
5.	Who else was involved on this occasion – and what they did. How I involved or worked with others.	
6.	The outcomes of my actions or involvement.	
7.	What worked well on this occasion?	

8.	What lessons did I learn from this occasion?	
9.	What would I do differently on another occasion?	
10.	How typical this example is of my life or work experience.	
11.	Brief details of a recent (or second) example.	
12.	Brief details of a third, preferably contrasting, example.	
13.	How could this competence be applied to other situations?	
14.	How do I measure my success for this competence?	

References

Beaver, D. (1998) *NLP for Lazy Learning* (Shaftesbury, Dorset, and Boston, Mass.: Element).

Belbin, M. R. (1996a) *Management Teams: Why They Succeed or Fail* (London: Butterworth-Heinemann).

Belbin, M. R. (1996b) *Team Roles at Work* (London: Butterworth-Heinemann).

Benson, J. F. (1987) *Working More Creatively with Groups* (London: Tavistock).

Boud, D., Keogh, R. and Walker, D. (1985) *Reflection: Turning Experience into Learning* (London: Kogan Page).

Bright, J. and Earl, J. (2000) *Brilliant CV: What Employers Want to See and How to Say It* (London: Prentice-Hall).

Butterworth, G. (1992) 'Context and cognition in models of cognitive growth'. In P. Light and G. Butterworth (eds), *Context and Cognition* (London: Harvester).

Buzan, T. (1993) *The Mind Map Book* (London: BBC Books).

Chapman, A. (2001) *The Monster Guide to Jobhunting: Get the Perfect Job, Double Click* (London and Edinburgh: Pearson Education).

Chase, W. G. and Simon, H. A. (1973) 'Perception in chess'. *Cognitive Science*, **13**, 145–82.

Cottrell, Stella (2003) *The Study Skills Handbook*, 2nd edn (Basingstoke: Palgrave Macmillan).

Cottrell, Stella (2001) *Teaching Study Skills and Supporting Learning* (Basingstoke: Palgrave Macmillan).

Covey, S. R. (1999) *The Seven Habits of Highly Effective People: Restoring the Character Ethic* (London: Simon and Schuster).

Committee of Vice-Chancellors and Principals/Department for Education and Employment (1998) *Skills Development in Higher Education, Short Report* (London: Committee of Vice-Chancellors and Principals).

Davidson, J. (2000) *The Ten-Minute Guide to Project Management* (Indianapolis: Alpha).

Dearing, R. (1997) *The Summary Report of the National Committee of Inquiry into Higher Education* (London: HMSO).

De Bono, E. (1994) *De Bono's Thinking Course*, revised and updated (London: BBC Books).

De Bono, E. (1995) *Teach Yourself to Think* (London: Penguin).

Dilts, R., Hallbom, T. and Smith, S. (1990) *Beliefs: Pathways to Health and Well-being* (Portland, OR: Metamorphous Press).

Donaldson, M. (1978) *Children's Minds* (London: Fontana).

Dryden, W. and Gordon, J. (1993) *Peak Performance: Become More Effective at Work* (Didcot, Oxon: Mercury Business Books).

Dunn, R., Griggs, S., Olson, J., Beasley, M. and Gorman, B. (1995) 'A meta-analytic validation of the Dunn and Dunn model of learning style preferences'. *Journal of Educational Research*, **88** (6), 353–62.

Ellis, A. (1994) *Reason and Emotion in Psychotherapy*, revised and updated (New York: Birch Lane Press).

Egan, D. and Schwartz, B. (1979) 'Chunking in recall of symbolic drawings'. *Memory and Cognition*, **7**, 149–58.

Fennell, M. (1999) *Overcoming Low Self-esteem: A Self-help Guide using Cognitive Behavioural Techniques* (London: Robinson).

Goleman, D. (1995) *Emotional Intelligence* (London: Bloomsbury).

Graham, R. J. (1989) *Project Management as if People Mattered* (Bala Cynwyd, PA: Primavera Press).

Greenfield, S. (2001) *The Human Brain: A Guided Tour* (London: Phoenix).

Hallows, J. (1997) *Information Systems Project Management* (New York: Amacom).

Heerkens, G. R. (2002) *Project Management* (New York: McGraw-Hill).

Heron, J. (1992) *Feeling and Personhood* (London: Sage Publications).

Hodgson, S. (2002) *Brilliant Answers to Tough Interview Questions* (London: Prentice-Hall).

Honey, P. and Mumford, A. (1992) *The Manual of Learning Styles Questionnaire* (Maidenhead, Berks: Peter Honey).

Jackson, T. and Jackson, E. (1997) *The Perfect CV: How to Get the Job You Really Want*, revised and updated (London: Piaktus).

Kozubska, J. (1997) *The 7 Keys of Charisma: The Secrets of Those Who Have It* (London: Kogan Page).

Lawrence, G. (1995) *People Types and Tiger Stripes*, 3rd edn (Gainesville, FL: Centre for Applications of Psychological Type).

Lazarus, R. S. (1999) *Stress and Emotion* (London: Free Association Books).

Luft, J. (1984) *Group Processes: An Introduction to Group Dynamics* (Mayfield, CA: Mountain View).

McCormick, R. and Paechter, C. (1999) *Learning and Knowledge* (London: The Open University).

McGill, I. and Beaty, L. (1992) *Action Learning: A Practitioner's Guide* (London: Kogan Page).

Mezirow, J. (ed.) (1990) *Fostering Critical Reflection in Adulthood: A Guide to Transformative and Emancipatory Learning* (San Francisco, CA: Jossey-Bass).

Mingus, N. (2002) *Teach Yourself Project Management in 24 Hours* (Indianapolis: Alpha).

Neenan, M. and Dryden, W. (2002) *Life Coaching: A Cognitive-Behavioural Approach* (New York: Brunner-Routledge).

Nolan, V. (ed) (2000) *Creative Education: Educating a Nation of Innovators. Papers by Members of the Synetics Education Initiative* (Buckinghamshire: Synetics Education Initiative).

Palmer, S. and Dryden, W. (1995) *Counselling for Stress Problems* (London: Sage).

Perry, W. G. (1970) *Forms of Intellectual and Ethical Development in the College Years: A Scheme* (New York: Holt, Rhinehart and Winston).

Piaget, J. (1952) *The Origins of Intelligence in Children* (New York: International Universities Press).

Piaget, J. (1975) *The Development of Thought: Equilibration of Cognitive Structures* (Oxford: Blackwell).

Popovich, I. (2000) *Winning at Job Interviews* (London: Hodder and Stoughton).

Project Management Institute (2000) *A Guide to the Project Management Body of Knowledge* (Newtown Square, PA: Project Management Institute).

Quality Assurance Agency for Higher Education (2000) http://www.qaa.ac.uk/Heprogressfile (30/5/2000).

Qualifications and Curriculum Authority (2000) *Improving Your Own Learning and Performance*, Key Skills Unit (London: QCA).

Qualifications and Curriculum Authority (2000) *Problem Solving*, Key Skills Unit (London: QCA).

Ribbens, G. and Thompson, R. (2001) *Understanding Body Language* (Abingdon: Gower).

Rossett, A. and Sheldon, K. (2001) *Beyond the Podium: Delivering Training and Performance to a Digital World* (San Francisco, CA: Jossey-Bass/Pfeiffer).

Sapadin, L. (1997) *It's about Time* (New York: Penguin).

Saven-Baden, M. (2000) *Problem-based Learning in Higher Education: Untold Stories* (Buckingham: SRHE and Open University Press).

Schon, D. A. (1989) *The Reflective Practitioner: How Professionals Think in Action* (London: Temple Smith).

Siegler, R. S. (1991) *Children's Thinking* (Englewood Cliffs, NJ: Prentice-Hall).

Skills and Enterprise Network, (2001) *Update: A Digest of Recent Labour Market, Research and Evaluation Reports and Developments*, no. 1, February (Sheffield: Skills and Enterprise Network).

Stordy, J. B. (2000) 'Dark adaptation, motor skills, docosahexaenoic acid and dyslexia'. *American Journal of Clinical Nutrition*, **71** (supplement), 323–26.

Taylor, R. and Humphrey, J. (2002) *Fast Track to the Top: Skills for Career Success* (London: Kogan Page).

TMP Worldwide Research (1998) *Soft Skills: Employers' Desirability and Actual Incidence* (32, Aybrook St, London, W1M 3JL).

Van Oech, R. (1990) *A Whack on the Side of the Head: How to be More Creative* (London: Thorsons).

Resources

Skills needs

www.skillsbase.dfes.gov.uk

Career guidance

www.prospects.ac.uk	advice and jobs for graduates
www.drjob.co.uk	advice and jobs for graduates
www.gradunet.co.uk	advice and jobs for graduates
www.hobsons.com	guidance and jobs for school leavers, young people and graduates
www.insidecareers.co.uk	guidance and jobs for graduates

Employment companies

www.bloomberg.com	international and entrepreneur site
www.companieshouse.gov.uk	lists all UK public companies
www.vault.com	what it is like to work for named companies

Employment: job hunting

www.career-index.com	lists job sites
www.gisajob.com	general
www.eteach.com	teaching
www.fish4jobs.co.uk	regional jobs
www.jobhunter.co.uk	adverts that appear in newspapers
www.jobshark.com	adverts and accepts electronic CVs
www.monster.co.uk	job adverts and career advice
www.planetrecruit.com	international jobs
www.stepstone.co.uk	UK and European jobs
www.tempz.com	temporary jobs
www.topgrads.co.uk	graduate jobs; accepts electronic CVs

Employment rights

www.cre.gov.uk	Commission for Race Equality
www.emplaw.co.uk	employment law
www.adviceguide.org	Citizens' Advice Bureau
www.hse.gov.uk	health and safety
www.i-resign.com/uk/home	leaving your job

Disability issues

www.ability.org/emp.html	disability charity
www.skill.org.uk	disability charity
www.disability.gov.uk	government's disability issues site

Adult Dyslexia and Skills Development Centre, 5 Tavistock Place, London, WC1H 9SN
Adult Dyslexia Organisation, 336 Brixton Road, London, SW9 7AA; www.futurenet.co.uk/charity/ado
British Dyslexia Association (BDA), 98 London Road, Reading, Berkshire, RG1 5AU; tel: 0118 966 8271

Index